Approaches to Class Analysis

Few themes have been as central to sociology as "class" and yet class remains a perpetually contested idea. Sociologists disagree not only on how best to define the concept of class but on its general role in social theory and indeed on its continued relevance to the sociological analysis of contemporary society. Some people believe that classes have largely dissolved in contemporary societies; others believe class remains one of the fundamental forms of social inequality and social power. Some see class as a narrow economic phenomenon whilst others adopt an expansive conception that includes cultural dimensions as well as economic conditions. This book explores the theoretical foundations of six major perspectives of class with each chapter written by an expert in the field. It concludes with a conceptual map of these alternative approaches by posing the question "If 'class' is the answer, what is the question?"

ERIK OLIN WRIGHT is Vilas Distinguished Professor at the Department of Sociology, University of Wisconsin. His recent books include *Deepening Democracy: Institutional Innovations in Empowered Participatory Governance* (2003) and *Class Counts: Comparative Studies in Class Analysis* (Cambridge, 1997).

Approaches to Class Analysis

Edited by

Erik Olin Wright

CAMBRIDGE
UNIVERSITY PRESS

CAMBRIDGE UNIVERSITY PRESS
Cambridge, New York, Melbourne, Madrid, Cape Town, Singapore, São Paulo

Cambridge University Press
The Edinburgh Building, Cambridge CB2 2RU, UK

www.cambridge.org
Information on this title: www.cambridge.org/9780521603812

First published 2005

Printed in the United Kingdom at the University Press, Cambridge

A catalogue record for this book is available from the British Library

Library of Congress Cataloguing in Publication data

Approaches to class analysis / edited by Erik Olin Wright
      p. cm.
   Includes bibliographical references and index.
   ISBN 0-521-84304-9 – ISBN 0-521-60381-1 (pb.)
   1. Social classes. 2. Sociology. I. Wright, Erik Olin.
   HT 609.A65 2005
   305.5–dc22   2004065036

ISBN-13 978-0-521-84304-1 hardback
ISBN-10 0-521-84304-9 hardback

ISBN-13 978-0-521-60381-2 paperback
ISBN-10 0-521-60381-1 paperback

To the Memory of
Aage B. Sørensen
1941–2001

Contents

Figures

Tables

Contributors

RICHARD BREEN is Official Fellow in Sociology at Nuffield College, Oxford University

DAVID GRUSKY is Professor of Sociology at Stanford University

JAN PAKULSKI is Professor of Sociology and Dean of Arts at the University of Tasmania

AAGE B. SØRENSEN[†], formerly Professor of Sociology at Harvard University

ELLIOT B. WEININGER is Assistant Professor of Sociology, State University of New York-Brockport

ERIK OLIN WRIGHT is Vilas Distinguished Professor, University of Wisconsin-Madison

Introduction

Erik Olin Wright

In March 2001, on the BBC Radio 4 *Today* program, a report was presented discussing a new seven-category class scheme being used in the British Census. Listeners were invited to the BBC website to see what class they were in. Within a few days there were over 50,000 hits on the site, a record for this sort of thing. At least for the segment of the British population that listens to the BBC morning news, class remains a salient issue.

In the broadcast a number of people were interviewed. One police inspector responded to being told that he was now classified in class I along with doctors, lawyers, and chief executives of corporations, by saying, "Does it mean now I have to wear tennis whites when I go out to do my gardening?... I don't see myself socially or economically in the same class as them." In a subsequent "live chat" program with Professor David Rose of Essex University, the principal designer of the new Census categories, many people called up complaining about the coding scheme. A truck driver objected to being in class VII on the grounds that his job was quite skilled and he had to use new information technologies and computers in his work. David Rose explained that the classification was meant to capture differences in the nature of the employment contract and conditions of work, not the skill level of jobs, and truck drivers typically had quite insecure conditions of employment. Another person asked, "How can you have a sense of solidarity and consciousness when you're 'Five' or 'Seven'? Can you imagine the *Communist Manifesto* written by the University of Essex? 'The history of all hitherto existing societies is the history of little internecine wars between class groups 1 and 2 and class groups 3 to 7?' Doesn't have the same ring does it?"

These comments by listeners on the BBC reflect the general ambiguity of the term "class" in the popular imagination. To some people it connotes lifestyle and tastes, the wearing of tennis whites while gardening. To others it is mainly about social status, esteem and respect: to be reclassified "down" the class hierarchy is seen as demeaning. Some see classes as social categories engaged in collective forms of conflict, shaping the

1

destiny of society. Politicians call for "middle-class tax cuts" by which they simply mean "tax cuts for people in the middle range of the income distribution." And many people, like David Rose, see class as identifying the basic determinants of a person's economic prospects.

These ambiguities in popular usages are also present in more academic discussions of class. The *word* class is deployed in a wide range of descriptive and explanatory contexts in sociology, just as it is in popular discourse, and of course, depending upon the context, different *concepts* of class may be needed. Given this diversity of the explanatory and descriptive tasks within which the word class appears, it is easy to see why debates over class are often confusing. Sometimes, of course, there is a genuine debate: alternative proposals for what concepts are needed to answer the same question are in dispute. Other times, however, the debate simply reflects different agendas. Some sociologists proclaim that class is disappearing, by which they mean that people are less likely to form stable identities in class terms and thus less likely to orient their political behavior on the basis of class, while others proclaim that class remains an enduring feature of contemporary society, by which they mean that a person's economic prospects in life continue to depend significantly on their relationship to economically valuable assets of various sorts.

The central objective of this book is to clarify the complex array of alternative conceptualizations of class rooted in different theoretical traditions of class analysis. Each of the authors in the book has written extensively on problems of class and inequality within different traditions of class analysis. Each has been given the assignment of writing a kind of theoretical manifesto for a particular kind of class analysis. The goal is to clarify the theoretical foundations of their preferred approach: lay out the underlying assumptions, systematically define each conceptual element, demarcate the explanatory ambitions of the concept and, where possible, differentiate their approach from others. While to a greater or lesser extent most of the approaches have their roots in an intellectual tradition linked to some classical social theorist – Marx, Weber, Durkheim – the chapters are not primarily discussions of the concept of class within the texts of these founding figures. Nor are they meant to be authoritative canonical statements about what counts as genuine "Marxist" or "Weberian" or any other kind of class analysis. Each of these traditions has considerable internal variation and, accordingly, the concept of class will be elaborated in different ways by different scholars all claiming to be working within the same broad current of thought. The authors were also instructed not to present the kind of extended "reviews of the literature" one might find in a sociological textbook on social class. What each chapter attempts to do is elaborate the analytical foundations of the conceptualization of class within each author's body of work, and by doing so, clarify the broader terrain of variation within class analysis.

Six different perspectives are presented. Chapter 1, by Erik Olin Wright, explores an approach to class analysis within the Marxist tradition. Here the central idea is defining the concept of class in terms of processes of exploitation and linking the concept to alternative systems of economic relations. Chapter 2, by Richard Breen, examines a form of class analysis linked to the Weberian tradition and associated with the work of the British sociologist John Goldthorpe. The central concern here is developing a concept of class built around the economic life chances of people, more specifically around the character of the employment relations available within labor markets and work organizations. Chapter 3, by David Grusky, develops a class analysis that he sees as located within the Durkheimian tradition of sociological theory. The guiding principle is the ways in which detailed locations within the occupational division of labor create homogeneous effects on the lives of people. Class locations are then identified with these highly disaggregated categories within systems of stratification. Chapter 4, by Elliot Weininger, lays out the central principles of class analysis identified with the French sociologist Pierre Bourdieu. In Bourdieu's framework, class is defined with respect to a variety of dimensions of "capital," where capital is understood as a multidimensional space of power-conferring resources that shape both the opportunities and the dispositions of actors. Chapter 5, by Aage Sørensen, presents an approach to class analysis that draws heavily on the reasoning of neoclassical economics, especially the notion of economic "rents." In this conceptualization of class, classes would not exist at all in a perfectly competitive market with complete information. Classes occur only where there are the kinds of market imperfections that create rents that can be captured by some groups of actors and not others. In Chapter 6, Jan Pakulski elaborates the foundations of what might be termed a "post-class analysis." He argues that class, especially as understood in the Marxist and Weberian traditions, is no longer an empirically useful category. Inequality may continue to be an important issue in contemporary society, but inequality, in his view, is no longer organized along class lines. Finally, the Conclusion to the book discusses how different traditions of class analysis are anchored in different central questions, and how this difference in questions underlies many of the differences in their concepts of class.

1 Foundations of a neo-Marxist class analysis

Erik Olin Wright

The concept of class has greater explanatory ambitions within the Marxist tradition than in any other tradition of social theory and this, in turn, places greater burdens on its theoretical foundations. In its most ambitious form, Marxists have argued that class – or very closely linked concepts like "mode of production" or "the economic base" – was at the center of a general theory of history, usually referred to as "historical materialism."[1] This theory attempted to explain within a unified framework a very wide range of social phenomena: the epochal trajectory of social change as well as social conflicts located in specific times and places, the macro-level institutional form of the state along with the micro-level subjective beliefs of individuals, large-scale revolutions as well as sit-down strikes. Expressions like "class struggle is the motor of history" and "the executive of the modern state is but a committee of the bourgeoisie" captured this ambitious claim of explanatory centrality for the concept of class.

Most Marxist scholars today have pulled back from the grandiose explanatory claims of historical materialism (if not necessarily from all of its explanatory aspirations). Few today defend stark versions of "class primacy." Nevertheless, it remains the case that class retains a distinctive centrality within the Marxist tradition and is called upon to do much more arduous explanatory work than in other theoretical traditions. Indeed, a good argument can be made that this, along with a specific orientation to radically egalitarian normative principles, is a large part of what defines the continuing distinctiveness and vitality of the Marxist tradition as a body of thought, particularly within sociology. It is for this reason that I have argued that "Marxism as class analysis" defines the core agenda of Marxist sociology.[2]

---

[1] The most systematic and rigorous exposition of the central tenets of historical materialism is Cohen (1978).

[2] For a more extended discussion of Marxism as class analysis, see Burawoy and Wright (2001) and Wright, Levine, and Sober (1993).

4

The task of this chapter is to lay out the central analytical foundations of the concept of class in a way that is broadly consistent with the Marxist tradition. This is a tricky business, for among writers who identify with Marxism there is no consensus on any of the core concepts of class analysis. What defines the tradition is more a loose commitment to the importance of class analysis for understanding the conditions for challenging capitalist oppressions and the language within which debates are waged – what Alvin Gouldner aptly called a "speech community" – than a precise set of definitions and propositions. Any claims about the theoretical foundations of Marxist class analysis which I make, therefore, will reflect my specific stance within that tradition rather than an authoritative account of "Marxism" in general or of the work of Karl Marx in particular.[3]

There will be two principal punchlines to the analysis: first, that the ingredient that most sharply distinguishes the Marxist conceptualization of class from other traditions is the concept of "exploitation," and second, that an exploitation-centered concept of class provides theoretically powerful tools for studying a range of problems in contemporary society. The goal of this chapter is to make these claims both intelligible and – hopefully – credible. Part I lays out what is the fundamental point of class analysis within Marxism, what it tries to accomplish. This is above all a question of clarifying the normative agenda to which class analysis is linked. In Part II we will carefully go through a series of conceptual clarifications that are needed to frame the specific analysis of class and exploitation. Some people may find this section a little pedantic, a bit like reading a dictionary in places, but I feel that it is necessary in order for the reasoning on which these concepts are based to be transparent. Part III specifies the core *common* explanatory claims of class analysis in both the Marxist and Weberian traditions. This will be helpful in setting the stage for the discussion in Part IV of the distinctive hallmark of the Marxist concept that differentiates it from its Weberian cousins and anchors the broader theoretical claims and agenda of Marxist class analysis. This will involve, above all, elaborating the concept of exploitation, one of the crucial causal mechanisms through which Marxists claim that class relations generate social effects. Finally, in Part V I will briefly lay out what I see as the pay-offs of the Marxian-inspired form of class analysis.

---

[3] There is a very large literature both of exegesis of Marx's own work on class and on varieties of class analysis within the broadly construed Marxist tradition. For an exegesis of Marx's treatment of class, see Cotreel (1984, Ch. 2). For a general review of alternative Marxist approaches, see Wright (1980b). For examples of Marxist class analyses that differ substantially from the approach outlined in this chapter, see Poulantzas (1975); Carchedi (1977); Resnick and Wolff (1987).

The big picture: what the Marxist concept of class is all about

At its core, class analysis within the Marxist tradition is rooted in a set of normative commitments to a form of radical egalitarianism. Historically, Marxists have generally been reluctant to systematically argue for these moral commitments. Marx himself felt that talk about "justice" and "morality" was unnecessary and perhaps even pernicious, believing that ideas about morality really just reflected material conditions and interests of actors. Rather than defend socialism on grounds of social justice or other normative principles, Marx preferred to simply argue that socialism was in the interests of the working class and that it was, in any case, the historical destiny of capitalism. Nevertheless, Marx's own writing is filled with moral judgment, moral outrage and moral vision. More significantly for present purposes, the Marxist tradition of class analysis gets much of its distinctive thrust from its link to a radical egalitarian normative agenda. In order to fully understand the theoretical foundations of the concept of class in the Marxist tradition, it is necessary, if only briefly, to clarify this normative dimension.

The underlying radical egalitarianism within Marxist class analysis can be expressed in terms of three theses. I will state these in a stripped-down form, without elaborate qualifications and amendments, since our purpose here is to clarify the character of the agenda of Marxist class analysis rather than to provide a defense of the theory itself:

Radical Egalitarianism thesis: Human flourishing would be broadly enhanced by a radically egalitarian distribution of the material conditions of life.[4] This thesis is captured by the classical distributional slogan advocated by Marx, "To each according to need, from each according to ability" and by the ideal of a "classless" society. This is the way material resources are distributed within egalitarian families: children with greater needs receive more resources, and everyone is expected to contribute as best they can to the tasks needed by the family. This is also the way books are distributed in public libraries: you check out what you need, not what you can afford. The radical egalitarianism of the Marxist tradition affirms that human flourishing in general would be enhanced if these principles could be generalized to the society as a whole.[5]

---

[4] The radical egalitarianism thesis as stated here is not, in and of itself, a thesis about *justice*. The claim is that human beings will generally flourish better under such egalitarian conditions than under conditions of inequality and hierarchy, but it does not stipulate that it is a requirement of justice that such flourishing be promoted. I believe that this is a question of social justice, but that belief is not necessary in the present context.

[5] The question of precisely what is meant by "egalitarianism" and on what grounds this is a justified normative principle has been the subject of considerable debate, some of it

Historical possibility thesis: Under conditions of a highly productive economy, it becomes materially possible to organize society in such a way that there is a sustainable radically egalitarian distribution of the material conditions of life. Egalitarian normative principles within the Marxist tradition are thought not simply to reflect some kind of timeless human value, although they may be that as well, but are also meant to be embodied in a practical political project. Central to the Marxist theoretical project is thus the attempt to understand the conditions under which these moral ideals can feasibly be translated into social practice. Here the basic idea is that radical egalitarianism becomes increasingly feasible as a practical principle of social organization as the productive capacity of a society increases and absolute scarcity is reduced. In the strongest version of this thesis, the egalitarian ideals are strictly impossible to implement and sustain until material scarcity is largely overcome; in weaker versions all that is claimed is that high productivity makes a basic egalitarianism of material conditions of life more feasible.

Anti-capitalism thesis: Capitalism blocks the possibility of achieving a radically egalitarian distribution of the material conditions of life. One of the great achievements of capitalism is to develop human productive capacity to such an extent that it makes the radical egalitarianism needed for human flourishing materially feasible, yet capitalism also creates institutions and power relations that block the actual achievement of egalitarianism. This sets the stage for the great drama and tragedy of capitalist development: it is a process which continually enhances the material conditions for an expanded scope of human flourishing while simultaneously blocking the creation of the social conditions for realizing this potential. The political conclusion of classical Marxism is that these obstacles can only be overcome by destroying capitalism through a revolutionary rupture. More social democratic currents within the Marxist tradition accept the idea that capitalism is the enemy of equality, but reject the ruptural vision of change: capitalism can be transformed from within in ways which gradually move in the direction of a more profoundly egalitarian social order. The full realization of the radical egalitarian ideal may, of course, be a utopian fantasy. But even if "classlessness" is unachievable, "less classness" can be a central political objective, and this still requires challenging capitalism.

Each of these theses is controversial and in need of extended defense, but here I will treat them as assumptions that define the broadest context

informed by the Marxist tradition. For a general overview of the issues see Swift (2001). For a penetrating discussion of an egalitarian theory of justice infused with Marxist sensibilities, see Cohen (1995).

for thinking about the concept of class.[6] Whatever else the concept of class is meant to accomplish, within Marxist class analysis it is meant to facilitate understanding the conditions for the pursuit of this normative agenda. This means that the concept needs to be linked to a theory of capitalism, not just inequality, and it needs to be able to play a role in clarifying the dilemmas and possibilities of egalitarian alternatives to existing institutions.

Let us now turn to the elaboration of the conceptual components with which we can build a concept of class suitable for this agenda.

Conceptual components of class analysis

The word "class" is used both as a noun and as an adjective. As a noun, one might ask the question "What class do you think you are in?" and the answer might be "The working class." As an adjective, the word class modifies a range of concepts: class relations, class structure, class locations, class formation, class interests, class conflict, class consciousness. In general, as will become clear from the analysis that follows, I think the term class is much more productively used as an adjective. Indeed, I think it is usually the case that when people use the term as a noun, they are speaking elliptically. An expression such as "the working class," for example, is often just a shorthand for a more cumbersome expression such as "working-class locations within capitalist class relations," or perhaps "working-class collective organizations within class conflicts." In any case, I will generally use the term as an adjective and only use the generic term "class" when I am referring to the general conceptual field within which these more specific terms are located.

In order to lay the foundations of Marxist class analysis, therefore, we need to figure out exactly what we mean by this adjective. Here the pivotal concepts are class *relations* and class *structure*. Other terms in the

---

[6] The objections to these theses are fairly familiar. Against the *Radical Egalitarianism thesis* two sorts of arguments are frequently raised: First, even if it is true that equality promotes human flourishing, the redistribution of resources needed for material equality is unjust since it deprives some people of material advantages which they have rightfully acquired; and second, far from creating conditions for a flourishing of human potential, radical material equality would generate passivity, laziness, and uniformity. Against the *historical possibility thesis*, many people argue that high levels of economic productivity can only be sustained when people have significant material incentives to invest, both in skills and capital. Any significant move towards radical material equality, therefore, would be unsustainable since it would lead to a decline in material abundance itself. Finally, against the *anti-capitalism thesis*, critics argue that while it may be true that capitalism blocks radical moves towards equality of material conditions of life, it does not block human flourishing; to the contrary, capitalism offers individuals the maximum opportunity to make of their lives what they wish.

conceptual menu of class analysis – class conflict, class interests, class formation, class consciousness – all derive their meanings from their link to class relations and class structure. This does not mean that for all problems in class analysis, the purely structural concepts of class are more central. It can certainly be the case, for example, that in trying to explain variations over time and place in state policies across capitalist societies, the variations in class formation and class struggle will turn out to be more important than the variations in class structure as such. Still, at the conceptual foundation of class analysis is the problem of understanding class relations and class structure, and thus it is on this issue that we will focus here.

In what follows we will examine eight clusters of conceptual issues: 1. the concept of social relations of production; 2. the idea of class relations as a specific form of such relations; 3. the meaning of "variations" of class relations; 4. the problem of complexity in class relations; 5. the meaning of a "location" within class relations; 6. complexity in specifying class locations; 7. the distinction between micro- and macro-levels of class analysis; 8. class "agency." While, taken as a whole, these conceptual problems are particularly relevant to elaborating the concept of class within the Marxist tradition, many of them will be relevant to other agendas of class analysis as well.

Social relations of production

Any system of production requires the deployment of a range of assets or resources or factors of production: tools, machines, land, raw materials, labor power, skills, information, and so forth. This deployment can be described in *technical* terms as a production function – so many inputs of different kinds are combined in a specific process to produce an output of a specific kind. This is the characteristic way that economists think of systems of production. The deployment can also be described in *social relational* terms: the people that participate in production have different kinds of rights and powers over the use of the inputs and over the results of their use.[7] The actual ways in which inputs are combined and used

---

[7] By "powers" over productive resources I mean *effective control over the use and disposition* of the resources in question. The term "rights" provides the additional idea that these powers are viewed as legitimate and enforced by the state. The expression "property rights" thus means "effective powers over the use of property enforced by the state." In most contexts in a stable system of production relations there is a close connection between rights and powers, but it is possible that people have effective, durable control over resources without that control being recognized in formal legal terms as a property right. In any case, for most of the analysis proposed here it will not be necessary to emphasize the distinction between rights and powers, and thus I will generally use the terms together as a couplet.

in production depends as much on the way these rights and powers are wielded as it does on the strictly technical features of a production function. The sum total of these rights and powers constitutes the "social relations of production."

It is important to keep in mind that these rights and powers over resources are attributes of social relations, not descriptions of the relationship of people to things as such: to have rights and powers with respect to land, for example, defines one's social relationship to other people with respect to the use of the land and the appropriation of the fruits of using the land productively. This means that the power relations involved in the social relations of production concern the ways in which the activities of people are regulated and controlled, not simply the distribution of a range of valuable things.

Class relations as a form of relations of production

When the rights and powers of people over productive resources are unequally distributed – when some people have greater rights/powers with respect to specific kinds of productive resources than do others – these relations can be described as class relations. The fundamental contrast in capitalist societies, for example, is between owners of means of production and owners of labor power, since "owning" is a description of rights and powers with respect to a resource deployed in production.

The rights and powers in question are not defined with respect to the ownership or control of things in general, but only of resources or assets *insofar as they are deployed in production*. A capitalist is not someone who simply owns machines, but someone who owns machines, deploys those machines in a production process, hires owners of labor power to use them, directs the process by which the machines are used to produce things, and appropriates the profits from the use of those machines. A collector of machines is not, by virtue of owning those machines, a capitalist. To count as a class relation it is therefore not sufficient that there be unequal rights and powers over the sheer possession of a resource. There must also be unequal rights and powers over the appropriation of the results of the use of that resource. In general this implies appropriating income generated by the deployment of the resource in question.

Variations in class relations

In some ways of using the term "class," it makes little sense to talk about qualitatively different *kinds* of class relations. Classes are simply identified with some universal, generic categories like "the haves" and "the have nots." There can still be *quantitative* variation of course – the gap between the rich and poor can vary as can the distribution of the population into these categories. But there is no theoretical space for *qualitative* variation in the nature of class relations.

One of the central ideas in the Marxist tradition is that there are many kinds of class relations, and pinpointing the basis of this variation is of central importance. The basic idea is that different kinds of class relations are defined by the kinds of rights and powers that are embodied in the relations of production. Consider, for example, three kinds of class relations that are often distinguished in the Marxist tradition: *slavery, feudalism*, and *capitalism*. In slave class relations, to say that a slave owner "owns" the slave is to specify a range of rights and powers that the slave owner has over one particular resource used in production – people. In the extreme case, the slave owner has virtually absolute property rights in the slave. In capitalism, in contrast, ownership of other people is prohibited. People are allowed to privately own land and capital, but they are prohibited from owning other people. This is one of the great accomplishments of capitalism: it has achieved a radically egalitarian distribution of this particular asset – everyone owns one unit of labor power, themselves.

In these terms, what is commonly called "feudalism" can be viewed as a society within which feudal lords and serfs have *joint* ownership rights in the labor of the serf. The conventional description of feudalism is a society within which the peasants (serfs) are forced to work part of each week on the land owned by the lord and are free to work the rest of the week on land to which they have some kind of customary title. This obligation to work part of the week on the lord's land means, in effect, that the lord has property rights in the serf which take the form of the right to use the labor of the serf a certain proportion of the time. This ownership is less absolute than that of the slave owner – thus the expression "joint ownership" of the serf by the lord and serf. When a serf flees the land for the town attempting to escape these obligations, the lord has the right to forcibly go after the serf and bring him or her back. In effect, by fleeing the land the serf has stolen something that belongs to the lord: the rights to part of the labor of the serf.[8] Just as a factory owner in capitalism would have the right to have the police retrieve machines stolen from the factory by workers, the feudal lord has the right to use coercive powers to retrieve labor stolen from the manor by the serf.

---

[8] The common expression for describing the right of lords to coercively bring peasants back to the land is that the peasant is "tied to the land" by feudal obligations. Since the pivot of this tying to the land is the rights the lord has in the labor of the peasant (or at least the fruits of labor when this takes the form of rents), the content of the class relation really centers on rights and powers over the ownership of labor power.

The problem of complexity in concrete class relations

Much of the rhetoric of class analysis, especially in the Marxist tradition, characterizes class relations in fairly stark, simplified, polarized terms. Class struggles are portrayed as battles between the bourgeoisie and the proletariat, between lords and serfs, between slave masters and slaves. This simplified image does capture, at an abstract level, something fundamental about the nature of class relations: they do indeed, as we shall see, generate antagonisms of interests that underlie overt conflicts. But this polarized image is also misleading, for in concrete societies located in time and space class relations are never this simple. One of the tasks of class analysis is to give precision to complexity and explore its ramifications.

Two kinds of complexity are especially important. First, in most societies a variety of different kinds of class relations coexist and are linked together in various ways.[9] In the American South before the Civil War, for example, slave class relations and capitalist class relations coexisted. The specific dynamics and contradictions of that society came from the way these distinct principles of class relations were combined. Certain kinds of sharecropping in the United States in the early twentieth century contained striking elements of feudalism, again combined in complex ways with capitalist relations. If we are willing to describe state-bureaucratic ownership of the means of production as constituting a distinctive kind of class relation, then many advanced capitalist societies today combine capitalism with such statist class relations. To fully understand the class relations of actual societies, then, requires identifying the ways in which different forms of class relations are combined.

Second, as we have already seen in our brief discussion of feudalism, the rights and powers people can have with respect to a given resource are actually complex bundles of rights and powers, rather than simple, one-dimensional property rights. It is common when people think about variations in the rights and powers over various factors of production to treat these rights and powers as having a simple, binary structure: you either own something or you do not. In the ordinary everyday use of the term, "ownership" seems to have this absolute character: if I own a book I can do anything I want with it, including burning it, using it to prop

---

[9] A technical term that is often used to describe a situation in which distinct forms of class relations coexist in different units of production is "articulation of modes of production." Typically in such situations the articulation takes the form of exchange relations between the distinct forms of class relations. In the American South before the Civil War, slavery existed on plantations and capitalism in factories. The plantation provided cotton to factories, and the factories provided agricultural machinery to the plantation.

open a door, giving it away, selling it, and so on. In fact, even ownership of ordinary things is generally much more complex than this. Some of the rights and powers are held by the "owner" and some are held by other people or collective agencies. Consider, for example, the machines in a capitalist factory. In conventional language, these are "owned" by the capitalists who own the business in the sense that they purchased them, can sell them, can use them to generate profits, and so on. But this does not mean that the capitalists have absolute, complete rights and powers over the use of those machines. They can only set them in motion, for example, if the machines satisfy certain safety and pollution regulations imposed by the state. If the factory exists in a highly unionized social setting, the capitalist may only be able to hire union members to use the machine. In effect, both state regulations of the machines and union restrictions in the labor market mean that some dimensions of the property rights in the machines have been transferred from the capitalist to a collective agency. This means that absolute capitalist property rights in the means of production have been at least partially "socialized."[10]

These kinds of complexity are pervasive in contemporary capitalism: government restrictions on workplace practices, union representation on boards of directors, co-determination schemes, employee stock-options, delegations of power to managerial hierarchies, etc. all constitute various ways in which the property rights and powers embodied in the idea of "owning the means of production" are decomposed and redistributed. Such redistribution of rights and powers constitutes a form of variation in class relations. Such systems of redistributed rights and powers move class relations considerably away from the simple, abstract form of perfectly polarized relations. This does not mean that the class relations cease to be *capitalist* – the basic power over the allocation of capital and command of profits remains, in spite of these modifications, under private control of capitalists – but it does mean that capitalist class structures can vary considerably depending on the particular ways these rights and powers are broken down, distributed, and recombined.

One of the objectives of class analysis is to understand the consequences of these forms of variation of class relations. Such complexity, however,

---

[10] This can also be described as a situation in which capitalist class relations and socialist class relations *interpenetrate*. If *articulation* of different class relations refers to a situation in which distinct class relations exist in distinct units of production and then interact through external relations, *interpenetration* of different class relations is a situation in which within a single unit of production the distribution of rights and powers over assets combines aspects of two distinct types of class relations.

is still complexity in the form of class relations, not some other sort of social relation, since the social relations in question are still constituted by the unequal rights and powers of people over economically relevant assets.

Class locations

Much of the sociological debate about class becomes in practice a debate about the optimal inventory of class *locations* – or some equivalent expression like "class categories" – rather than class *relations* as such. To a significant extent, this is because much empirical research, particularly quantitative research, revolves around data that are tagged onto individuals and it thus becomes important to be able to locate the individual within the social structure. In the case of class analysis, this implies assigning them a location within class relations. As a practical matter, any such exercise requires that one decide which criteria are going to be deployed to differentiate among class locations and "how many" class categories are to be generated using those criteria.

There is nothing wrong in using the concept of class in research in this way. But, at least within the Marxist tradition, it is important not to lose sight of the fact that "class locations" designate the social positions occupied by individuals within a particular kind of social relation, class relations, not simply an atomized attribute of the person. The premise behind the idea of social relations is that when people go about their lives in the world, when they make choices and act in various ways, their actions are systematically structured by their relations to other people who are also making choices and acting.[11] "Social relation" is a way of talking about the inherently structured interactive quality of human action. In the specific case of class relations, the claim is that the rights and powers people have over productive resources are important for the structured interactive quality of human action. To talk about a "location" within a class relation, then, is to situate individuals within such structured patterns of interaction.

---

[11] To say that people make choices and act in structured relations with other choosing/acting individuals leaves open the best way to theorize choosing and acting. There is no implication, for example, that choices are made on the basis of some process of rational maximization, or even that all actions are consciously chosen. There is also no implication, as methodological individualists would like to argue, that the explanation of social processes can be reduced to the attributes of the individuals choosing and acting. The relations themselves can be explanatory. The concept of social relation being used here, therefore, does not imply rational choice theory or reductionist versions of methodological individualism.

Complexity in class locations

At first glance it might seem that the problem of specifying class locations is pretty straightforward. First you define the concept of class relations and then you derive the inventory of class locations from these relations. In capitalism the central class relation is the capital/labor relation and this determines two class locations, capitalists and workers.

As in our discussion of the problem of complexity in class relations themselves, for some problems it might be sufficient to distinguish only two class locations in capitalist societies. But for many of the questions one might want to ask for which the problem of class locations figures in the answer, such a single, binary model of class locations seems woefully inadequate. If we want to understand the formation of people's subjective experience within work, or the dilemmas faced by union organizers on the shop floor, or the tendencies for people to form different kinds of coalitions within political conflicts, or the prospects for living a comfortable material existence, then knowing that they are a capitalist or a worker within a polarized model of class relations is unlikely to tell us everything we want to know.

Given this explanatory inadequacy of the two-location model, we face two basic kinds of choices. One option is to retain the simple two-location model (often called the "two-class model"), and then add additional complexities to the analysis that are not treated as complexities in *class* locations as such. Thus, for example, to understand the formation of the subjective experience of people within work we can introduce a set of concrete variations in working conditions – degrees of autonomy, closeness of supervision, levels of responsibility, cognitive complexity of tasks, physical demands of work, promotion prospects, and so on – which are relevant to understanding work experience. These would then be treated as sources of variation in experience among people occupying working-class locations within class relations, where working-class locations are defined in the simple binary terms of the two-location model. Alternatively, we can note that some of these variations in "working conditions" are actually variations in the concrete ways in which people are located within class relations. The degree of authority an employee has over other employees, for example, can be viewed as reflecting a specific form of distribution of the rights and powers over the process of production.

In my work in class analysis I have opted for the second of these strategies, trying to incorporate a considerable amount of complexity directly into the account of class locations. I do this (hopefully) not in the stubborn belief that we want to engineer our class concepts in such a way that class locations as such explain as much as possible, but because I believe that many of these complexities are in fact complexities in the concrete ways in which rights and powers over economic resources and activities are distributed across locations within relations.

The trick is to introduce complexity into the analysis of class locations in a systematic and rigorous manner rather than seeing complexity as haphazard and chaotic. This means trying to figure out the principles through which complexity is generated and then specifying the implications of these principles for the problem of locating people within class relations. Five sources of such complexity seem especially important for class analysis:

1. Complexity of locations derived from complexity *within* the relations themselves: unbundling the rights and powers of class relations
2. Complexity in the allocation of individual persons to locations: occupying multiple class locations at the same time
3. Complexity in the temporal aspects of locations: careers vs slots
4. Strata within relations
5. Families and class relations

Unbundling of rights and powers. If the rights and powers associated with class relations are really complex bundles of decomposable rights and powers, then they can potentially be partially unbundled and reorganized in complex ways. This can generate class locations which I have referred to as "contradictory locations within class relations."[12] Managers within corporations, for example, can be viewed as exercising some of the powers of capital – hiring and firing workers, making decisions about new technologies and changes in the labor process, etc. – and in this respect occupy the capitalist location within the class relations of capitalism. On the other hand, in general they cannot sell a factory and convert the value of its assets into personal consumption, and they can be fired from their jobs if the owners are unhappy. In these respects they occupy the working-class location within class relations. The assumption behind this analytical strategy for understanding the class character of managers, then, is that the specific pattern of rights and powers over productive resources that are combined in a given location defines a set of real and significant causal processes.

Another candidate for a kind of "contradictory class location" is rooted in the ways in which certain kinds of skills and credentials confer upon their holders effective rights and powers over many aspects of their work.[13] This is particularly true for employed professionals whose control over

---

[12] For a discussion of the development of this concept, see Wright (1985, Ch. 2) and Wright *et al.* (1989, Ch. 1).

[13] Control over the conditions of employment constitutes a redistribution of the rights and powers of capital–labor relations insofar as employers no longer have the capacity to

their conditions of work constitutes a distinct form of employment relation with their employers, but aspects of these empowered employment relations also characterize many highly skilled nonprofessional jobs.[14]

Allocating people to class locations. Individuals can hold two jobs which are differently located within social relations of production: a person can be a manager or a worker in a firm and self-employed in a second job. Such a person in effect is simultaneously in two class locations. A factory worker who moonlights as a self-employed carpenter is located within class relations in a more complex way than one who does not. Furthermore, some people within working-class locations within a capitalist firm may also own stocks (either in the firm in which they work or in other firms), and thus occupy, if only to a limited extent, a capitalist location as well. Workers in a firm with a real Employee Stock Ownership Plan (ESOP) do not thereby cease to be "in" working-class locations within the class relations of capitalism, but they are no longer *merely* in those locations: they are simultaneously in two class locations.

Temporality of locations. Some jobs are part of career trajectories – sequences of orderly job changes over time – in which there is a reasonable probability that the class character of these jobs will change over time. In some work organizations, for example, most managers begin work in nonmanagerial positions with the full expectation of moving into management after a kind of shop-floor apprenticeship and subsequently of moving up managerial hierarchies. Even though they may for a time be working alongside ordinary workers, their "jobs" are, from the start, connected to managerial careers. Why should this matter for understanding the class character of such jobs? It matters because both the interests and experiences of people in such jobs are significantly affected by the likely future tied to their job. This means that the location within class relations of people within such careers has what might be termed temporal complexity. Furthermore, since the future is always somewhat uncertain, the temporal dimension of class locations also means that a person's location

---

effectively direct the laboring activity of such employees and are forced to offer them fairly secure long-term contracts with what John Goldthorpe has called "prospective rewards." In the extreme case, as Philippe Van Parijs has argued in Wright *et al.* (1989, Ch. 6), this comes close to giving employees something like property rights in their jobs. John Goldthorpe describes this kind of employment relation as a *service* relation to distinguish it from the ordinary wage labor relation characteristic of people in working-class locations.

[14] I have formulated the quality of the contradictory class location of these kinds of positions in different ways at different times. In my early work (Wright 1978) I called them "semi-autonomous employees," emphasizing the control over the conditions of work. In later writing (Wright 1985, 1997) I referred to them as "experts," emphasizing their control over knowledge and credentials and the way in which this affected their relationship to the problem of exploitation.

within class relations can have a certain degree of temporal indeterminacy or uncertainty.

Strata and class locations. If class locations are defined by the rights and powers people have with respect to productive resources and economic activities, then another source of complexity within class locations centers on the amount of resources and scope of activities subjected to these rights and powers. There are capitalists who own and control vast quantities of capital employing thousands of workers all over the world, and capitalists who employ a small number of people in a single location. Both are "capitalists" in relational terms, but vary tremendously in the amount of power that they wield. Among people in working-class locations, workers vary in their skills and in their associated "market capacity," their ability to command wages in the labor market. If their skills are sufficiently scarce, they may even be able to command a significant "rent" component within their wages. Both skilled and unskilled workers occupy working-class locations insofar as they do not own or control means of production and must sell their labor power in order to obtain their livelihood, but they vary the amount of one specific resource, skill. These kinds of quantitative variations among people who occupy a similar relational location can be referred to as strata within class locations.

Families and class locations. People are linked to class relations not simply through their own direct involvement in the control and use of productive resources, but through various other kinds of social relations, especially those of family and kinship. The reason we care about a person's class "location" is because we believe that through a variety of mechanisms their experiences, interests, and choices will be shaped by how their lives intersect class relations. If you are married to a capitalist, regardless of what you yourself do, your interests and choices will be partially conditioned by this fact. And this fact is a fact about your "location." This particular dimension of the problem of class locations can be called "mediated locations within class relations."[15] Mediated locations are especially important for understanding the class locations of children, of retired people, of housewives, and of people in two-earner households. Mediated locations add particularly interesting complexities to class analysis in cases in which a person's direct class location – the way in which they are inserted into class relations through their own jobs – and their mediated class locations are different. This is the case, for example, of a female typist in an office married to a corporate manager. As the proportion of married women in paid employment and the length of time they spend in the labor force increases, the existence of such "cross-class

[15] See Wright (1997, Ch. 10).

households," as they are sometimes called, becomes a more salient form of complexity in class locations.[16]

These kinds of complexities in specifying class locations make certain common ways of talking about class problematic. People often ask the question "how many classes are there?" My own work on class structure, for example, has been described as offering a "twelve-class model" since in some of my research I have constructed a twelve-category class variable in order to study such things as class consciousness or class mobility. Within the framework I am proposing here, this kind of question is, I think, misconstrued. A class "location" is not "*a* class"; it is a location-within-relations. The number of such locations within an analysis of class structure, then, depends upon how fine-grained an account is needed for the purposes at hand.[17] For some research questions, a relatively fine-grained differentiation of locations within class relations is desirable, since the precise ways in which persons are connected to rights-and-powers-over-resources may be of explanatory importance. In my research on the relationship between class location and class consciousness, for example, I felt that a fairly refined set of categories would be relevant.[18] For other problems, a more coarse-grained description of locations-within-relations may provide more insight. In my work on the problem of class compromise I felt a much simpler two-location class model consisting only of workers and capitalists was appropriate.[19]

Macro- and micro-class analysis

Class analysis is concerned with both macro- and micro-levels of analysis. The basic concept for macro-class analysis is *class structure*. The sum total of the class relations in a given unit of analysis can be called the "class structure" of that unit of analysis. One can thus speak of the class structure of a firm, of a city, of a country, perhaps of the world. Traditionally, the nation-state has been the favored unit of analysis for the specification of class structure. This has been justified, in part, because of the importance of the state as the institution for enforcing the pivotal rights and powers over assets that constitute the stuff of class relations.

---

[16] In the 1980s, roughly a third of dual-earner families in the United States would be classified as cross-class households, which meant around 12 percent of the adult population lived in such households. See Wright (1997, pp. 226–7).

[17] My views on the problem of the "number" of class locations are very similar to those of Erickson and Goldthorpe, who write that "the only sensible answer [to the question 'How many classes are there?'] is, we would believe, 'as many as it proves empirically useful to distinguish for the analytical purposes at hand.'" Erikson and Goldthorpe (1993, p. 46).

[18] See Wright (1997, Ch. 14).

[19] See Wright (2000, pp. 957–1002).

Nevertheless, depending upon the problem under investigation, other units of analysis may be appropriate.

The macro-level of class analysis centers on the effects of class structures on the unit of analysis in which they are defined. The analysis of how the international mobility of capital constrains the policy options of states, for example, constitutes a macro-level investigation of the effects of a particular kind of class structure on states. The analysis of how the concentration or dispersion of ownership of capital in a particular sector affects the conditions for union organizing would be a macro-level investigation of class formation.

The micro-level of class analysis attempts to understand the ways in which class impacts on individuals. At its core is the analysis of the effects of class locations on various aspects of individual lives. Analyses of labor market strategies of unskilled workers, or the effects of technological change on class consciousness, or political contributions of corporate executives would be examples of micro-level class analysis.

Micro- and macro-levels of class analysis are linked in complex ways. On the one hand, class structures are not disembodied wholes generating macro-level effects independently of the actions and choices of individuals: macro-processes have micro-foundations. On the other hand, the micro-processes through which a person's location in class relations shapes their opportunities, consciousness and actions occur in macro-contexts which deeply affect the ways in which these micro-processes operate: micro-processes are mediated by macro-contexts. Class analysis, like all sociological analysis, seeks to understand both the micro- and macro-levels and their interactions.

Class "agency"

The issues we have so far addressed have been almost entirely *structural* in character. That is, we have examined the nature of the social relations in which people live and act and how these can be understood in class terms, but we have not said much about action itself. Marxist class analysis is ultimately about the conditions and process of social change, and thus we need a set of categories in terms of which the actions of people that reproduce and transform these social relations can be understood. Five concepts are particularly relevant for this purpose: class interests, class consciousness, class practices, class formations and class struggle.

- Class *interests*: These are the material interests of people derived from their location-within-class-relations. "Material interests" include a range of issues – standards of living, working conditions, level of toil, leisure, material security, and other things. To describe the interests people have with respect to these things as "class" interests is to say that the opportunities and trade-offs people face in pursuing these interests are structured by their class locations. An account of these interests provides the crucial theoretical bridge between the description of class relations and the actions of individuals within those relations.

- Class *consciousness*: The subjective awareness people have of their class interests and the conditions for advancing them.
- Class *practices*: The activities engaged in by individuals, both as separate persons and as members of collectivities, in pursuit of class interests.
- Class *formations*: The collectivities people form in order to facilitate the pursuit of class interests. These range from highly self-conscious organizations for the advance of interests such as unions, political parties, and employers associations, to much looser forms of collectivity such as social networks and communities.
- Class *struggle*: Conflicts between the practices of individuals and collectivities in pursuit of opposing class interests. These conflicts range from the strategies of individual workers within the labor process to reduce their level of toil, to conflicts between highly organized collectivities of workers and capitalists over the distribution of rights and powers within production.

The explanatory claims: the fundamental metathesis of class analysis

The fundamental metathesis of class analysis is that class (i.e. class relations, class locations, and class structure), understood in the above way, has systematic and significant consequences both for the lives of individuals and for the dynamics of institutions. One might say "class counts" as a slogan. At the micro-level, whether or not one sells one's labor power on a labor market, whether or not one has the power to tell other people what to do in the labor process, whether or not one owns large amounts of capital, whether or not one possesses a legally certified valuable credential, etc. have real consequences in the lives of people. At the macro-level it is consequential for the functioning of a variety of institutions whether or not the rights over the allocation and use of means of production are highly concentrated in the hands of a few people, whether or not certain of these rights have been appropriated by public authority or remain privately controlled, whether or not there are significant barriers to the acquisition of different kinds of assets by people who lack them, and so on. To say that "class counts," then, is to claim that the distribution of rights and powers over the basic productive resources of a society have significant, systematic consequences at both the micro- and macro-levels of social analysis.

At the core of these kinds of claims is a relatively simple pair of more specific propositions about the effects of class relations at the micro-level of individual lives:

> *Proposition 1.*   What you *have* determines what you *get*.
> *Proposition 2.*   What you *have* determines what you *have to do to get*
> *what you get.*

The first of these concerns, above all, the distribution of *income*. The class analysis claim is, therefore, that the rights and powers people have over productive assets are a systematic and significant determinant of their standards of living: *what you have determines what you get*. The second of these causal processes concerns, above all, the distribution of economic *activities*. Again, the class analysis thesis is that the rights and powers over productive assets are a systematic and significant determinant of the strategies and practices people engage in to acquire their income: whether they have to pound the pavement looking for a job; whether they make decisions about the allocation of investments around the world; whether they have to worry about making payments on bank loans to keep a farm afloat. *What you have determines what you have to do to get what you get.* Other kinds of consequences that are linked to class – voting patterns, attitudes, friendship formation, health, etc. – are second-order effects of these two primary processes. When class analysts argue, for example, that class locations help explain voting, this is usually because they believe that class locations shape the opportunities for standards of living of people and these opportunities affect political preferences, or because they believe class location affects the lived experience of people within work (i.e. the experiences generated by the activities of work) and these in turn affect preferences.

These are not trivial claims. It could be the case, for example, that the distribution of the rights and powers of individuals over productive resources has relatively little to do with their income or economic activities. Suppose that the welfare state provided a universal basic income to everyone sufficient to sustain a decent standard of living. In such a society what people get would be significantly, although not entirely, decoupled from what they own. Similarly, if the world became like a continual lottery in which there was virtually no stability either within or across generations to the distribution of assets, then even if it were still the case that relations to such assets *statically* mattered for income, it might make sense to say that class didn't matter very much. Or, suppose that the central determinant of what you have to do to get what you get was race or sex or religion and that ownership of economically relevant assets was of marginal significance in explaining anyone's economic activities or conditions. Again, in such a society, class might not be very explanatory (unless, of course, the main way in which gender or race affected these outcomes was by allocating people to class positions on the basis of their race and gender). The sheer fact of inequalities of income or of domination and subordination within work is not proof that class counts; what has to be shown is that the rights and powers of people over productive assets has a systematic bearing on these phenomena.

Marxist class analysis[20]

As formulated above, there is nothing uniquely Marxist about the explanatory claims of class analysis. "What people get" and "what people have to do to get what they get" sound very much like "life chances." Weberian class analysts would say very much the same thing. It is for this reason that there is a close affinity between Marxist and Weberian concepts of class (although less affinity in the broader theoretical frameworks within which these concepts figure or in the explanatory reach class is thought to have).

What makes class analysis distinctively Marxist is the account of specific mechanisms that are seen as generating these two kinds of consequences. Here the pivotal concept is *exploitation*. This is the conceptual element that anchors the Marxist concept of class in the distinctive Marxist agenda of class analysis.

Exploitation is a complex and challenging concept. It is meant to designate a particular form of interdependence of the material interests of people, namely a situation that satisfies three criteria:

(1) *The inverse interdependent welfare principle*: The material welfare of exploiters causally depends upon the material deprivations of the exploited. This means that the interests of actors within such relations are not merely *different*, they are *antagonistic*: the realization of the interests of exploiters imposes harms on the exploited.

(2) *The exclusion principle*: This inverse interdependence of the welfare of exploiters and exploited depends upon the exclusion of the exploited from access to certain productive resources.

(3) *The appropriation principle*: Exclusion generates material advantage to exploiters because it enables them to appropriate the labor effort of the exploited.

Exploitation is thus a diagnosis of the process through which the inequalities in incomes are generated by inequalities in rights and powers over productive resources: the inequalities occur, in part at least, through the

---

[20] Parts of this section are drawn from Wright (1997, pp. 9–19).

ways in which exploiters, by virtue of their exclusionary rights and powers over resources, are able to appropriate surplus generated by the effort of the exploited.

If the first two of these principles are present, but not the third, what might be termed *nonexploitative economic oppression* may exist, but not exploitation. In nonexploitative economic oppression, it is still true that the welfare of the advantaged group is at the expense of the disadvantaged, and this inverse relationship is itself based on the ownership and control over economic resources. But in nonexploitative oppression there is no appropriation of labor effort, no transfer of the fruits of labor from one group to another.

The crucial implication of this difference between these two types of inequality is that in nonexploitative economic oppression the privileged social category does not itself *need* the excluded category. While their welfare does depend upon the exclusion principle, there is no ongoing interdependence of their activities. In the case of exploitation, the exploiters actively need the exploited: exploiters depend upon the effort of the exploited for their own welfare. Consider, for example, the contrast between the treatment of indigenous people by European settlers in North America and in Southern Africa. In both places the material welfare of the white settlers was secured through a process of exclusion of the indigenous people from access to the land. The welfare of the settlers was therefore causally linked to the deprivations of the indigenous people, and this causal link centered on control of resources. The two cases differ sharply, however, on the third criterion. In South Africa white settlers depended significantly on the labor effort of indigenous people, first as tenant farmers and farm laborers and later as mineworkers. In North America the European settlers did not rely on the labor of Native Americans. This meant that in North America when resistance by Native Americans to their dispossession from the land was encountered by white settlers, a strategy of genocide could be pursued. There is an abhorrent American folk expression, popular in the nineteenth century, which reflects this reality of the nonexploitative economic oppression of Native Americans: "the only good Indian is a dead Indian." It is no accident that there is no expression of the form "the only good worker is a dead worker." One might say "the only good worker is an obedient worker or a conscientious worker," but not "a dead worker." Exploitation, in a sense, imposes constraints on the exploiter, and this is captured in the contrast between the fate of indigenous people in North America and Southern Africa.[21]

---

[21] One of the pivotal differences between the conception of exploitation offered here and that in Aage Sørensen's strategy of class analysis (Chapter 5 in this volume) centers on the

This deep interdependence makes exploitation a particularly explosive form of social relation for two reasons: First, exploitation constitutes a social relation which simultaneously pits the interests of one group against another and which requires their ongoing interactions; and second, it confers upon the disadvantaged group a real form of power with which to challenge the interests of exploiters. This is an important point. Exploitation depends upon the appropriation of labor effort. Because human beings are conscious agents, not robots, they always retain significant levels of real control over their expenditure of effort. The extraction of effort within exploitative relations is thus always to a greater or lesser extent problematic and precarious, requiring active institutional devices for its reproduction. Such devices can become quite costly to exploiters in the form of the costs of supervision, surveillance, sanctions, etc. The ability to impose such costs constitutes a form of power among the exploited.

Exploitation, as defined here, is intimately linked to the problem of *domination*, that is, the social relations within which one person's activities are directed and controlled by another. Domination occurs, first, in the exclusion principle: "owning" a resource gives one power to prevent other people from using it. The power exercised by employers to hire and fire workers is the clearest example of this form of domination. But domination also occurs, in most instances, in conjunction with the appropriation principle, since the appropriation of the labor effort of the exploited usually requires direct forms of subordination, especially within the labor process, in the form of bossing, surveillance, threats, etc. Together exploitation coupled with domination defines the central features of the structured interactions within class relations.

In Weberian class analysis, just as much as in Marxist class analysis, the rights and powers individuals have over productive assets define the material basis of class relations. But for Weberian-inspired class analysis, these rights and powers are consequential primarily because of the ways they shape *life chances*, most notably life chances within market exchanges, rather than the ways they structure patterns of exploitation and domination. Control over resources affects bargaining capacity within processes

distinction between nonexploitative oppression and exploitative oppression. Sørensen rejects this distinction arguing with respect to my analysis of European settlers in North America that "the European settlers clearly created antagonistic interests that brought about conflict, so it is not clear what is added by the requirement of transfer of the fruits of labor." The appropriation principle would not matter if all we are concerned with is the sheer presence or absence of "antagonistic interests," for in both exploitative and nonexploitative oppression there is surely deep antagonism. But the dynamic of antagonism is quite different in the two contexts: *exploiters depend upon and need the exploited* in a way that is not true for nonexploitative oppressors. Sørensen's treatment of exploitation does not distinguish between a situation in which an exclusion from access to resources simply imposes a harm on the excluded and a situation in which the welfare of the advantaged category also depends upon ongoing interactions with the excluded.

I. Simple Gradational Class Analysis

II. Weberian Class Analysis

III. Marxist Class Analysis

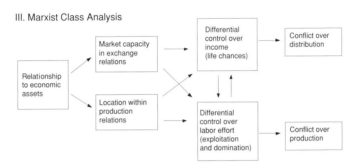

Figure 1.1 Three models of class analysis

of exchange and this in turn affects the results of such exchanges, especially income. Exploitation and domination are not centerpieces of this argument.

This suggests the contrast between Marxist and Weberian frameworks of class analysis illustrated in figure 1.1. Both Marxist and Weberian class analysis differ sharply from simple gradational accounts of class in which class is itself directly identified within inequalities in income, since both begin with the problem of the social relations that determine the access of people to economic resources. In a sense, therefore, Marxist and Weberian definitions of class relations in capitalist society share the same basic operational criteria. Where they differ is in the theoretical elaboration and specification of the implications of this common set of criteria: the Marxist model sees two causal paths being systematically generated by these relations – one operating through market exchanges and the other through the process of production itself – whereas the Weberian model traces only one causal path; and the Marxist model elaborates the mechanisms of these causal path; in terms of exploitation and domination as well as bargaining capacity within exchange, whereas the Weberian model only deals with the bargaining within exchange. In a sense, then, the Weberian strategy of class analysis is nested within the Marxist model.

This nesting of the Weberian concept of class within the Marxist means that for certain kinds of questions there will be little practical difference between Marxist and Weberian analyses. This is especially the case for micro-questions about the impact of class on the lives of individuals. Thus, for example, if one wants to explain how class location affects standards of living of people, there is no particular reason for the concept of class location used in the analysis to differ within a Marxist or a Weberian approach. Both treat the social relationship to income-generating assets, especially capital and skills, as central to the definition of class locations.[22]

Of course, any Weberian can include an analysis of class-based domination and exploitation within any specific sociological inquiry. One of the attractions of the Weberian analytical framework is that it is entirely permissive about the inclusion of additional causal processes. Such an inclusion, however, represents the importation of Marxist themes into the Weberian model; the model itself does not imply any particular importance to these issues. Frank Parkin once made a well-known quip in a book about class theory that "Inside every neo-Marxist is a Weberian struggling to get out." The argument presented here suggests a complementary proposition, that "Inside every leftist neo-Weberian is a Marxist struggling to stay hidden."

---

[22] Of course, the operational criteria adopted may differ between any two scholars faced with the inevitable difficulties of making pragmatic choices. For example, in both John Goldthorpe's approach to class analysis and my own, large capitalists, corporate executives, and "high-grade" professionals occupy distinct kinds of locations within class relations because they differ in the kinds of resources they control and the nature of the employment relations in which they are located. But we differ in our operational choices about how to treat these categories in our empirical work: whereas I keep these three categories separate as distinct kinds of class locations, Goldthorpe merges them into a more heterogeneous class I for largely pragmatic reasons. This is not fundamentally because my work is rooted in the Marxist tradition and his has a closer link to the Weberian tradition, since both traditions regard professors and capitalists as occupying different class locations. It is because of a pragmatic judgment about where it is important to maintain close operational congruence with abstract categories and where it is not. For the questions Goldthorpe wishes to address he feels that since there are so few proper capitalists in his samples anyway, nothing much is lost by merging them with professionals into a single class category.

The pay-off: what are the advantages of the Marxist strategy of class analysis?

Exploitation and domination are both normatively loaded terms. To describe class relations this way is to affirm the egalitarian critique of those relations. For someone committed to the radical egalitarian vision of the Marxist tradition, this is an attraction, but of course not everyone who is interested in the study of class in capitalist society accepts the radical egalitarianism of the Marxist normative agenda. What if one believes that emancipatory transformations of capitalism, however morally attractive, are utopian fantasies? Or even more critically, what if one believes that capitalism isn't especially oppressive? If one rejects the relevance of the Marxist normative agenda, does this necessarily imply a complete rejection of the Marxist conceptualization of class as well? I think not. There are a number of reasons that elaborating the concept of class in terms of exploitation and domination has theoretical pay-offs beyond the specific normative agenda of Marxist class analysis itself:

1. *Linking exchange and production.* The Marxist logic of class analysis affirms the intimate link between the way in which social relations are organized within exchange and within production. This is a substantive, not definitional, point: the social relations which organize the rights and powers of individuals with respect to productive resources systematically shape their location both within exchange relations and within the process of production itself. This does not mean, of course, that there is no independent variation of exchange and production, but it does imply that this variation is structured by class relations.

2. *Conflict.* One of the standard claims about Marxist class analysis that it foregrounds conflict within class relations. Indeed, a conventional way of describing Marxism in sociological textbooks is to see it as a variety of "conflict theory." This characterization, however, is not quite precise enough, for conflict is certainly a prominent feature of Weberian views of class as well. The distinctive feature of the Marxist account of class relations in these terms is not simply that it gives prominence to class conflict, but that it understands conflict as generated by *inherent properties of those relations* rather than simply contingent factors. Exploitation defines a structure of inter-dependent antagonistic interests in which advancing the interests of exploiters depends upon their capacity to impose harms on the exploited. This is a stronger antagonism of interests than simple competition, and it underwrites a strong prediction within Marxist class analysis that class systems will be conflict ridden.

3. *Power.* At the very core of the Marxist construction of class analysis is
not simply the claim that class relations generate deeply antagonistic
interests, but that they also give people in subordinate class locations
forms of power with which to struggle for their interests. As already
noted, since exploitation rests on the extraction of labor effort, and
since people always retain some measure of control over their own
effort, they always confront their exploiters with capacities to resist
exploitation.[23] This is a crucial form of power. It is reflected in the complex counter-strategies exploiting classes are forced to adopt through
the elaboration of instruments of supervision, surveillance, monitoring, and sanctioning. It is only by virtue of this inherent capacity for
resistance – a form of social power rooted in the inter-dependencies
of exploitation – that exploiting classes are forced to devote some of
their resources to insure their ability to appropriate labor effort.

4. *Coercion and consent.* Marxist class analysis contains the rudiments of
what might be termed an endogenous theory of the formation of consent. The argument is basically this: The extraction of labor effort
in systems of exploitation is costly for exploiting classes because of
the inherent capacity of people to resist their own exploitation. Purely
coercively backed systems of exploitation will often tend to be subopti-
mal since under many conditions it is too easy for workers to withhold
diligent performance of labor effort. Exploiting classes will therefore
have a tendency to seek ways of reducing those costs. One of the ways
of reducing the overhead costs of extracting labor effort is to do things
that elicit the active consent of the exploited. These range from the
development of internal labor markets which strengthen the identification and loyalty of workers to the firms in which they work to
the support for ideological positions which proclaim the practical and
moral desirability of capitalist institutions. Such consent-producing
practices, however, also have costs attached to them, and thus systems
of exploitation can be seen as always involving trade-offs between coercion and consent as mechanisms for extracting labor effort.

This argument implies a specific prediction about the kinds of ideologies that are likely to emerge under conditions of exploitative class
relations and conditions of nonexploitative oppression. In nonexploitative oppression, there is no dependency of the oppressing group on the
extraction of labor effort of the oppressed and thus much less need to

---

[23] It is important to note that one need not accept the normative implications of the concept
of "exploitation" to recognize the problem of the "extraction of labor effort." This is one
of the central themes in discussions of principal/agent problems in transaction costs
approaches to organization. For a discussion of class and exploitation specifically in
terms of p/a issues, see Bowles and Gintis (1990).

elicit their active consent. Purely repressive reactions to resistance – including in some historical situations genocidal repression – are therefore feasible. The central ideological problem in such a situation is likely to be the moral qualms within the oppressive group, and thus ideologies are likely to develop to justify this repression *to the oppressors*, but not to the oppressed. The slogan "the only good Indian is a dead Indian" was meant for the ears of white settlers, not Native Americans. Within exploitative class relations, on the other hand, since the cooperation of the exploited is needed, ideologies are more likely to attend to the problem of creating consent, and this puts pressure on ideologies to incorporate in one way or another the interests of the exploited group.

5. *Historical/comparative analysis*. As originally conceived, Marxist class analysis was an integral part of a sweeping theory of the epochal structure and historical trajectory of social change. But even if one rejects historical materialism, the Marxist exploitation-centered strategy of class analysis still provides a rich menu of concepts for historical and comparative analysis. Different kinds of class relations are defined by the specific mechanisms through which exploitation is accomplished, and these differences in turn imply different problems faced by exploiting classes for the reproduction of their class advantage and different opportunities for exploited classes to resist. Variations in these mechanisms and in the specific ways in which they are combined in concrete societies provide an analytically powerful road map for comparative research.

These are all reasons why a concept of class rooted in the linkage between social relations of production on the one hand and exploitation and domination on the other should be of sociological interest. Still, the most fundamental pay-off of these conceptual foundations is that way it infuses class analysis with moral critique. The characterization of the mechanisms underlying class relations in terms of exploitation and domination focuses attention on the moral implications of class analysis. Exploitation and domination identify ways in which these relations are oppressive and create harms, not simply inequalities. Class analysis can thus function not simply as part of a scientific theory of interests and conflicts, but of an emancipatory theory of alternatives and social justice as well. Even if socialism is off the historical agenda, the idea of countering the exploitative logic of capitalism is not.

2 Foundations of a neo-Weberian class analysis

Richard Breen

Introduction

In the broad project of "class analysis" a great deal of effort goes into defining class and delineating the boundaries of classes. This is necessarily so, because class analysis is "the empirical investigation of the consequences and corollaries of the existence of a class structure defined *ex-ante*" (Breen and Rottman 1995b, p. 453). By starting from a particular definition, sociologists can assess the extent to which such things as inequality in life chances among individuals and families are structured on the basis of class. This approach stands in contrast to one that discovers a class structure from the empirical distribution of inequality in society (Sørensen 2000 labels this the "nominal classifications" approach). In class analysis the theoretical underpinnings of the version of class that is being used have to be made clear at the outset, and the concept of class has to be operationalized so as to allow claims about class to be tested empirically. If we examine the two main varieties of contemporary class analysis – namely Marxist class analysis, particularly associated with the work of Erik Olin Wright and his associates, and the neo-Weberian class analysis linked to the use of the class schema devised by John Goldthorpe – we find that these two tasks are central to both.

In this chapter I will discuss some of the issues involved in seeking to pursue class analysis within a broadly Weberian perspective. I begin by outlining Weber's own views on social class, as these are presented in *Economy and Society*. This serves to set out the broad parameters within which Weberian class analysis operates and to suggest the extent and limits of its explanatory ambitions. I go on to discuss, in very general terms, what sort of operationalization of class is suggested by the work of Weber and then to outline the Goldthorpe class schema, which is widely held to be Weberian in conception (for example, Marshall *et al.* 1988, p. 14). The chapter concludes with a discussion of some of what I see as the fundamental objections to a neo-Weberian approach to class analysis and with some clarifications about exactly what we might expect a neo-Weberian class classification to explain.

Social class in the work of Max Weber

In capitalism the market is the major determinant of life chances. Life chances can be understood as, in Giddens's terms, "the chances an individual has for sharing in the socially created economic or cultural 'goods' that typically exist in any given society" (1973, pp. 130–1) or, more simply, as the chances that individuals have of gaining access to scarce and valued outcomes. Weber (1978 [1922], p. 302) writes that "a class situation is one in which there is a shared typical probability of procuring goods, gaining a position in life, and finding inner satisfaction": in other words, members of a class share common life chances. If this is what members of a class have in common, what puts them in this common position? Weber's answer is that the market distributes life chances according to the resources that individuals bring to it, and he recognizes that these resources could vary in a number of ways. Aside from the distinction between property owners and nonowners, there is also variation according to particular skills and other assets. The important point, however, is that all these assets only have value in the context of a market: hence, class situation is identified with market situation.

One consequence of Weber's recognition of the diversity of assets that engender returns in the market is a proliferation of possible classes, which he calls "economic classes." Social classes, however, are much smaller in number, being aggregations of economic classes. They are formed not simply on the basis of the workings of the market: other factors intervene, and the one singled out by Weber for particular attention is social mobility. "A social class makes up the totality of class positions within which individual and inter-generational mobility is easy and typical" (Weber 1978 [1922], p. 302). Weber suggests that, as a matter of empirical fact, four major social classes can be identified under capitalism, between which social mobility is infrequent and difficult but within which it is relatively common. The first distinction is between those who own property or the means of production, and those who do not, but both groups are "further differentiated . . . according to the kind of property . . . and the kind of services that can be offered in the market" (Weber 1978 [1922], p. 928). The resulting four classes are the "dominant entrepreneurial and propertied groups"; the petty bourgeoisie; workers with formal credentials (the middle class) and those who lack them and whose only asset is their labor power (the working class).

It is well known that Weber saw class as only one aspect of the distribution of power in society. In a famous definition, power is "the probability that one actor within a social relationship will be in a position to carry out his own will despite resistance, regardless of the basis on which this probability rests" (Weber 1978 [1922], p. 53), and status groups and parties, along with classes, are, for Weber, the major phenomena of the distribution of power in society. The distinction between them concerns the different resources that each can bring to influence the distribution of life chances. While membership of each will overlap, none of these dimensions can be wholly reduced to the other. Each of them can be a basis for collective action, but, according to Weber, status groups and parties are more likely to fulfil this role than are classes. For parties, collective action is their *raison d'être*, while membership of a status group is more likely to figure in individuals' consciousness, and thus act as a basis for collective action, than is membership of a class. Whether or not members of a class display "class consciousness" depends on certain contingent factors: it is "linked to general cultural conditions . . . and especially linked to the transparency of the connections between the causes and the consequences of the class situation" (Weber 1978 [1922], pp. 928–32). Different life chances, associated with social class membership, do not themselves give birth to "class action": it is only when the "real conditions and the results of the class situation" are recognized that this can occur.

This review of Weber's writings on social class serves, not least, to establish some limits to the ambitions of a Weberian class analysis. Perhaps most importantly there is no assumption that patterns of historical change can be explained in terms of the evolution of the relationship between classes, as is the case with Marxist historical materialism. Nor is there any supposition that classes are necessarily in a zero-sum conflict in which the benefits to one come at the (illegitimate) expense of the other. Indeed, there is no assumption in Weber that class will be the major source of conflict within capitalist society or that classes will necessarily serve as a source of collective action. Rather, the focus is on the market as the source of inequalities in life chances. But this is not to say that a Weberian approach takes market arrangements as given. Weber writes that markets are themselves forms of social action which depend, for their existence, on other sorts of social action, such as a certain kind of legal order (Weber 1978 [1922], p. 930). But in understanding how market arrangements come to be the way they are, one cannot simply focus on classes and the relationships between them. The evolution of social forms is a complex process that can be driven by a wide variety of factors, as Weber himself illustrates in *The Protestant Ethic and the Spirit of Capitalism*, where ideas are allotted a central role in the development of modern capitalism.

Weber's comments on class are rather fragmentary: there is, for example, very little in his work addressing questions of class conflict.[1] This being so, it may, on occasion, seem easier to define a Weberian approach by what it is not, rather than what it is, and almost any class schema that is not avowedly Marxist could be considered Weberian. Indeed, the boundaries between the Marxist and Weberian versions are themselves often rather less than sharp. But, as I hope to show, there is a distinctive element to a Weberian class schema, and this determines both how we should go about constructing it and how we should evaluate its performance as an explanatory factor in class analyses. But I see no virtue in seeking to follow Weber's writings "to the letter" (even supposing that it were possible to do so), and the approach I outline here, which I call neo-Weberian, may not be the only one to which Weber's own rather unsystematic remarks on class could give rise.

The aims of class analysis

Understood as a general project, class analysis sees class as having the potential to explain a wide range of outcomes. A principal aim, of course, is to examine the relationship between class position and life chances, but class analysis is seldom restricted to this. Class is commonly held to have various possible consequences. Because a set of individuals shares a common class position they tend to behave in similar ways: class position is a determinant of the individual's conditions of action and similar actions could be expected among those who have similar conditions of action (see Weber 1978 [1922], p. 929). But this might be distinguished from class-conscious behavior. This can occur when, as Weber says, individuals become aware of "the connections between the causes and the consequences of the class situation."

In principle, then, not just variation in life chances but in a whole range of action, behavior, attitudes, values, and so forth can be taken as objects that class might help to explain. But the link between classes and their consequences cannot simply be an empirical matter: there must be some theory or argument for why classes, defined in a given way, are salient for

---

[1] See Weber (1978 [1922], pp. 302–5). The development of neo-Weberian ideas of "class closure" and of exclusion and usurpation, associated with the work of Parkin (1979) and Murphy (1988), draws much more on Weber's discussion of status groups rather than classes. He writes that "not much of a general nature can be said about the more specific kinds of antagonism between classes" (1978 [1922], p. 930) – which I take to mean that, although there are conflicts between classes, these do not follow a general form but are, instead, conditioned by specific historical circumstances.

the explanation of these outcomes, and, in particular, for the explanation of variation in life chances. This is a point we shall revisit in this chapter. But now I turn to the question of how Weber's ideas on social class might be operationalized.

The development of a Weberian class schema

To a Weberian, class is of interest because it links individuals' positions in capitalist markets to inequality in the distribution of life chances. As we have seen, variations in market position arise on the basis of differences in the possession of market-relevant assets. One possible approach to constructing a Weber-inspired class schema might be to group together individuals possessing the same or similar assets. After all, Weber defines "class situation" as the sharing of a "specific causal component of . . . life chances" (1978 [1922], p. 927) and it might therefore seem reasonable to define classes in terms of such causal components of life chances. In this sense, the explanatory variables in a neoclassical earnings function would serve to delineate at least some classes.

In fact, such an approach to the study of class in not usually adopted – because what is important is not the possession of assets *per se* but their implementation in the market. For many reasons there is not a deterministic relationship between the resources that individuals bring to the market and what they receive in return. So the focus shifts to market situation and to identifying a set of structural positions that can be grouped together as classes. As Sørensen (1991, p. 72) puts it, classes are "sets of structural positions. Social relationships within markets, especially within labor markets, and within firms define these positions. Class positions exist independently of individual occupants of these positions. They are 'empty places.'" The question for all forms of class analysis is how – on what basis – we should distinguish these positions.

One way of approaching this question would be to start by asking what it is that class is meant to explain. If the primary purpose of a class schema is to capture how social relationships within markets and firms shape life chances, then classes could be defined so as to maximize the statistical association between them and the distribution of life chances. Such an approach might be seen as being half-way between purely inductive ("nominal" in Sørensen's term) class classifications and the approach more usually adopted in class analysis. I am not aware of any class schema that follows this practice, but something similar has been suggested as a method for constructing social distance or social dominance scales (Prandy 1999, Rytina 2000). Alternatively, the principle on which classes are defined could be viewed as a theory about how relationships in markets and firms are linked to the distribution of life chances. In either case, the boundaries that we draw to categorize positions in firms and labor markets should have a claim to being the classification that best captures the distinctions that are relevant to explain variation, in this case, in life chances. But this raises the possibility that if our purpose is to capture how position in the system of production influences, let us say, voting behavior, or some types of collective action, then a quite different principle might be appropriate.

The single defining characteristic of Weber-inspired class analysis is that classes are of interest insofar as they shape life chances, and so the latter strategy is the one that is followed in constructing a neo-Weberian schema. However, as an empirical fact, it emerges that such schemata do often prove to be good predictors of a wide range of behaviors, actions, attitudes, preferences, and so forth. Class analysis should therefore explain not only why certain distinctions of position within labor markets and firms lead to differences in life chances, but also why a categorization of positions developed for this purpose explains variations in a range of different outcomes. But before taking this issue any further, it may be useful to put the discussion on a more concrete basis by examining a class schema that is usually held to be neo-Weberian.

The Goldthorpe class schema

The class schema developed by John Goldthorpe and his associates (Goldthorpe 1980; Erikson, Goldthorpe, and Portocarero 1979; Erikson and Goldthorpe 1992) has been extensively used in empirical class analysis during the past twenty years.[2] Initially, the schema was presented as distinguishing occupations on the basis of their market and work situations. Market situation refers to an occupation's sources and levels of income, its associated conditions of employment, degree of economic security, and chances, for its holders, of economic advancement. Work situation refers to an occupation's location within systems of authority and control in the production process (Goldthorpe 1980, p. 40). Occupations that typically share common market and work situations were held to constitute classes and occupants of different classes were held to enjoy different life chances.

In his later work, however, Goldthorpe has provided a slightly different set of principles on which the same class schema is based. "The aim of the class schema is to differentiate positions within labor markets and

---

[2] There are very many descriptions of the Goldthorpe schema, but the clearest and most detailed is to be found in Erikson and Goldthorpe (1992, Ch. 2), while Goldthorpe (2000, Ch. 10) provides an extended discussion of the schema's rationale.

production units or, more specifically ... to differentiate such positions in terms of the employment relations that they entail" (Erikson and Goldthorpe 1992, p. 37). Now classes are held to capture two main distinctions: between those who own the means of production and those who do not, and, among the latter, according to the nature of their relationship with their employer. The important dichotomy here is between positions that are regulated under a labor contract, and those that are regulated by a "service" relationship with the employer. Under a labor contract there is a very specific exchange of wages for effort and the worker is relatively closely supervised, while the service relationship is more long-term and involves a more diffuse exchange.

The basis for this distinction is the problem that employers face of ensuring that their employees act in the best interests of the firm. Employees always have at least some discretion about how they carry out their job – how hard they work, what degree of responsibility or initiative they exercise and so on (Goldthorpe 2000, p. 212) – and so the issue for the employer is to ensure that this discretion is exercised in the service of the employer. How this is done depends on the type of work that the employee undertakes, and thus the solution to the problem is the establishment of employment contracts tailored to different kinds of work.

The crucial dimensions along which work is differentiated are, according to Goldthorpe, the degree of "asset-specificity" involved and the extent of monitoring difficulty (Goldthorpe 2000, p. 213). Asset-specificity refers to the extent to which a job calls for job-specific skills, expertise, or knowledge, in contrast to jobs that require general, non-specific skills. In the former case, an employee has to be persuaded to invest in these skills, despite the fact that they may be of no value to her in another firm or occupation. But equally, once an employee has gained these skills, the employer needs to ensure, as far as possible, that the skilled employee is retained, since these skills cannot be bought on the open labor market. Monitoring difficulties arise when the employer cannot, with any reasonable degree of clarity, assess the extent to which the employee is acting in the employer's interests. This is the classical "principal/agent problem." In certain jobs the employee has appreciable autonomy and discretion about exactly how to carry out the tasks that the job calls for, and thus, while the employee (the agent) knows whether he or she is working in the interests of the firm, the employer (the principal) does not. This informational asymmetry establishes an incentive for the agent to act in her interests when these conflict with the interests of the principal.

Problems of asset-specificity and monitoring are countered by setting up, through the service relationship, incentives to persuade employees to act in the employer's interest. These incentives must align the interests of the two parties, and this is done by establishing a link "between employees' commitment to and effective pursuit of organizational goals and their career success and lifetime material well-being" (Goldthorpe 2000, p. 220). To secure this, prospective elements in the employment contract play a major role: "for example, salary increments on an established scale, assurances of security...pension rights...and...well defined career opportunities" (Erikson and Goldthorpe 1992, p. 42). As far as monitoring difficulties are concerned this solution is one which is familiar in the game theory literature: the temptation to defect and gather a short-term gain is offset by the prospect of extended and long-term pay-offs as a reward for cooperation.

The labor contract is found where neither asset-specificity nor monitoring problems occur. In this case, even if the work tasks require skills, these will be general and readily available in the labor market. Monitoring problems are largely absent because what the employee does in the service of the employer and what he or she actually produces is readily observable. There is then no need for the kinds of incentives established in the service relationship, and, according to Goldthorpe, the two defining characteristics of the labor contract are payment for discrete amounts of work and the absence of any attempts to secure a long-term relationship between the parties.

What does the resulting class schema look like? There is one class of the self-employed and small employees (petty bourgeoisie), labeled class IV (the classification uses Roman numerals). This is subdivided first on a sectoral basis, so that IVc comprises farmers and "other self-employed workers in primary production," and secondly between non-agricultural employers and the self-employed: IVa comprises small proprietors with employees,[3] IVb those without employees. The remaining classes are comprised of employee positions, and thus the shape of this part of the class structure depends on which occupations are characterized by one, both or neither of asset-specificity and monitoring difficulties. Classes I and II are made up of those occupations that most clearly have a service relationship: the distinction between them is a matter of degree. So class I comprises higher-grade, and class II lower-grade, professionals, administrative and managerial workers. In these occupations problems arise of both monitoring and asset-specificity. At the other extreme, members of classes VI (skilled manual workers) and VII (unskilled manual workers) most clearly have a labor contract with their employer. Class VII is itself also divided sectorally: VIIb is non-skilled agricultural workers, VIIa is non-skilled workers outside agriculture. The labor contract is also shared by workers in what are termed "lower-grade," routine nonmanual

---

[3] When applied to the United Kingdom this means less than twenty-five employees.

occupations (Class IIIb). These occupations include "the lowest grades of employment in offices, shops, and other service outlets – machine operators, counter staff, attendants, etc" (Erikson and Goldthorpe 1992, p. 241). The remaining classes, IIIa (higher-grade routine nonmanual occupations) and V (lower technical and manual supervisory occupations), "comprise positions with associated employment relationships that would appear characteristically to take on a very mixed form" (Erikson and Goldthorpe 1992, p. 43). But this mixed form occurs for different reasons in each case. The occupations in IIIa (typically clerks, secretaries, and other routine administrative personnel) typically require no asset-specificity but do present some difficulties of monitoring, while those in class V have the opposite combination. Class IIIa occupations enjoy many elements of the service relationship but often lack any clear career structure, while class V occupations enjoy such a career structure but are relatively closely monitored and paid according to the number of hours they work. The possible combinations of asset-specificity and monitoring difficulties and the classes characterized by each are shown in figure 2.1, taken from Goldthorpe (2000, p. 223). In developing this account, Goldthorpe has drawn heavily on literature in organizational economics and, indeed, there are many similarities between the "efficiency wage" (Akerlof 1982) and the service contract. Employment contracts are viewed as a means by which the parties try to ensure the viability of the enterprise and to increase the total value of the contract to the benefit of both (Goldthorpe 2000, p. 210). One criticism that might be made of this approach is that it gives too much weight to efficiency arguments and neglects questions concerning the balance of power between employers and employees. Put in the form of a simple example, a particular occupation or group of occupations might enjoy some elements of the service relationship not because this maximizes efficiency, but because the bargaining strength of the workers allows them to capture these elements in the form of a rent. It seems quite plausible to suggest that changes over the past twenty years in the terms and conditions of employment governing many jobs – and, in some cases, the loss of some aspects of the service relationship – is attributable to the generally weaker bargaining position of workers vis-à-vis employers as much as it is to, say, changes in the skill requirements of these jobs or in the possibilities of monitoring them (Breen 1997). If these arguments are correct, they suggest that the class allocation of an occupation does not follow quite so unproblematically from a consideration of efficiency and that, in explaining any particular class structure, attention also needs to be paid to other, historically contingent factors.

In its most disaggregated form the Goldthorpe schema identifies eleven classes. In Goldthorpe's work on England and Wales, and in many

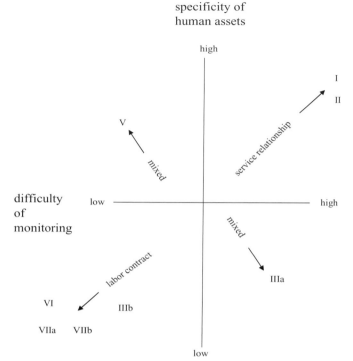

Figure 2.1 Dimensions of work as sources of contractual hazard, forms of employment contract, and location of employee classes of the schema (from Goldthorpe 2000, p. 223, figure 10.2)

other applications, a seven-category version is employed, while the most aggregated version that nevertheless would seem to preserve the essential distinctions of the schema is probably a four-category classification of the service (I and II), intermediate (IIIa and V), petty-bourgeois (IV), and labor contract (IIIb, VI, and VII) classes. These various aggregations of the schema are shown in Table 2.1.[4] What is strikingly absent from the schema is a class of large employers – the haute bourgeoisie. Nowadays

---

[4] It may seem strange that the seven-category version of the schema puts classes IIIa and IIIb together. However, this version was initially used by Goldthorpe in his analysis of social mobility among men in England and Wales. The version used later by Erikson and Goldthorpe, although it differed slightly from the seven categories shown in Table 2.1, also amalgamated IIIa and IIIb, but, once again, this was developed for the analysis of men's mobility. Relatively few men occupy positions in IIIb, and those positions that are occupied by men are typically closer to those in IIIa than are the positions occupied by women. Thus in their chapter analyzing women's mobility, Erikson and Goldthorpe (1992, Ch. 7) place class IIIb together with class VII.

Table 2.1 *Possible aggregations of the Goldthorpe class schema*

Eleven-class (maximally disaggregated) version	Seven-class version	Four-class version
I Upper service class	**I** Upper service class	**I + II** Service class
II Lower service class	**II** Lower service class	
IIIa Routine nonmanual employees, higher grade	**III** Routine nonmanual	**IIIa + V** Intermediate class
IIIb Routine nonmanual employees, lower grade		**IIIb + VI + VII** Manual class
IVa Small proprietors with employees	**IV** Petty bourgeoisie	**IV** Petty bourgeoisie
IVb Small proprietors without employees		
IVc Farmers and other self-employed workers in primary production		
V Lower-grade technicians and supervisors of manual workers	**V** Technicians and supervisors	**IIIa + V** Intermediate class
VI Skilled manual workers	**VI** Skilled manual	**IIIb + VI + VII** Manual class
VIIa Semi- and unskilled manual workers (not in agriculture)	**VII** Nonskilled manual	
VIIb Semi- and unskilled manual workers in agriculture		

large employers tend to be organizations rather than individuals, but those individual large employers that exist are placed in class I. Erikson and Goldthorpe (1992, pp. 40–1) justify this practice on two grounds. First, such individuals are usually owners of enterprises that differ from those of the petty bourgeoisie in legal rather than substantive terms. They are placed in class I rather than IV because "in so far as such large proprietors tend to be quite extensively involved in managerial as well as entrepreneurial activities, they may be regarded as having a yet greater affinity with those salaried managers to be found in class I who have a substantial share in the ownership of the enterprises in which they work." But this argument is rather unconvincing for the simple reason that large proprietors do not have the service relationship with an employer that defines this class. On this basis they might better be placed in class IV. Secondly, large proprietors or employers account for "around 5 per cent of all men allocated to the service class (i.e. Classes I and II) in Western industrial societies, and cannot...be realistically seen as members of a capitalist elite...Rather, they turn out on examination to be most typically the owners of stores, hotels, restaurants, garages, small factories or transportation firms" (Goldthorpe 1990, p. 435). Presumably the share of female proprietors in the service class would be even smaller. But this argument too tends to reinforce the view that class IV, rather than I, is the appropriate location. Of course, as a practical matter (and assuming that the frequency of large proprietors in survey data reflects their frequency in the population) large proprietors are sufficiently scarce that their assignment to class I or class IV is hardly likely to be consequential for any conclusions that might be drawn about, say, inequalities in mobility chances. Nonetheless, placing them in class I (rather than, say, in a new sub-class in class IV) does lead to an inconsistency between the theoretical postulates of the schema and its implementation.

The change from the early to the later formulation of the Goldthorpe class schema has no operational consequences: that is, the assignment of occupations to classes has remained unchanged (this is discussed below). Furthermore, one might argue that the two formulations can be reconciled at the theoretical level, since it is differences between positions in the nature of the employment contract that give rise to the variations in market and work situation that were relevant in the earlier version. In both cases, the distinctions captured in the schema are held to produce differences in life chances: class position is a determinant of "experiences of affluence or hardship, of economic security or insecurity, of prospects of continuing material advance, or of unyielding material constraints" (Erikson and Goldthorpe 1992, p. 236).

Despite Goldthorpe's protestations, there is some justification in labeling his schema "neo-Weberian" inasmuch as it shares the Weberian focus on life chances and the Weberian modesty about the scope of class analysis.[5] The purpose of the schema is to allow exploration of the "interconnections defined by employment relations in labor markets and production units...the processes through which individual and families are distributed and redistributed among these positions over time; and the consequences thereof for their life-chances" (Goldthorpe and Marshall 1992, p. 382). Furthermore, the class schema makes no claims to identifying groups that act as "the engine of social change," nor does it suppose

---

[5] Goldthorpe's reluctance to identify his class schema as Weberian is well known. While acknowledging that the principles of the schema have been largely adopted from Marx and Weber, he writes "our own approach has often been referred to and discussed as 'Weberian,' but we would not regard this as particularly informative or otherwise helpful:...it is consequences, not antecedents, that matter" (Erikson and Goldthorpe 1992, p. 37, fn. 10).

that the classes stand in an exploitative relationship one to another, nor that the members of classes will automatically develop class consciousness and engage in collective action (Goldthorpe and Marshall 1992, pp. 383–4).

The boundary problem in neo-Weberian class analysis

A neo-Weberian class schema is a set of principles that allocates positions to classes so as to capture the major dimensions of differentiation in labor markets and production units that are consequential for the distribution of life chances. In assessing a neo-Weberian, or indeed any class schema, it is important to draw a distinction between criticisms leveled at its conceptualization or theoretical basis, on the one hand, and, on the other, its specific implementation, even though objections of both kinds might ultimately be adjudicated empirically. A frequent objection to class classifications is the following: given the apparently enormous diversity of positions in labor markets and economic organizations, how can a class schema, such as Goldthorpe's, especially one with a relatively small number of classes, claim to capture the salient distinctions among positions that are consequential for the distribution of life chances among those who occupy them?[6]

One response to this is to say that variation in life chances among individuals or families in the same class is not in itself a theoretical objection to a neo-Weberian class schema since the life chances that someone enjoys depend on a variety of factors apart from class position. From this perspective, differences in life chances among those in the same class should be seen not as class differences *per se* but as differences based on other factors. But the further objection might be advanced that the chosen set of principles is not optimal: that is, there exists another set of principles that does this job better (and this might, but need not, lead to a finer classification of occupations). It might be argued, for instance, that a scale of occupational prestige better captures distinctions among positions that are salient for life chances. Or occupations themselves could be held to be groups whose life chances are more sharply distinct than is true of classes. Addressing this objection would require both conceptual clarification and empirical analysis. First, one could ask what mechanisms explain variation in life chances arising from these sources. In the case

---

[6] Weber overcomes this objection by employing two sets of criteria. Members of a class share common life chances, but social classes are made up of those classes between which mobility is common. Breiger (1982) applies this idea to analyze a seventeen-occupational group mobility table, in which both the pattern of mobility and the underlying class structure (an aggregation of the original seventeen categories) are tested for their goodness-of-fit with the original data. However, his approach has not been widely followed.

of Goldthorpe's schema, the form of employment relationship is consequential for life chances because of the different rewards and incentives that are associated with each type of contract. Secondly, one could ask how positions come to be differentiated in this way. In Goldthorpe's schema the two kinds of employment contract are attempted solutions to the problems of asset-specificity and employee monitoring that confront employers. Alternative principles for the construction of classes should then have underlying mechanisms of both these sorts that had at least the same degree of plausibility. Lastly, we could move to empirical tests. Given the choice between two theoretically grounded classifications an empirical analysis would ask which of them was the stronger predictor of life chances, while taking into account the trade-off between explanatory completeness and explanatory parsimony.

Objections like this are fundamental, and are distinct from those that could be leveled against a particular operationalization of a set of underlying principles on which both the critic and the defender might agree. Indeed, in their work, Erikson and Goldthorpe (1992) move between seven-, five- and three-class versions[7] of the Goldthorpe class schema and never, in fact, employ the full eleven categories. They note that "while preserving the underlying idea of the schema that classes are to be defined in terms of employment relations . . . the differentiation [of classes] . . . could obviously be much further extended, were there good reason to do so" (Erikson and Goldthorpe 1992, p. 46, fn. 18). This is consistent with their assertion that the class schema is an *instrument du travail* rather than a definitive map of *the* class structure.

Despite the fact that positions are put into classes according to their relationship to the means of production and then to the kind of employment relationship they display, the Goldthorpe schema has never, in fact, been operationalized by measuring these characteristics of positions and assigning them to classes on this basis. Instead, occupations are assigned to classes on the basis of knowledge about their typical employment relations. This has been done for pragmatic reasons. One important benefit is that data that have already been collected can be coded into the schema. This was the case with the national data sets used in the CASMIN (Comparative Analysis of Social Mobility in Industrial Nations) project, which led to *The Constant Flux* (Erikson and Goldthorpe 1992). But this is not to say that the same occupations need always be assigned to the same

---

[7] The five-class version groups together I, II and III into a white-collar class; IVa and IVb into a petty bourgeoisie; IVc and VIIb into farm workers; V and VI into skilled workers; and VIIa is left as the class of non-skilled workers. The three-class version then places IVa and IVb with I, II and III in a nonmanual workers class; V, VI and VII in a manual workers class; and retains the farm workers class (IVc and VIIb).

classes. Occupations could change their class location over time and the same occupation could be placed in different classes in different countries (something that seems to have been allowed for in the CASMIN project: see Erikson and Goldthorpe 1992, pp. 50–1).

But because the type of employment relationship is defined by a number of different features (salary increments, pension rights, and assurances of security are among features of the service relationship listed by Erikson and Goldthorpe), the question arises of the extent to which they do in fact occur together within occupations. If, for example, these dimensions of employment relationships were only weakly related to one another this would call into question the operationalization of the underlying concepts in the form of classes. Evans and Mills (1998) address this issue using British survey data collected in 1984 to analyze the relationship between nine indicators of the employment relationship. These include whether or not the job requires the employee to clock on at a set time, the way in which the employee is paid (piece rate, by the hour, performance related, etc.), whether the job is on a recognized career ladder, and whether the employee can decide on how fast the work is done. They apply latent class analysis to these indicators and find four latent classes. This is a reasonably good indication, then, that these various aspects of the employment relationship do not vary independently: rather they mainly co-occur in four combinations. Furthermore, inspection of the pattern of the response probabilities for each item within each latent class suggests to Evans and Mills that these four classes correspond approximately to a white-collar salariat; a class of lower-level managers and supervisors; a routine nonmanual class; and a class of manual wage workers. For example, the probability of clocking on is .05 in the first and third of these classes, while it is .54 in the purported lower-level managers and supervisors class and .65 in the manual wage workers class. The first and last of these classes might be taken as the two polar types of service and wage labor relationship, with the others representing intermediate classes. And, indeed, Evans and Mills find that there is a very good match between these latent classes and the respondents' Goldthorpe classes: "78 per cent of latent type 1 can be found in Goldthorpe I and II, 95 per cent fall into I, II and IIIa. Similarly, no less than 89 per cent of latent type 4 are to be found in Goldthorpe VI and VIIab, 96 per cent in VI, VIIab and V" (Evans and Mills 1998, p. 95). They argue that these results point to the schema's high criterion validity: that is, the extent to which it succeeds in dividing 'the occupational structure in such a way as to identify important cleavages in the job characteristics which are considered theoretically significant by Goldthorpe and his colleagues' (Evans 1992, p. 213).

In a later analysis, Evans and Mills (2000) use a much larger and more recently collected (in 1996) set of British data and a similar, though not identical, set of eight indicators of the employment relationship. The results of their latent class analysis this time reveal

A small latent class (1), between 8 and 13 per cent of the population, that are predominantly remunerated with a salary plus some other form of bonus or additional payment; have very high probabilities of not receiving overtime payments; have to give a month or more notice of resignation; and have control over start and quit times. At the other end of the spectrum we find a class (3), between 35 and 45 per cent with the opposite characteristics . . . . Between these two groups are a class (2), between 45 and 52 per cent, which are predominantly salaried, tend to receive overtime payments, have to give more than one month notice to quit and are somewhat mixed with regard to their control over their working hours. (Evans and Mills 2000, p. 653)

Not surprisingly they identify latent classes 1, 2 and 3 with a service, intermediate and labor contract respectively. But, in this case, when they turn to the question of the criterion validity of the scheme, Evans and Mills (2000, p. 657) conclude that there are some problems with the operationalization of the schema.

The majority of Goldthorpe's class II do not have a "service" type of employment contract. The dividing line between the service and the intermediate classes appears to run through class II rather than between class II and class IIIa. We also estimate that about a third of class I employees do not have a "service" contract.

This casts doubt on the sustainability of the practice of continuing to rely wholly on occupational titles as the basis of the empirical classification, at least in the British case, and at least for the purpose of locating the service class.[8] The interval of twelve years between the collection dates of the two data sets used by Evans and Mills suggests that there has been some recent slippage between occupational titles and the Goldthorpe service class. One plausible assumption is that an inflation of occupational titles may have led to their becoming poorer indicators of the nature of the employment relationship, as in the increasing use of titles such as "manager" for a growing diversity of occupations. Moving to the use of direct measures of the employment relationship might, in any case, confer a benefit. It would allow researchers to determine which of the elements of the relationship were most strongly associated with particular class

---

[8] One difficulty with these analyses that should be mentioned, however, is that they elicit information from employees, whose responses may well relate more to their own position and experiences than to the characteristics of the position that they occupy (for example in questions about the likelihood of promotion). Information about positions might be better collected from employers.

outcomes, and this would be of obvious value in the search to specify the mechanisms that link class position to these outcomes. Indeed, the absence of any precise explanation of what mechanisms link the type of employment relationship to variations in life chances is a notable weakness of the schema. The work of Evans and Mills has shown the extent to which the schema captures distinctions in the employment relationship, and a great deal of research has shown that class position is associated with differences in life chances (and in other outcomes). But what has generally been absent is a theoretical account of how such differences can be explained as the consequence of these distinctions and, following from this, attempts to subject these to empirical test. This problem has been recognized by Goldthorpe and others (Erikson and Goldthorpe 1992, Ch. 11; Breen and Rottman 1995b), and Goldthorpe (2000, Ch. 11) has recently sought to address it. In order for these explanatory mechanisms to support the particular theory of class being advanced, however, they have to discriminate between alternative theories. In other words, the purported mechanisms should not be of such generality that they would serve equally well to explain the link between outcomes and more than one theory of class. This "specificity requirement" as we might call it, may prove to be the most difficult condition to meet in developing a persuasive neo-Weberian theory of class.

The unit of class analysis

So far classes have been discussed as aggregations of positions, rather than individuals. The implicit mechanism that links class position and life chances is then, simply, that the individual's life chances derive from the particular class position that he or she occupies (or, taking a lifetime perspective, from the sequence of positions he or she occupies). But not all individuals occupy one of these positions and, in these cases, life chances are held to derive through the relationship between such individuals and others who do occupy a position in the class structure. A child's class position is then derived from its parents and the class position of a married woman is conventionally considered to derive from the position occupied by her husband. But the life chances of someone who does not occupy a position in the class structure, such as a child or a married woman who does not work outside the home, will depend not only on the position occupied by her parents or husband, but also on the nature of the relationship between her and her parents or husband. In other words intra-familial and intra-household relationships intervene between the market and the individual's life chances. This issue is, of course, exactly the same as that which arises in studies of income inequality where considerations of the within-household distribution of income are rarely addressed empirically.

Notwithstanding these arguments, treating all the members of a household as occupying a single class position has long been standard among theorists of class. This is relatively unproblematic when only one member of a household occupies a position in the labor market, as in the male-breadwinner arrangement, but difficulties arise when both spouses work outside the home. Some authors (such as Heath and Britten 1984) want to retain the idea of a single class position for a household, but one that is determined by the class position of both spouses. Others (for example, Stanworth 1984) argue that spouses should be considered to have their own class position and, rather than the family occupying a single position in the class structure, its fate should be treated as a function of both. Goldthorpe and his collaborators have argued against both these points of view. They suggest that, because women typically have discontinuous labor market careers, analyses of female mobility will tend, as a result, to record a great deal of class mobility, much of which is artefactual. The appropriate unit of class analysis is therefore the household, and the class to which it and its members belong should be determined by the class position of whichever spouse has the more enduring attachment to the labor market. One way of measuring the latter is the so-called "dominance" approach (Erikson 1984). Empirically it is the case that it is usually the male partner who proves to have the more enduring attachment to the labor market. "However, there is no presumption that this will always be the case . . . it is not difficult to envisage the circumstances . . . under which the application of the dominance approach might lead to many more families being assigned to a class on the basis of the woman's occupation" (Breen and Rottman 1995a, pp. 166–7).

One way of conceptualizing these competing approaches is to recast them in a slightly more formal way. Assume that our goal is to explain variation in some outcome, Y, measured at the individual or family level (such as a person's educational attainment or the standard of living of a family) in terms of social class, X, of which we have two possible measures (one for each spouse in a household), labeled X_m and X_w. Then the issues discussed above reduce to the question of the functional form of the relationship between Y and X_m and X_w. This can be written very generally as $Y = f(g(X_m, X_w))$. Here f specifies the form of the relationship between Y and $g(X_m, X_w)$ while g determines how X_m and X_w are treated in the analysis. The individual approach to class membership argues for a model that sets $g(X_m, X_w)$ equal to X_m and X_w, whereas so-called conventional approaches would specify g as a two-to-one mapping from (X_m, X_w) to X. In the dominance approach, for example, $g(X_m, X_w)$ is the function that picks out whichever of X_m and X_w is dominant. Written in this way it becomes clear that many functions could serve for g: for example, it could specify a relationship between a latent class, X, and two indicators, X_m and X_w. This slight formalization provides a way of resolving these problems empirically. Given that a neo-Weberian class analysis is concerned with the distribution of life chances, one might seek to determine, conditional on the choice of f, which of the possible functional forms for g best accounts for variation in individuals' life chances.

Conclusion

A neo-Weberian approach to class analysis rests on the construction of a schema based on principles that capture the major dimensions of positional differentiation in labor markets and production units that are important for the distribution of life chances. The chosen principle is the theoretical basis, and the corresponding class schema is its operationalization. Given this, at least two important lines of empirical inquiry can be pursued. On the one hand, we might want to know how substantively important class is in explaining variation in life chances, particularly in comparison with other bases of social inequality such as ethnic group membership, gender, and so on. And of course such an inquiry can be extended to make comparisons in the strength of class effects between countries and through time. On the other hand, the existence and strength of the relationship between class and other outcomes are also matters for empirical investigation. But if the classes are meant to capture distinctions that are primarily relevant for the distribution of life chances, then members of a class may or may not behave similarly, hold similar attitudes, or engage in collective action, and so on. Inasmuch as variation in these or other outcomes can be causally traced to variation in life chances, or insofar as those aspects of the organization of labor markets and the production process that shape life chances are also determinants of these other outcomes, then we will find a relationship between them and class. Very often the causal link between life chances and an outcome like collective action will be contingent on other circumstances and then, as Weber recognized, there may or may not be a relationship with class. But in many cases there will be a consistent link between life chances and other outcomes. To revert to a point I made earlier: if life chances determine the conditions under which certain types of action are undertaken – including the interests that people have (and which they may express in, say, voting) and the resources they can bring to bear (and which may be important in, say, shaping their children's educational attainment) – then variations in these actions will be structured according to class position.

But suppose that in a given case we find no relationship, as when classes are found not to be a basis of any common or collective identity. Should we therefore conclude that class is not important or that the particular classification is inadequate? My answer is that we should conclude that those distinctions that lead to differences in life chances are not ones that serve as a basis for collective identity. But the important point is that these latter sorts of outcome are not constitutive of a neo-Weberian class schema. For example, what are termed *gemeinschaftlich* ideas of class – that is, classes as subjectively real communities – are not a necessary part of the neo-Weberian approach.[9]

But even if these other outcomes are not constitutive of class understood in the neo-Weberian sense, the importance of class as a sociological concept will certainly depend upon how strongly it is related to them, as well as to life chances. If class did not predict significant outcomes it would be of little interest. What is clear, however, is that in many of the areas central to sociological endeavor there is little evidence that the influence of class is declining and, indeed, some evidence that its influence is growing. Shavit and Blossfeld's (1993) edited collection shows that the influence of class origins on children's educational attainment showed no decline over the course of the twentieth century in thirteen developed nations. The papers in Evans (1997) demonstrate that the much vaunted "general decline of class voting" is an inaccurate description of the rather complex and cross-nationally varying trends in this phenomenon. Class voting seems to have weakened in Scandinavia, but in Germany, France, and elsewhere no such temporal change is evident. Lastly, in the area of social mobility, Breen and Goldthorpe (2001) show that in Britain, during the last quarter of the twentieth century, there has been no change in the extent to which class origins help shape class destinations. This holds true even controlling for educational attainment and measures of individual ability. This result may then be added to the evidence of longer-term temporal stability in patterns of class mobility in Europe reported by Erikson and Goldthorpe (1992).

---

[9] Indeed, in Goldthorpe's own work, and that of those who use his class schema, relatively little attention is now paid to issues of demographic class formation and their consequences (in contrast, for example, to Goldthorpe's [1980] earlier work on mobility in England and Wales). Rather, the class schema is now mainly employed as a means of capturing inequalities in life chances.

3   Foundations of a neo-Durkheimian
class analysis

David Grusky in collaboration with Gabriela Galescu

The class analytic tradition has come under increasing attack from post-modernists, anti-Marxists, and other commentators who argue that the concept of class is an antiquated construction of declining utility in under-standing modern or postmodern inequality.[1] In large part, this state of affairs might be blamed on class analysts themselves, as they have invari-ably represented the class structure with highly aggregate categories that, for all their academic popularity, have never been deeply institutionalized in the world outside academia and hence fail the realist test. By default-ing to nominalism, the class analytic tradition becomes especially vulner-able to critique, with postmodernists in particular arguing that academics have resorted to increasingly arcane and complicated representations of the class structure because the site of production no longer generates well-organized classes that academics and others can easily discern.

The purpose of this chapter is to outline a neo-Durkheimian alterna-tive to such postmodernism that points to the persistence of class-like structuration at a more disaggregate level than class analysts have typ-ically appreciated. It follows that class analysis is well worth salvaging; that is, rather than abandoning the site of production and concentrating exclusively on other sources of attitudes and behavior (e.g., race, ethnic-ity, gender), one should recognize that the labor market is indeed orga-nized into classes, albeit at a more detailed level than is conventionally allowed. The great virtue of disaggregating is that the nominal categories

We are grateful to Erik Wright and the students in his graduate seminar for their exceed-ingly detailed and insightful reactions to an earlier draft of this chapter. We have also received helpful comments on a related paper from Julia Adams, Jeffrey Alexander, Vivek Chibber, Dalton Conley, Paul DiMaggio, Kathleen Gerson, Guillermina Jasso, Michèle Lamont, Jeffery Paige, Philip Smith, Margaret Somers, George Steinmetz, Kim Wee-den, Bruce Western, and Yu Xie. In drafting this chapter, we have drawn on previously published materials in Grusky and Sørensen (1998), Grusky and Weeden (2001), and Grusky, Weeden, and Sørensen (2000). The research reported here was supported in part by the National Science Foundation (SBS-9906419).

[1] For examples, see Hall 2001; Pakulski and Waters 1996a, 1996b, 1996c, 1996d; Lee and Turner 1996; Clark 1996; Joyce 1995; Kingston 2000, 1994; Clark and Lipset 2001, 1991; Pahl 1989.

of conventional class analysis can be replaced by *gemeinschaftlich* "micro-classes" that are embedded in the very fabric of society and are thereby meaningful not merely to sociologists but to the lay public as well.

As shall be evident, our neo-Durkheimian approach motivates us to come out foursquare in favor of realist classifications, where these are defined as schemes in which the constituent categories are institutionalized in the labor market.[2] By contrast, scholars working within a nominalist tradition seek to construct class categories that reflect social processes, forces, or distinctions that are regarded as *analytically* fundamental, even though the categories implied by such approaches may be only shallowly institutionalized. In some cases, a theory of history has been grafted onto such nominalist models, thus generating the side-claim that currently "latent" (but analytically fundamental) class categories may ultimately come to be appreciated by actors, serve as bases for collective action, or become institutionalized groupings that bargain collectively on behalf of their members. There is of course much variability across scholars in the particular processes or forces (e.g., exploitation, authority relations, terms of employment, life chances) that are regarded as fundamental and hence generative of classes that may in the future become more deeply institutionalized. As is well known, it can be extremely difficult to adjudicate between these competing models, especially when they are grounded in a theory of history that requires scholars to withhold judgment until some (potentially) distant future. It is high time, we think, to attend to the empirically more viable task of characterizing such structures at the site of production as can currently be found.[3]

This line of argumentation has distinctly Durkheimian roots that have not been adequately drawn out in our prior work.[4] In some of this work, we have duly acknowledged our intellectual debt to Durkheim (especially Grusky and Sørensen 1998, pp. 1,192, 1,196, 1,219), but the relationship between our micro-class approach and the developmental arguments

---

[2] This definition glosses over a number of complications, including (a) the operational difficulty that analysts face in discerning institutionalized categories and the consequent inevitability of analyst-imposed "constructions" (even when the objective is to best represent institutionalized categories), and (b) the typical insistence of scholars working within the nominalist tradition that their preferred categories rest on causal forces or processes (e.g., exploitation) that are altogether "real" regardless of whether such categories are presently institutionalized in the labor market. We shall return to these complications in subsequent sections of this chapter.

[3] The categories of a realist scheme will, by virtue of their institutionalization, tend to be recognized by the lay public and appreciated as meaningful. However, our formal definition of realist approaches relies entirely on the criterion of institutionalization, and the tendency for realist categories to become subjectively salient thus becomes a (possible) empirical result that falls outside the definition *per se*.

[4] See, for instance, Grusky and Sørensen (1998, 2001), Grusky and Weeden (2002, 2001), Grusky, Weeden, and Sørensen (2000).

of Durkheim might still be usefully elaborated. There is good reason to take on this task now. After all, few scholars have so far rushed in to offer a retooled Durkheimian approach to class analysis, even though many Marxian models have fallen out of favor and Durkheimian ones arguably offer an alternative that captures much of the institutional reality of contemporary class systems (see Parkin 1992, p. 1; Pearce 1989, p. 1; Müller 1993, p. 106; cf. Lee 1995; Fenton 1980; Lehmann 1995). This is obviously not to suggest that theorists have ignored Durkheim altogether; however, contemporary exegesis focuses increasingly on *The Elementary Forms of Religious Life*, providing as it does the requisite classical source for the cultural turn in sociology (see Smith and Alexander 1996; Meštrović 1992). Moreover, when contemporary class analysts *have* engaged with *The Division of Labor in Society*, it has often been for the negative purpose of refuting Durkheimian or neo-Marxian class models rather than advancing some positive analysis.[5]

This state of affairs may seem puzzling given the long and venerable tradition of stratification scholarship treating occupations as the "backbone" of the class system (esp. Parkin 1971; Featherman, Jones, and Hauser 1975; Duncan 1968, pp. 689–90; Parsons 1954, pp. 326–9). In understanding why Durkheim has nonetheless been ignored, it bears noting that stratification scholars have typically preferred to scale occupations in terms of a socioeconomic gradient, and the work of Durkheim does not provide any obvious justification for such a procedure. If mention of Durkheim is, then, conspicuously absent from present-day commentary on class, it is largely because his project cannot be seen as presaging any conventional class analytic approaches, including those that map occupations or jobs into aggregate classes as well as those that map them into socioeconomic scales.

We will develop a class analytic approach that rests explicitly on the technical division of labor and thus has a more distinctly Durkheimian heritage. In this regard, it is striking that class analysts have not only ignored the *Division of Labor*, but have more generally eschewed *any* analysis of the technical division of labor, even a non-Durkheimian one. Indeed, Wright (1979) commented over twenty-five years ago on the "relatively few sustained theoretical reflections on the logic of linking

---

[5] See, for instance, Mouzelis (1993), Bottomore (1981), Tiryakian (1975), Dahrendorf (1959, pp. 48–51), Zeitlin (1968), cf. Pope and Johnson (1983), Hawkins (1994), Müller (1993), Thompson (1982), Lukes (1973), Nisbet (1952), Giddens (1971, 1972, 1978), Watts Miller (1996), Filloux (1993). The recent work of Lockwood (1992) is a notable exception to this claim. In his pathbreaking book, Lockwood (1992) shows that the Durkheimian model treats instrumental action as an unanalyzed residual, whereas the Marxian model conversely treats normative action as an unanalyzed residual. These models may therefore be regarded as incomplete in complementary ways.

class to positions within the technical division of labor" (p. 12), and the same conclusion probably holds with equal force today. We will seek to repair this state of affairs by discussing (a) how Durkheim developed, rather unwittingly, a class analysis grounded in the technical division of labor, (b) how this class analytic approach might be modified to address developments that Durkheim did not fully anticipate, and (c) how the resulting approach, while arguably an advance over conventional forms of class analysis, nonetheless leaves important problems unresolved.

Durkheim and the class structure: a selective exegesis

We begin, then, by considering how Durkheim approached issues of class and occupation, relying not only on his famous preface to the *Division of Labor* but also on related commentary in *Suicide* and elsewhere (see, especially, Hawkins 1994 for a comprehensive treatment). In the secondary literature on such matters, it is often noted with some disapproval that Durkheim treated class conflict as a purely transitory feature of early industrialism, thereby "ignoring . . . the [enduring] implications of class cleavages" (Zeitlin 1968, p. 235; also, see Lockwood 1992, p. 78; Bottomore 1981). As is well known, Durkheim indeed argued that class conflict in the early industrial period would ultimately dissipate because (a) the growth of state and occupational regulation should impose moral control on the conflict of interests (i.e., the "institutionalization" of conflict), and (b) the rise of achievement-based mobility should legitimate inequalities of outcome by making them increasingly attributable to differential talent, capacities, and investments rather than differential opportunities (i.e., the rise of "equal opportunity"). In light of current developments, it is not altogether clear that such emphases within the work of Durkheim should still be regarded as an outright defect, foreshadowing as they do important developments in the transition to advanced industrialism. The twin forces of normative regulation and meritocratic allocation have, in fact, been featured in much subsequent discussion about the "institutionalization" of class conflict (e.g., Dahrendorf 1959), even though the early work of Durkheim has not always been accorded a properly deferential place in this commentary.

This institutionalization of conflict has motivated contemporary class theorists to de-emphasize macro-level theories of history and related developmental narratives (see Holton and Turner 1989), preferring instead to deploy class categories for the more modest academic task of explaining micro-level behavior in the present day (e.g., voting behavior, lifestyles). The obvious question that then arises is whether the class categories devised by Marx and others for macro-level purposes are also optimal for this more limited micro-level explanatory agenda (Grusky and Weeden 2001). For the most part, scholars of contemporary class relations have concluded that they are not, leading to all manner of attempts to increase the explanatory power of class models by introducing further distinctions within the category of labor. The main failing, however, of such efforts is that the posited categories have been only shallowly institutionalized, with scholars seeking to defend their competing schemes with all imaginable criteria save the seemingly obvious one that the posited categories should have some institutional veracity.

In this context, the scholarship of Durkheim is again instructive, as it refocuses attention on the types of intermediary groups that have emerged in past labor markets and will likely characterize future ones. This is to suggest, then, that Durkheim contributed to class analysis on two fronts, simultaneously providing (a) a negative macro-level story about the social forces (e.g., institutionalization of conflict) that render big classes unviable in the long run, and (b) a positive micro-level story about the "small classes" (i.e., *gemeinschaftlich* occupations) that are destined to emerge at the site of production and shape individual values, life chances, and lifestyles. The latter micro-level story, which is typically dismissed as irrelevant to class analysis, is the focus of our commentary here. We feature this story because small classes can be shown to take on properties that class analysts have conventionally (but mistakenly) ascribed to big classes.

In laying out this micro-level story, it has to be conceded that Durkheim is (famously) silent on the proximate mechanisms by which occupational associations will emerge, as he simply presumes, by functionalist fiat, that outcomes that putatively serve system ends will ultimately win out. This approach leads Durkheim to equate "the normal, the ideal, and the about-to-happen" (Lukes 1973, p. 177). By contrast, Marx and most neo-Marxians put forward analyses that are mechanism-rich, relying on such forces as exploitation, opposed interests, and conflict as proximate sources bringing about the postulated end-states. In some of his writings, Durkheim does hint at proximate mechanisms, but for the most part he is correctly taken to task for failing to "proceed to an investigation of causes" (Bottomore 1981, p. 911). It is nonetheless worth asking whether the end-state that Durkheim describes captures some of the developmental tendencies within contemporary systems of inequality.

How, then, might one characterize Durkheim's view of the "normal, ideal, and about-to-happen" (Lukes 1973, p. 177)? We take on this question below by describing the three forms of micro-level organization that, according to Durkheim, are destined to emerge at the site of production.

The rise of occupational associations

The *Division of Labor* is most instructively read as an extended discourse on the level (i.e., class or "micro-class") at which the site of production will come to be organized.[6] When class analysts summarize this work, they typically emphasize the argument that big classes are purely transitory and will fade away as "normal" forms of adaptation emerge (i.e., the "negative macro-level story"), while the predicted rise of social organization at the local occupational level (i.e., the "positive micro-level story") is disregarded or viewed as irrelevant. By contrast, we think that the micro-level story in Durkheim is worth considering more carefully, not merely because local organization can take on class-like properties (as argued below), but also because it can crowd out or substitute for class formation of a more aggregate sort. Indeed, Durkheim argued that occupational associations are destined to become the main organizational form "intercalated between the state and the individual" (1960 [1893], p. 28), supplanting both Marxian classes and other forms of intermediary organization (e.g., the family). Although Durkheim emphasized the informal ties and bonds that were cultivated in occupational associations, he also laid out a variety of formal functions that such associations were likely to assume, including (a) establishing and administering a system of occupational ethics, (b) resolving conflicts among members and with other associations, and (c) serving as elemental representative bodies in political governance (see Durkheim 1960 [1893], pp. 26–7; also, see Durkheim 1970a [1897], pp. 372–82). The foregoing functions are best carried out at the local level because an "activity can be efficaciously regulated only by a group intimate enough with it to know its functioning [and] feel all its needs" (Durkheim 1960 [1893], p. 5).

These associations find their historical precedent in medieval guilds and bear some resemblance to the professional and craft associations that are now so ubiquitous. For Durkheim, it is revealing that occupational associations have a long history that extends well into ancient times, with early forms evidently appearing "as soon as there are trades" (Durkheim 1960 [1893], p. 7). If occupational associations have surfaced throughout recent history, Durkheim reasoned that they must have a "timeless authenticity" (Parkin 1992, p. 77) suggestive of important underlying functions. Among these functions, Durkheim particularly stressed

---

[6] The views of Durkheim on occupational associations evolved and changed throughout his career (see Hawkins [1994] for an excellent exegesis). In the early 1890s, Durkheim began to lay out the positive functions of occupational associations, but at that time he regarded them as a largely "temporary antidote to contemporary social problems" (Hawkins 1994, p. 473). It was not until the late 1890s that his full-fledged "theory" of occupational associations was formulated.

that occupations can rein in excessive ambition and aspirations, if only by inducing workers to calibrate their aspirations for remuneration to the occupational norm rather than some less attainable standard. The egoism unleashed by the breakdown of the traditional social order can therefore be contained by subjecting workers to a new form of extra-individual authority at the occupational level (Durkheim 1960 [1893], p. 10). By implication, the macro-level and micro-level stories in the *Division of Labor* are closely linked, with the declining fortunes of big classes reflecting, in part, the institutionalization of occupations and the consequent legitimation of inequalities that both (a) undermine the unity of the working class, and (b) convince workers to regard occupational differences in remuneration (including those between big classes) as appropriate and acceptable. If there is a class analytic theory of history in Durkheim, it is clearly one that emphasizes the role of occupations in justifying inequality, making it palatable, and hence undermining the more spectacular theories of history that Marx and various neo-Marxians have advanced.

The "localization" of the collective conscience

The rise of occupational associations is also relevant to the "problem of order" and Durkheim's putative solution to it.[7] As traditional forms of organization wither away, there has been much concern in sociology (see Parsons 1967, 1968 [1937]) that the forces of differentiation and specialization might prove to be maladaptive, leading to excessive egoism, unrestrained individual action, and a diminished commitment to collective ends. This concern has, in turn, set off a search for countervailing processes that might contain or at least offset these individuating forces. When Durkheim is invoked in this literature, he is frequently credited with recognizing that the modern collective conscience has been transformed to encompass increasingly abstract and generalized sentiments, especially those stressing the dignity of individuals (i.e., the "cult of the individual") and their right to freely pursue opportunities unhampered by circumstances of birth (i.e., "equal opportunity"). In content, these beliefs form a deeply individualistic "religion" (Durkheim 1960 [1893], p. 172), but they are nonetheless shared across individuals and, as such, constitute the modern-day collective conscience.

The latter story remains, however, partial and incomplete without a parallel discussion of the rise of occupation-specific beliefs and how these

---

[7] As is well known, Parsons (1949; 1967) sought to interpret all of classical sociology, including the *Division of Labor*, as engaging directly with issues of social order. By contrast, other scholars (esp. Giddens 1983) have argued that Parsons imposed his own idiosyncratic problematic on the work of others, especially that of Durkheim.

also operate to suppress egoism, bind workers to an extra-individual community, and thereby counteract the forces of individuation.[8] To be sure, Durkheim appreciated that modern occupations will not develop the total, all-encompassing morality of traditional social systems (see Pope and Johnson 1983, p. 684; Hawkins 1994, p. 464), yet he was still impressed with how "imperative" (1960 [1893], p. 227) the rules of occupational morality have been in the past and would likely come to be in the future. This new form of solidarity links individuals to local subgroupings (i.e., occupations) rather than the larger society itself; and, consequently, the modern tendency is to move toward "moral polymorphism" (Durkheim (1958, p. 7), where this refers to the rise of multiple, occupation-specific "centers of moral life." At the level of values, the Durkheimian solution thus references not only the integrative effects of highly abstract system-wide sentiments, but also the "mechanical solidarity" that persists as more concrete and specialized sentiments are ratcheted down and reexpress themselves within occupational groupings (see Parsons 1968 [1937], p. 339).[9]

This line of argument has of course been carried forward by subsequent generations of French sociologists. For example, Bouglé (1971 [1927]) treated the Indian caste system as an extreme case of "moral polymorphism" in which the occupational communities are organized in deeply hierarchical terms, are especially well-protected against "polluting" interaction (e.g., intermarriage), and are self-reproducing to an unusual degree (i.e., hereditary closure). Although the Indian case represents, for Bouglé, the purest form of the caste system, it is but a "unique dilation of universal tendencies" (Bouglé 1971 [1927], p. 28) that generate profound occupational differentiation in all societies. Likewise, Halbwachs (e.g, 1992 [1945]) argued that occupations tend to breed distinctive traditions and forms of consciousness, with his examples of such polymorphism often drawing on detailed occupations (e.g., general, legislator, judge) as well as big classes (also, see Halbwachs 1958; Coser 1992, pp. 18–20). The Durkheimian imagery of "moral polymorphism" emerges yet more clearly in the (comparatively) recent work of Bourdieu (1984 [1979]). In *Distinction: A Social Critique of the Judgment of Taste*, Bourdieu (1984 [1979]) characterized the habitus and the distinctive

---

[8] See Durkheim (1960 [1893], pp. 2, 4–5, 10), Pope and Johnson (1983, pp. 682–4). See also Hawkins (1994) for a review of other relevant pieces.

[9] If the terminology of Durkheim is strictly applied, it is inappropriate to refer to "mechanical solidarity" in this context, as the latter term is reserved for traditional societies in which the collective conscience consists of beliefs and sentiments shared by all. We have appropriated the term here only because it clarifies that intra-occupational solidarity arises from similarities among individuals (see Pope and Johnson [1983]).

lifestyles it generates in terms of quite detailed occupations (e.g., professors, nurses), albeit with the proviso that such occupations provide only imperfect signals of "homogeneous conditions of existence" (1984, p. 101).

For class analysts, the practical implication of this Durkheimian formulation is that detailed occupations, more so than big classes, become the main site at which distinctive attitudes and styles of life are generated. As Durkheim puts it, occupations have their own cultures comprising "certain ideas, certain usages, and certain ways of seeing things" (1956 [1911], p. 68), and workers participate in them as naturally and inevitably as they "breathe the air" around them (1970b [1905], p. 286, translated in Watts Miller 1996, p. 125). These specialized cultures arise because (a) the forces of self-selection operate to bring similar workers into the same occupation (Durkheim 1960 [1893], p. 229), (b) the resulting social interaction with coworkers tends to reinforce and elaborate these shared tastes and sentiments (Durkheim 1960 [1893], pp. 228–9, 361), and (c) the incumbents of occupations have common interests that may be pursued, in part, by aligning themselves with their occupation and pursuing collective ends (Durkheim 1960 [1893], pp. 212–13). If communities of practice indeed become localized in this fashion, then the conventional micro-level objective of explaining class outcomes of all kinds (i.e., attitudes, behaviors, lifestyles) is best pursued at the local occupational level. In effect, Durkheim is describing a unification of class and *Stand* that, according to Weber (1968b [1922]), occurs only rarely in the context of conventional aggregate classes.

Occupations and organic solidarity

The Durkheimian solution to the problem of order comes in two parts, the first involving the emergence of occupation-specific sentiments that generate mechanical solidarity (as described above), and the second involving the rise of occupational interdependencies that generate organic solidarity. We turn to a consideration of the second part of the story and its implications for class analysis. As before, we shall find that detailed occupations play a central role in the Durkheimian vision, but now as the elementary units of interdependence (i.e., "organic solidarity") rather than as repositories of shared moral sentiments (i.e., "mechanical solidarity").

The natural starting point here is the long-standing concern (e.g., Smith 1991 [1776]; Comte 1988 [1830]) that the forces of occupational specialization and differentiation may be alienating because they render work increasingly routine and repetitive. By way of response, Durkheim

(1960 [1893]) suggests that such alienating effects can be countered when workers are in "constant relations with neighboring functions" (p. 372), thereby sensitizing them to their larger role within the division of labor and convincing them that their "actions have an aim beyond themselves" (pp. 372–3). In this sense, extreme specialization need not be intrinsically alienating, as individuals will come to recognize and appreciate their contribution to the collective enterprise, no matter how humble, repetitive, or mundane that contribution happens to be.[10] It bears emphasizing that Durkheim again has local organization working to undermine aggregate class formation; that is, constant contact with "neighboring functions" (p. 372) allows workers to appreciate interdependencies and to infuse their own work with some larger meaning, thus undermining any competing Marxian interpretation of work as exploitative and alienating. In the language of class analysis, Durkheim clearly has workers attending to the "relational features" of intermediary groupings, yet the relations of interest are those of visible cooperation and coordination at the micro-level rather than hidden exploitation at the macro-level.

For Durkheim, organic solidarity is also normatively expressed through the rise of occupational regulation that institutionalizes industrial conflict, most notably that between labor and capital. As before, the claim here is that occupational groupings will be the main impetus and carriers of normative regulation, since they are close enough to the activity being administered to "know its functioning, feel all its needs, and [understand its] variations" (Durkheim 1960 [1893], p. 5). It follows that occupational associations will increasingly devise codes of conduct and specify the terms under which labor is divided. In early industrial systems, such regulation is either lacking altogether (i.e., the "anomic division of labor") or is enforced without full consent of all parties (i.e., the "forced division of labor"), and conflict therefore remains unchecked and revolutionary ideologies become appealing. As the division of labor advances, Durkheim expects regulation to develop spontaneously through social intercourse and to become embodied in formal industrial law, with the initial appeal of socialist and other revolutionary programs accordingly undermined. The resulting normative regulation may again be seen as a form of micro-level organization that works to impede class development at the macro-level.

---

[10] Although the skeptic might reasonably ask whether the banal collective ends of everyday life are inspiring enough to infuse the most routine jobs with much meaning, the Durkheimian position does become easier to appreciate when collectivities are oriented to especially dramatic or uplifting objectives (e.g., fighting a war, building socialism) that could render even the smallest of contributions morally significant and rewarding.

Was Durkheim right?

It is useful at this point to consider whether the Durkheimian story about the rise of local organization has any contemporary relevance. Although class analysts routinely consider whether Marxian and Weberian formulations have been "borne out," the class analytic arguments of Durkheim have not typically been put to similar test. To the contrary, the *Division of Labor* is usually regarded as a quaint piece of disciplinary "prehistory" (Barnes 1995, p. 170), and class analysts have felt no real need to engage with it.

This fixation with Marx, Weber, and their followers is not especially sensible given the course of recent history. In many ways, the labor market has become increasingly "Durkheimianized," not merely because industrial conflict at the macro-class level has come to be regulated and contained, but also because occupational groupings have emerged as the elementary building blocks of modern and postmodern labor markets. As Treiman (1977) notes, contemporary workers routinely represent their career aspirations in occupational terms, while professional and vocational schools are organized to train workers for occupationally defined skills, and employers construct and advertise jobs in terms of corresponding occupational designations (also, see Parsons 1954; Wilensky 1966). This "occupationalization" of the labor market has been fueled by (a) a long-term growth in the size of the professional sector (with its characteristically strong occupational associations), (b) the rise of new quasi-professional occupations and associations built around emerging abstract skills in the division of labor, (c) the growing application of such devices as licensing, registration, and certification for the purposes of effecting (partial) closure around occupational boundaries, and (d) the strengthening of local labor unions (e.g., the American Federation of Teachers) as more encompassing visions of the labor movement unravel and "sectional self-interest ... becomes the order of the day" (Marshall *et al.* 1988, p. 7; also, Visser 1988, p. 167).[11] These considerations led Krause (1971) to conclude long ago that "there has historically been more occupation-specific consciousness and action than cross-occupational

---

[11] There is, to be sure, a contemporary literature on "post-occupationalism" that describes the gradual withering away of functionally defined positions. This literature rests on the claim that contemporary organizations are relying increasingly on teamwork, cross-training, and multi-activity jobs that break down conventional occupation-based distinctions (e.g., Casey 1995). These changes, if indeed they are underway, should be regarded as a recent and modest setback for the occupationalizing forces that have dominated the post-Durkheim period. Moreover, the post-occupationalist account is not without its critics, some of whom have argued that the "pressures for an occupational logic of organizing may in fact be rising" (Barley 1995, p. 40).

combination" (p. 87; also, see Freidson 1994, pp. 75–91; Van Maanen and Barley 1984, pp. 331–3; Dahrendorf 1959). Indeed, when the history of guilds, unions, and related production-based associations is reevaluated from the long view, it becomes clear that true classwide organization emerged for only a brief historical moment and that postmodern forms are reverting back to localism and sectionalism. The foregoing interpretation is consistent with the Durkheimian formula that micro-level organization crowds out and substitutes for class formation of a more aggregate sort.

This is not to suggest, of course, that the site of production has evolved entirely as Durkheim envisaged. As we see it, Durkheim was remarkably prescient in discerning the occupationalizing forces at work, but he clearly overstated the power of these forces and the consequent speed with which they might possibly play out. The Durkheimian formula is especially vulnerable on the three counts reviewed below.

Multifunctionalism and competing associational forms

In most of his relevant essays, Durkheim has occupational associations taking on a wide variety of functions, such as (a) regulating the labor market through norms governing pay, working conditions, and interoccupational relations, (b) providing a *gemeinschaftlich* setting in which workers can "lead the same moral life together" (Durkheim 1960 [1893], p. 15), and (c) serving as an "essential organ of public life" charged with electing parliamentary delegates (Durkheim 1960 [1893], p. 27). Relative to these expectations, contemporary occupational associations might well seem poorly developed, especially with respect to the political functions served. There is, to be sure, much political action at the detailed occupational level (see, e.g., Abbott 1988), but nowhere have occupations achieved the central, direct, and formal role in political governance that Durkheim outlined. Rather, occupations are typically consigned to the role of lobbying the state for highly specialized benefits, most notably the right to train and certify members and to otherwise establish control over the supply of labor. Even in this limited domain, occupational associations continue to compete with alternative associational forms, including most obviously labor unions. As Durkheim anticipated, the conflict between labor and capital has indeed been tamed and contained, but this has occurred as much by institutionalizing large unions as by replacing them with occupational associations or local craft unions. The resulting web of associational forms is inconsistent with the Durkheimian imagery of all-purpose associations that divide the workforce into mutually exclusive groups, squeeze out all competing organization, and accordingly become the *sole* intermediary between the individual and the state.[12]

Incomplete occupationalization

In some sectors of the class structure, occupational associations have simply failed to emerge, either because they have been overrun by competing forms (e.g., unions) or because social organization of all forms has proven unviable. For example, occupationalization has not yet taken hold in the lower manual sector, presumably due to low skill levels, limited investments in training, and relatively rapid changes in manufacturing process. It is unclear whether these poorly organized sectors will remain unorganized, will ultimately develop strategies allowing for some form of closure and occupationalization, or will continue to decline in size and eventually wither away. Although skill upgrading works to diminish the proportion of the workforce in poorly organized sectors, this process has of course played out only fitfully and may have reached its limit (e.g., Spenner 1995).[13] The contemporary class structure is best viewed, then, as a complex patchwork of moral communities and realist occupations interspersed with large regions of purely nominal categories in which occupationalization has yet to play out, if ever it will.[14]

Cross-national variation

There is also much cross-national variation in the extent to which the labor market has become occupationalized (see table 3.1; also, see Grusky and Weeden 2001, p. 210; Grusky and Sørensen 1998, pp. 1220–2). The German labor market, for example, is built directly on institutionalized occupational groupings and may therefore be seen as an especially successful realization of the Durkheimian formula.[15] As scholars have long stressed, Germany has well-developed systems of vocational training and

---

[12] Unlike Tocqueville (2000 [1835]), Durkheim regarded the proliferation of multiple and overlapping intermediary groupings as maladaptive, indicating "the absence or weakness of central authority" (see Hawkins 1994, p. 476).

[13] Moreover, even in regions of the occupational structure that are well organized, one often finds complex combinations of nested and overlapping occupational associations that belie the simpler structure that Durkheim seemed to anticipate.

[14] In conventional class analyses, the site of production is represented in *either* nominalist *or* realist terms, and the fundamentally hybrid character of modern class systems has therefore gone unappreciated.

[15] However, given that aggregate classes persist in Germany as well-developed and deeply institutionalized groupings, the correspondence with the Durkheimian formulation is imperfect at best (see table 3.1).

Table 3.1 *Countries classified by type and amount of class structuration*

	Disaggregate structuration	
Aggregate structuration	High	Low
High	Germany	Sweden
Low	US	Japan

apprenticeship, both of which serve to encourage occupation-specific investments and promote professional commitment and craftsmanship (e.g., Blossfeld 1992). In systems of this sort, workers must invest in a single trade early in their careers, and the correspondingly high costs of retraining produce relatively closed occupational groupings. The case of Japan reveals, to the contrary, the extent to which local structuration can be institutionally suppressed. The standard characterization of Japan emphasizes such distinguishing features as an educational curriculum that is generalist in orientation rather than functionally differentiated, a vocational training system that cultivates firm-specific "nenko skills" (Dore 1973) through teamwork and continuous job rotation, an organizational commitment to lifetime employment that further strengthens firm-specific ties at the expense of more purely occupational ones, and a weakly developed system of enterprise unions that cuts across functional specializations and hence eliminates any residual craft-based loyalties (Ishida 1993; Cole 1979; Dore 1973). This conjunction of forces thus produces a "post-occupational system" that some commentators (e.g., Casey 1995) might well regard as prototypically postmodern. Finally, the Swedish case is equally problematic for Durkheim, not merely because occupational solidarities have been suppressed through "active labor market" programs (Esping-Andersen 1988, pp. 47–53), but also because aggregate classes have become corporate actors in ways that Durkheim explicitly ruled out as developmentally abnormal. Arguably, Sweden provides the textbook case of class formation of the aggregate variety, given that craft unionism and guild organization have long been supplanted by classwide forms of collective bargaining. It follows that "abnormal" organizational forms have, at least in Sweden, had rather more staying power than Durkheim allowed.

The occupationalizing forces that Durkheim emphasizes have therefore been suppressed in some countries and sectors of the labor force. The main question that emerges is whether these zones of resistance (a) will ultimately be overcome by the forces for occupationalization, (b) will live on in current form as testimony to the diversity of solutions to contemporary organizational problems, or (c) are best regarded as signaling some fundamental defect in the Durkheimian formula that will ultimately reveal itself more widely and reverse previously dominant tendencies toward sectionalism, localism, and occupationalization. Although there is clearly much room here for debate and speculation, we are of course inclined toward (a) and (b) as the most plausible interpretations, all the more so because the distinctive institutional arrangements of Sweden and Japan are under increasing threat and are no longer as frequently held up by class analysts as alternatives to be emulated.

Contemporary class analysis

We have so far argued that Durkheim deserves some credit for anticipating both the demise of aggregate classes (i.e., the negative macro-level story) and the rise of local organization at the site of production (i.e., the positive micro-level story). If this Durkheimian interpretation of the course of recent history is accepted, it raises the question of how class analysis might now be pursued. We suggest that two changes in contemporary practice are warranted: (a) the search for big classes and the sociological principles underlying them should no longer be treated as the *sine qua non* of the class analytic enterprise, and (b) the focus of class analysis might usefully shift to a local level that has heretofore been dismissed as irrelevant to research and theorizing on social class. We develop below the case for each of these arguments.

The virtues of a realist account

As for the first point, our concern is that class analysis has become disconnected from the institutional realities of contemporary labor markets, with scholars positing class mappings that are represented as *analytically* meaningful even though they have no legal or institutional standing and are not salient to employers, workers, or anyone else (save a small cadre of academics). This criticism applies, for example, to such standard sociological categories as "semicredentialed supervisors" (Wright 1997), "operatives" (Featherman and Hauser 1978), "professionals and managers" (Ehrenreich and Ehrenreich 1977), and "routine non-manuals" (Erikson and Goldthorpe 1992). Although class categories of this conventional sort are only shallowly institutionalized in the labor market, the class analyst nonetheless attempts to build a case for them (a) by claiming that they are consistent with the class analytic "logic" of some revered theorist (i.e., the "exegetical" justification), (b) by arguing that such categories, while currently latent, will nonetheless reveal themselves in the future and ultimately become classes "*für sich*" (i.e., the "latency" claim), or (c) by suggesting that these categories capture much of the important variability in life chances, political behavior, or other outcomes of interest (i.e., the "explained variance" justification). The latter claim has at least the virtue of being testable, yet in practice the proffered tests have involved little more than demonstrating that the preferred class mapping has *some* explanatory value, leaving open the question of whether other mappings might perform yet better (e.g., Evans and Mills1998; Marshall *et al.* 1988; Hout, Brooks, and Manza 1993; cf. Halaby and Weakliem 1993).

This conventional "analytic" approach often rests on the logic that scholars should look beyond surface appearances and somehow discern more fundamental forces at work. It is no accident, we suspect, that surface appearances came to be seen as misleading just as aggregate categories began to wither away. After all, the modern analyst who continues to serve up aggregate schemes in the modern context has no choice but to justify them via some deeper logic, thereby converting what would appear to be a defect (i.e., shallow institutionalization) into a virtue. This approach, while now dominant, is of course peculiarly modern. In characterizing stratification systems of the past, sociologists have typically relied on categories that were deeply institutionalized (e.g., estates, castes), thus rendering them sensible and meaningful to intellectuals and the lay public alike.

If sociologists were to return to this strategy today, it would lead them directly to the micro-level of production, where Durkheim presciently argued that deeply institutionalized categories will be found. The starting point for a modern Durkheimian analysis is accordingly the "unit occupation," which may be defined as a grouping of technically similar jobs that is institutionalized in the labor market through such means as (a) an association or union, (b) licensing or certification requirements, or (c) widely diffused understandings (among employers, workers, and others) regarding efficient or otherwise preferred ways of organizing production and dividing labor. The unit occupations so defined are often generated through jurisdictional struggles between competing groups over functional niches in the division of labor (e.g., Abbott 1988). As Granovetter and Tilly (1988) note, "Our encrusted and reified sense that one task is for orderlies, another for nurses, and yet another for doctors . . . is the result of legal, political, and economic struggles, just as are the names of the professions themselves" (p. 190). We have thus defined unit occupations in terms of the social boundaries that are constructed through closure-generating devices of various kinds. By contrast, statisticians often describe the task of constructing occupational classifications in narrowly technical terms, as if the categories defined in such schemes were merely aggregates of positions sharing "general functions and principal duties and tasks" (International Labor Office 1990 [1968], p. 5; also, Hauser and Warren 1997, p. 180). Although all unit occupations do indeed comprise technically similar tasks, this constraint hardly suffices in itself to account for the classification decisions that are embodied in conventional occupational schemes, given that the criterion of technical similarity could justify an infinity of possible combinations and aggregations of jobs. This is not to imply, of course, that socially constructed boundaries are always to be found; to the contrary, the technical division of labor is clearly "occupationalized" to varying degrees, with some sectors remaining disorganized because of minimal skill barriers or other impediments (see "Incomplete occupationalization" above). In these sectors, the task of defining unit occupations is perforce difficult, involving as it does the identification of social boundaries that are, at best, in incipient form and may never come to be well defended.[16]

Should class analysts care about local organization?

The preceding hopefully makes the case that scholars have over-invested in the search for aggregate classes and under-invested in the study of more deeply institutionalized groupings at the disaggregate level. The critic might well counter, however, that the study of local organization is perfectly suitable for scholars of occupations and professions, but is hardly the heady stuff deserving of attention of class analysts proper (see Goldthorpe 2002; Kingston 2000). This reaction, while understandable, nonetheless fails to appreciate the class-like behavior that emerges at the local level. We have argued elsewhere (Grusky and Sørensen 1998, pp. 1,196–212) that occupations act collectively on behalf of their members, extract rent and exploit nonmembers, shape life chances and lifestyles, and otherwise behave precisely as class theorists have long thought aggregate classes should. If class analysts wish to demonstrate that advanced economies are "lumpy" amalgams of competing groups (rather than seamless neoclassical markets), they would accordingly do well to turn to the local level and analyze the occupational associations

---

[16] The concept of "unit occupation" is further an artifice given that one typically finds complex webs of nested and overlapping boundaries that are not easily reducible to an exhaustive set of mutually exclusive occupations. It follows that sociologists do violence to the data by assuming that each worker must be mapped into one and only one occupation. However, insofar as such simplifying assumptions continue to be relied upon, our approach requires class analysts to identify the dominant jurisdictional settlements at the disaggregate level.

that emerge around functional niches in the division of labor. The purpose of this section is to elaborate the above argument for each of the social organizational processes (i.e., identification, closure, collective action, proximate structuration) that class analysts have sought, largely unsuccessfully, to uncover at the aggregate level.

Identification and awareness: It is natural to begin by considering the subjective domain of class systems. Although both Marx and Durkheim anticipated a great clearing operation in which solidarities outside the productive realm (e.g., ethnic or regional ties) would wither away, they differed on whether aggregate or disaggregate groupings would be the main beneficiaries of this development. The aggregate account appears, of course, to have lost out. To be sure, some sociologists remain convinced that contemporary identities are strongly shaped by aggregate affiliations (e.g., Marshall *et al.* 1988), but the prevailing post-Marxist position is that big classes now have only a weak hold over workers. For example, Emmison and Western (1990) report that only 7 percent of all Australians choose a big class as a "very important" identity, while other commentators (e.g., Saunders 1989) have stressed that open-ended queries about class identification tend to yield confused responses, refusals to answer, and even explicit denials that classes exist. This evidence has led many sociologists to conclude that class is now a "passive identity" (Bradley 1996, p. 72) and that the realm of production is no longer the dominant or principal locus of identity formation (e.g., Hall 1988; Pakulski and Waters 1996a). As we see it, the latter conclusion is overstated and fails to appreciate the continuing power of class analysis, at least in the expanded form that we are proposing here. The Emmison-Western results are again revealing on this point, since they indicate that detailed occupational groupings continue to be one of the main social identities for contemporary workers (Emmison and Western 1990, pp. 247–8). Likewise, there is much qualitative research suggesting that individual identities and self-definitions are strongly affected by occupational affiliations, almost to the point of bearing out a Durkheimian "essentialist" view that such ties provide a master identity.[17] These results are hardly surprising given that occupational affiliations are so routinely solicited in everyday interactions. For example, firms often request occupational information from clients and customers, while individuals proceed likewise in their opening gambits at parties, business meetings, and other social gatherings. The state also collects detailed occupational information when marriages, births, or deaths occur, when state benefits are requested and taxes collected, when censuses and labor force surveys are

---

[17] See, for instance, Zabusky and Barley (1996), Mortimer and Lorence (1995), Freidson (1994, pp. 89–91).

administered, and when immigrants, citizens, and jurors are admitted or selected. The disaggregate "language of occupation" is accordingly well developed and widely diffused, whereas the aggregate language of class is spoken almost exclusively in academic institutions. This state of affairs, while perhaps too obvious to interest class analysts searching for deeper truths, is also too important to ignore when attention turns to the social organization of the labor market and subjective understandings of this organization.

Social closure: If subjectivist models of class were once dominant in sociology (e.g., Warner, Meeker, and Bells 1949), they have now been superseded by approaches that focus on the social processes by which class membership is restricted to qualified eligibles.[18] These models emphasize not only the institutionalized means by which closure is secured (e.g., private property, credentials, licenses) but also the efforts of excluded parties to challenge these institutions and the inequality that they maintain. While closure theory provides, then, a new sociological language for understanding inter-class relations, the actual class mappings posited by closure theorists have proven to be standard aggregate fare. The two-class solution proposed, for example, by Parkin (1979, p. 58) features an exclusionary class comprising those who control productive capital or professional services and a subordinate class comprising all those who are excluded from these positions of control. This tendency to default to aggregate mappings reveals the hegemony of big-class formulations and the consequent inability of class analysts, even those armed with closure theory, to imagine any alternatives. Indeed, if closure theory were somehow reinvented without the coloration of class analytic convention, its authors would likely emphasize that the real working institutions of closure (e.g., professional associations, craft unions) are largely local associations "representing the credential-holders themselves" (Murphy 1988, p. 174). In most cases, the underlying mechanisms of closure (e.g., licensing, credentialing, apprenticeships) do not govern entry to aggregate classes, but instead serve only to control entry (and exit) at the more detailed occupational level. By contrast, there are no analogous organizations that represent aggregate classes, nor are there jurisdictional settlements or closure devices that are truly aggregate in scope.[19]

---

[18] See Freidson (1994, pp. 80–84), Murphy (1988), Collins (1979), Parkin (1979), Weber (1968 [1922]).

[19] The forces for aggregate closure are arguably better developed outside the workplace. For example, post-secondary schools generate closure within a broadly defined professional-managerial class, both by virtue of (a) the generalist post-secondary degrees that are "redeemable" for positions throughout this class, and (b) the classwide constriction of interaction that occurs within campus settings. Similarly, residential segregation may be

Collective action: For most neo-Marxists, social closure is of interest not because it provides a vehicle for pursuing purely local interests (e.g., "trade union consciousness"), but rather because it allegedly facilitates the development of classwide interests and grander forms of inter-class conflict. The aggregate classes identified by contemporary sociologists have so far shown a decided reluctance to act in accord with such theorizing. This quiescence at the aggregate level initially prompted various neo-Marxian salvage efforts (e.g., Poulantzas 1974; Wright 1985; Korpi 1983) and then provoked a more radical postmodernist reaction in which interests were held to be increasingly defined and established outside the realm of production (e.g., Laraña, Johnston, and Gusfield 1994). The latter form of postmodernism, popular as it is, overlooks the simple fact that much collective action flows unproblematically out of structurally defined groupings, albeit only when those groupings are defined in less aggregate terms than is conventionally the case. The three principal types of collective action at the level of unit occupations are (a) downwardly directed closure strategies designed to restrict access to occupational positions, (b) lateral competitive struggles between occupational associations over functional niches in the division of labor, and (c) upwardly directed collective action oriented toward securing occupation-specific benefits (e.g., monopoly protection) from the state and from employers. This emphasis on instrumental action at the micro-level is not inconsistent with a Durkheimian formulation. To be sure, Durkheim glossed over all discussion of the instrumental pursuits of occupational associations, but this was largely because he took them for granted and sought to cast light on more subtle and complicated extra-economic functions (Durkheim 1960 [1893], p. 15). For Durkheim, the purely instrumental action of occupational associations had neither complicated nor profound effects, as it was oriented toward straightforward sectional interests (e.g., pay, working conditions) rather than transformative or revolutionary objectives.[20] While we might conclude, then, that disaggregate class analysis is an intellectually modest project, it bears noting that aggregate class analysts have likewise scaled back their ambitions and effectively discarded comprehensive class-based theories of history (e.g., Goldthorpe

---

seen as a force for aggregate closure, as neighborhoods typically are segregated by race, ethnicity, and income rather than detailed occupation. We are simply arguing here that such closure at the aggregate level produces boundaries that are blurrier, weaker, and less deeply institutionalized than those defining occupations and controlling entry into them.

[20] Although occupational associations typically pursue sectional objectives, the spread of such associations nonetheless has unintended systemic effects, most notably the "squeezing out" of alternative classwide solidarities. We have sought to emphasize this linkage between Durkheim's micro-level and macro-level stories throughout our essay.

and Marshall 1992, p. 385). As Holton and Turner (1989) have noted, such theories have by now been largely abandoned, with the typical fall-back position being a "reconceptualization of class around non-organic *gesellschaftlich* relations or a historicization of class analysis around the few contingent moments when economic class has seemed to correspond to social class" (p. 175; also, Holton 1996; Goldthorpe and Marshall 1992, pp. 383–5).

Proximate structuration: In this sense, the class analytic project has become more limited in its objectives, with most contemporary scholars now satisfied with merely documenting that class membership conditions individual-level outcomes of all kinds (e.g., attitudes, voting behavior, lifestyles). The resulting analyses of "proximate structuration" (Giddens 1973) proceed by examining either the categorical effects of aggregate classes or the gradational effects of variables that represent the many dimensions underlying jobs (e.g., "substantive complexity") or detailed occupations (e.g., socioeconomic status). Although these approaches have yielded important results, it is nonetheless troubling that they ignore the *gemeinschaftlich* character of (some) disaggregate occupations. As argued above, modern closure is secured principally at the detailed occu-pational level, with the resulting restriction of social interaction generating occupational subcultures that are correspondingly disaggregate. These constraints on interaction serve to preserve and elaborate occupation-specific cultures of the sort that Durkheim (1960 [1893]) described long ago (also, see Caplow 1954). By contrast, aggregate classes have no com-parable influence or authority over secondary socialization, and such aggregate cultures as emerge are accordingly more diffuse and abstract.[21] The great failing, then, of conventional analyses of lifestyles, dispositions, and attitudes is that *gemeinschaftlich* occupations are regarded as nomi-nal categories and are therefore blithely aggregated or dimensionalized. Indeed, when critics of class analysis complain that "class effects" tend to be weak (esp. Kingston 2000), this argument likely capitalizes on the blunt and highly aggregate operationalization of class more than any true weakness in the effects of the site of production (see Weeden and Grusky [2002] for substantiating evidence).

Where does this leave us? We have sought to establish that the social orga-nizational processes that are often ascribed to big classes in fact emerge more clearly at a lower analytic level. We have emphasized, for example, the tendency of occupational groupings to act collectively on behalf of

---

[21] See, for instance, Lamont (2000, 1992), Bourdieu (1984 [1979]), Bernstein (1971), Kohn and Slomczynski (1990).

their interests, to defend their boundaries and thereby secure (partial) closure, to define lifestyles and consumption practices that are binding on members, and to become subjectively meaningful categories through which workers perceive themselves as well as others. To be sure, class analysts are free to claim that such processes are of interest only when revealed at aggregate levels, but doing so closes off an important route for revitalizing class analysis and protecting it from postmodernists who have exploited the characteristic weakness of big classes to (misleadingly) advance broader claims about the irrelevance of the site of production. If class analysts can see beyond their obsession with big groupings and own up to the rise of smaller class-like groupings, it may become possible to develop more powerful accounts of social behavior (e.g., Weeden and Grusky 2002), to build more realistic models of social mobility and social closure (e.g., Sørensen and Grusky 1996), and to otherwise tend to the micro-level business of class analysis in much more persuasive ways (see Grusky and Weeden [2001] for details).

Is there a Durkheimian model of exploitation and rent?

The preceding discussion suggests that disaggregate occupations can be meaningful sociopolitical communities of precisely the sort that class analysts have long sought. By contrast, it has proven difficult to find equally well-developed sociopolitical communities at the aggregate level, and class analysts have accordingly adopted the more limited objective of mapping out aggregate "structural locations" that are alleged to have the potential to become such communities in the future. Under this for-mulation, much attention is conventionally focused on identifying the underlying axes of exploitation, since these are assumed to constitute the "objective bases of antagonistic interests" (see Wright 1985) that may ultimately come to be recognized and pursued through more established sociopolitical communities. The two objectives of the present section are to explore whether Durkheim anticipated such models of exploitation and to examine how they might be usefully adapted or modified in light of his work.

A Durkheimian provenance?

For these objectives, the substantial literature on skill-based exploitation is especially relevant, and we shall therefore focus on it. In the context of this literature, Wright (1985) and others (Sørensen 1994, 2000) have equated skill-based exploitation with the extraction of rent, where the lat-ter refers to the returns to skill that are secured by limiting opportunities for training and thus artificially restricting the supply of qualified labor. If this definition is adopted, one can then test for exploitation by calculating whether the cumulated lifetime earnings of skilled labor exceed those of unskilled labor by an amount larger than the implied training costs (e.g., school tuition, foregone earnings). In a perfectly competitive market, labor will presumably flow to the most rewarding occupations, thereby equalizing the lifetime earnings of workers and eliminating exploitative returns (after correcting for training costs).[22] However, when opportunities for mobility are limited by constructing barriers that preclude workers from freely assuming highly remunerative or otherwise desirable jobs, the equilibrating flow of labor is disrupted and the potential for rent-extraction and exploitation occurs. The relatively high pay of doctors, for example, may be understood as arising from "artificial" restrictions on the number of training positions offered through medical schools.

Although skill-based exploitation of this type is sometimes represented as a generalized form of classical Marxian exploitation, the concept also has a Durkheimian provenance that has gone largely unappreciated. This becomes apparent, for example, when Durkheim (1960 [1893], pp. 374–88) rails against the constraints on free mobility that emerge either because of (a) norms or laws placing restrictions on the occupations that certain individuals may assume (e.g., caste systems, gender typing of occupations), or because of (b) economic barriers or entry costs that preclude lower-class workers from considering jobs that involve extended search or training time. The effect of both types of "forced mobility" is to reduce the bargaining power of the affected workers by eliminating or weakening their exit threat. As Durkheim (1960 [1893]) puts it, "If one class of society is obliged, in order to live, to take any price for its services, while another can abstain from such action thanks to resources at its disposal . . ., the second has an unjust advantage over the first" (p. 384). The resulting potential for exploitation can be addressed by opening up mobility opportunities through direct or indirect interventions in the labor market. That is, Durkheim would have us equalize market opportunities not only by directly removing normative and legal restrictions on the free flow of labor (e.g., removing prohibitions on the mobility of caste members), but also by prohibiting parents from transmitting wealth and assets that indirectly advantage their children in the competition for desirable jobs (Durkheim 1960 [1893], pp. 30–1, 374–88).[23]

[22] We are ignoring here the inequality that arises by virtue of effort, native ability, and compensating differentials.

[23] It is conventional at this point to criticize Durkheim for failing to appreciate how upper-class parents also transmit social and cultural resources to their children. This critique clearly has merit, but also ought not be overstated. Although Durkheim does not emphasize noneconomic inequalities to the extent that contemporary sociologists would, he does appreciate that some "illegitimate" inequalities would perforce persist even if economic inheritance were eliminated (see Lehmann [1995] for a relevant discussion).

This formulation anticipates contemporary understandings of exploitation insofar as it recognizes that the bargaining power of workers is a function of the supply and demand for labor within their occupations. At the same time, the modern conception of rent is only partly and imperfectly anticipated, not merely because Durkheim emphasized the unfairness and inefficiency of "forced mobility" more than the exploitative wage terms that it allowed, but also because he focused on the wages foregone by workers trapped in undesirable occupations more than the rent extracted when privileged workers act to restrict the supply of competitors.

Improving contemporary models of skill-based exploitation

Although Durkheim thus fell well short of anticipating a systematic model of rent, his emphasis on local organization is nonetheless instructive when considering how contemporary models of skill-based exploitation might be improved. Indeed, given that modern institutions of closure (e.g., professional associations, craft unions) generate local rather than class-wide restrictions on labor supply, the logic of the Durkheimian position suggests that rent is principally extracted at the local level. As we have stressed, Durkheim was especially interested in the extra-economic functions of occupational associations, yet he appreciated that such associations also provided their members with the "force needed to safeguard their common interests" (Durkheim 1960 [1893], p. 11). This force may be used to restrict the number of new entrants to an occupation, to prohibit competing occupations from performing similar functions, and to otherwise generate pockets of monopoly control within the division of labor. For the most part, neo-Marxians have instead argued for big "exploitation classes" that encompass and cut across many occupations, with the rationale for such aggregation being the usual analytic one that workers in structurally similar positions are equivalently exploited, have interests that are accordingly shared, and may ultimately come to form solidary crosscutting groups to press such shared interests. This approach is problematic because the posited classes typically have no institutional or social organizational standing; that is, the working institutions of closure are organized largely at the occupational level (see "Social closure" above), and the potential for rent therefore emerges at that level. As a result, the elementary units of skill-based exploitation are occupations themselves, while neo-Marxian classes are heterogeneous aggregations of jobs and occupations that have structurally similar capacities for exploitation. It is always possible, of course, that rent-extracting exploiters with "structurally similar" capacities will ultimately band together to protect the credentialing institutions that make closure and rent possible (see Grusky and Sørensen 1998, pp. 1,211–12). In this sense, disaggregate class mappings serve to characterize the contemporary structure of rent-extraction, whereas conventional big-class mappings serve as hypotheses about how that structure might simplify in the future.

The more fundamental question, of course, is whether the underlying structure of rent-extraction will come to shape how interests are understood and pressed. From a neo-Durkheimian standpoint, the conventional definition of skill-based rent might well be critiqued as too arcane and academic to become widely diffused, especially given that countervailing stories about the appropriateness and legitimacy of occupational wage differentials are so widely accepted. As Durkheim saw it, consensual beliefs about the "level of reward ... appropriate to the various occupational groups" (Parkin 1992, p. 62) will inevitably emerge in all societies, with such beliefs holding sway even when forced mobility and exploitation account for the observed differentials (see, especially, Durkheim 1951 [1897], p. 126). The occupational structure should be regarded, then, as a double-edged sword that works simultaneously to create closure and extract rent (i.e., the "rent-extraction" side) and to legitimate that rent and convince us that it is appropriate and unproblematic (i.e., the "rent-legitimation" side). The latter legitimating efforts may rest on beliefs about the importance of filling the most important occupations with the best workers (i.e., "functionalism"), about the sacredness or inviolability of market-determined rewards (i.e., "market legitimation"), or about the appropriateness of compensating workers for completing difficult or unpleasant tasks (i.e., "compensating differentials").

Whatever the story, the result is that inter-occupational differentials in earnings are typically regarded as acceptable, whereas intra-occupational differentials are closely scrutinized and are sometimes taken as evidence of discrimination (especially when correlated with race, gender, or ethnicity). It is no accident, for example, that anti-discrimination legislation has flourished just as comparable worth legislation has languished. In explaining this outcome, we need only appreciate that anti-discrimination legislation seeks to outlaw intra-occupational disparities in wages, whereas comparable worth legislation seeks to prohibit entrenched inter-occupational disparities that are legitimated with cultural stories about functional importance, market forces, and compensating differentials (see Nelson and Bridges 1999). The institutionalization of an occupational classification scheme thus trains us to regard between-category disparities as appropriate and legitimate. Indeed, there is much rhetoric in Durkheim 1951 [1897] about the importance of developing well-legitimated "classification schemes," precisely because they rein in potentially disruptive aspirations and prevent the weakest from "endlessly multiplying their protests" (p. 383; also, see Zeitlin 1968, p. 275). For many sociologists, a more palatable value-free position is simply that these legitimating forces are exceedingly well-developed, thus calling into question any theory of rent suggesting that rent-extraction will ultimately become exposed and activate antagonistic interests that were previously latent.

The upshot, then, of our commentary is that big-class formulations cannot be salvaged by simply shifting over to rent-based definitions of class. When conventional definitions of skill-based rent are applied, a neo-Durkheimian should immediately point out that (a) such rent is extracted at a more local level than most class analysts appreciate, and (b) the very institutionalization of occupational classification schemes works to legitimate occupational wage differentials and to suppress the development of antagonistic interests. It follows that the categories of a micro-class scheme may never come to be invested with those antagonistic properties that class analysts have long sought.

Is more disaggregation always better?

In arguing for our neo-Durkheimian approach, we have referred to all competing class analytic models in quite generic terms, labeling them variously as "big-class," aggregate, or gradational approaches. Although it has been convenient to treat conventional approaches as a whole, it is worth considering at this point whether all class models are equally vulnerable to the criticisms that we have been advancing. As indicated in table 3.2, six general types of categorical schemes and scales may be usefully distinguished, each combining a particular level of measurement (i.e., continuous, categorical) with a preferred unit of analysis (i.e., unit occupation, occupational aggregate, job-level aggregate). In the foregoing sections, we have principally focused on models that either scale occupations (i.e., Type A and C models) or aggregate them (i.e., Type D models), making it possible to pitch our critique in terms of the heterogeneity that is suppressed when "similar" unit occupations are coded into a single class or into similar levels on a gradational scale. This emphasis is justifiable given that most sociologists default to class models of these general types (i.e., Types A, C, and D).[24] At the same time, some analysts have of course sought to understand the social organization of production by treating jobs (rather than occupations) as the elementary

---

[24] In their recent work, Erikson and Goldthorpe (1992) have sought to motivate their class scheme with reference to job-level properties (i.e., terms of employment), even though the scheme itself has always been operationalized at the occupational level.

Table 3.2 *Models of social organization at the site of production*

Level of measurement	Type of aggregation or disaggregation		
	Unit occupations	Occupational aggregates	Job-level aggregates
Continuous	*Type A Models*: Prestige, socioeconomic, and cultural capital scales (e.g., Hauser and Warren 1997; Bourdieu 1984 [1979])	*Type C Models*: Hollingshead occupational scale (e.g., Hollingshead and Redlich 1958)	*Type E Models*: Scales of working conditions and job desirability (e.g., Kohn and Slomczynski 1990; Jencks, Perman, and Rainwater 1988)
Categorical	*Type B Models*: Neo-Durkheimian micro-classes (Grusky and Sørensen 1998)	*Type D Models*: Neo-Weberian classes (e.g., Erikson and Goldthorpe 1992; Featherman and Hauser 1978)	*Type F Models*: Neo-Marxian "exploitation classes" (e.g., Wright 1985)

unit of analysis, thus raising the question of whether our concerns and arguments apply equally to such alternative approaches.

We may define a job as the "specific and sometimes unique bundle of activities carried out by a person in the expectation of economic remuneration" (Hauser and Warren 1997, p. 180). In conventional labor markets, there are at least as many jobs as there are workers, and analysts of job-level data can therefore choose to disaggregate even more radically than we have been advocating. We might usefully ask whether a neo-Durkheimian should be attracted to the possibility of such extreme disaggregation. In addressing this question, it should be recalled that unit occupations are socially constructed through various closure-generating mechanisms, such as associations, unions, and licensing or certification. It is this "social clothing" worn by functionally similar jobs that makes unit occupations relatively homogeneous categories. The sources of such homogeneity are threefold: (a) unit occupations select for workers who are consistent with pre-existing occupational "stereotypes" (e.g., sociology attracts left-leaning recruits); (b) explicit training regimens introduce further homogeneity in the attitudes, behaviors, and worldviews of prospective incumbents (e.g., graduate school, vocational training, apprenticeships); and (c) social interaction occurs disproportionately within occupational boundaries and thus reinforces occupation-specific attitudes, values, and lifestyles. At some point, the explanatory returns to disaggregation should accordingly diminish, as the inveterate splitter disaggregates beyond the occupational boundaries that are institutionalized in the labor market and that generate homogeneity.

The class analysts advocating Type E or F models will concede that some aggregation or dimensionalizing of jobs is required, but they of course opt against aggregating up to socially constructed occupational boundaries. Instead, an "analytical" approach is again preferred, with the objective thus being to identify the technical conditions of work (e.g., substantive complexity, autonomy) that structure interests, affect processes of social interaction, or otherwise condition the outcomes of interest. This approach has obviously yielded important results. However, because jobs that share the same abstract technical conditions (e.g., substantive complexity) are not socially organized into meaningful groups, such homogeneity as is found arises from the direct effects of technical conditions rather than the additional socially induced effects of selection, shared training, and interactional closure. The explanatory losses involved in foregoing these social effects may be substantial.

The limitations of analytic approaches can be more closely examined by considering the familiar case of sociologists and their seemingly distinctive "habitus" (Bourdieu 1984 [1979]). In seeking, for example, to account for the humanist, antimaterialist, and otherwise left-leaning culture and lifestyle of sociologists, a neo-Durkheimian would emphasize (a) the left-leaning reputation of sociology and the consequent self-selection of left-leaning recruits, (b) the liberalizing effects of lengthy professional training and socialization into the sociological worldview, and (c) the reinforcing effects of social interaction with like-minded colleagues. To be sure, sociologists also labor under distinctive working conditions (e.g., high autonomy, high complexity), but the effects of such abstract technical conditions would appear to be swamped by the foregoing social forces. The case of economists provides an instructive contrast here; after all, economists labor under quite similar job conditions (e.g., high autonomy, high complexity), yet are nonetheless comparatively conservative in their politics and lifestyles. It would be difficult to account for such conservatism without recognizing that economists are self-selected for conservatism, that their graduate training in neoclassical approaches only reinforces this pre-existing affinity for conservatism, and that their subsequent interaction with fellow economists further protects against any ideological "straying." The conservatism of economists would appear, then, to be socially produced rather than attributable to the technical conditions under which they labor.

The purely analytic approach of Type E and F models is thus weakened because the posited class categories are not held together by the homogenizing effects of selection, socialization, and interactional closure. This line of argumentation is of course identical to that earlier advanced against Type A, C, and D models. Although our preferred micro-classes are not nested within job-level class categories (and hence the rhetoric of "disaggregation" cannot be strictly applied), this in no way alters or affects our larger argument about the virtues of sociological realism.

Conclusions

In his celebrated preface to the *Division of Labor*, Durkheim (1960 [1893], p. 28) predicted that corporate occupations would gradually become "intercalated between the state and the individual," thereby solving the problem of order by regulating and institutionalizing industrial conflict and by creating new forms of solidarity at the detailed occupational level. This account is ritually rehearsed by scholars of Durkheim but has never been treated as a credible developmental model by class analysts. As neo-Marxian class models are subjected to increasing attack, class analysts have typically fallen back to some version of neo-Weberianism or postmodernism, neither of which pays much attention to the occupation-level structuration that Durkheim emphasized. There is, then, much room for exploring a neo-Durkheimian third road that refocuses attention on local organization within the division of labor.

This "third road" involves opening up new research questions more than providing ready or stock answers. As a sampling of such research, we list below five empirical questions of interest, each of which speaks to standard areas of inquiry within the class analytic tradition (see Grusky and Weeden [2001] for more details).

Are the effects of social class adequately captured by big-class categories? Although we have suggested that conventional classes fail to exploit the explanatory power available at the site of production, we have not provided any empirical evidence on behalf of this claim; and the burden of proof necessarily rests with scholars who seek to improve on existing approaches. In many conventional class schemes, the posited categories are merely aggregations of detailed occupations (see table 3.2), and it becomes possible to test such aggregations by examining whether much explanatory power is lost by imposing them (see Weeden and Grusky 2002). These tests should of course be carried out for "class correlates" of all kinds (e.g., attitudes, consumption practices, life chances, lifestyles).

Is aggregation more defensible in some sectors of the class structure than in others? The costs of aggregation may be especially high in some classes. For example, the lifestyles of nonmanual workers are likely to be quite heterogeneous, since occupations in the nonmanual sector are well formed and their incumbents are accordingly exposed to distinctive cultures and socializing experiences. The lower manual sector, by contrast, is typically represented as a relatively homogeneous zone in which occupationalization is only weakly developed. As plausible as it is, this standard account has not been pitted against any number of alternatives, most notably the null hypothesis that academics are simply more sensitive to occupational distinctions in sectors of the class structure with which they are most familiar.

Are some occupations especially well formed? The contours of disaggregate structuration are likewise of interest. The conventional story here is that craft occupations are paradigmatic in their fusing of work and lifestyle (Mills 1956, p. 223), but we suspect that well-developed lifestyles also exist elsewhere in the occupational structure. The available evidence, such as it is, suggests that disaggregate structuration will be most pronounced when (a) training is harsh or lengthy (e.g., doctors, professors), (b) workers are isolated or stigmatized (e.g., sanitation workers, loggers, carnival workers), or (c) recruitment is highly self-selective by virtue of social networks (e.g., actors), economic barriers to entry (e.g., capitalist), or the unusual tastes and skills that an occupation requires (e.g., morticians). These hypotheses can be pursued by examining the heterogeneity of lifestyles and behaviors within unit occupations.

Are social classes decomposing as postmodernists allege? In postmodern circles, the main debates of interest implicitly address issues of trend, with the most extreme accounts implying that all forms of structure at the site of production are withering away. The evidence amassed in support of this claim is nonetheless quite limited. Indeed, virtually all relevant research pertains to trends in aggregate structuration, and even here the available evidence refers principally to voting behavior (e.g., Evans 1997), life chances (e.g., Erikson and Goldthorpe 1992), and a few other standard outcomes (see Grusky and Weeden 2001). The evidence thus falls well short of substantiating a "class destructuration" thesis in the broad and encompassing terms that it usually takes.

Is the underlying structure of social mobility misrepresented by big-class models? If social closure is secured mainly at the unit occupational level, then conventional aggregate analyses may underestimate the extent of rigidity and persistence in mobility regimes (Sørensen and Grusky 1996; Rytina 2000). Moreover, given that much of the cross-national variability in local structuration is concealed through aggregation, we may find that standard convergence hypotheses are no longer plausible once mobility data are disaggregated. The existing literature on social mobility, massive though it is, has been especially beholden to big-class formulations and is accordingly vulnerable when revisited at the micro-class level.

We are thus arguing that conventional research on "class effects" can be usefully revisited. Although big-class formulations will likely remain dominant, the discipline should at least consider the possibility that a wrong turn has been taken and that much explanatory action will be found within big classes. It is well to bear in mind that big-class models were initially devised to account for macro-level transformative events and large-scale social change (see Grusky, Weeden, and Sørensen 2000). As class conflict became institutionalized, class theorists have gradually de-emphasized these macro-level theories of history and related developmental narratives (Holton and Turner 1989), preferring instead to deploy class categories for the more modest academic task of explaining contemporary micro-level behavior (e.g., voting behavior, lifestyles). The contemporary fascination with tinkering, adapting, and revising big-class formulations may be understood as the flailing efforts of a subfield coming to terms with this new agenda. It is altogether possible, of course, that no amount of tinkering will suffice. If the contemporary micro-level agenda is taken seriously, it may require new micro-class models that go beyond big-class nominalism and exploit such local social organization as can be found.

4   Foundations of Pierre Bourdieu's class analysis

Elliot B. Weininger

At the time of his death in January 2002, Pierre Bourdieu was perhaps the most prominent sociologist in the world (see Calhoun and Wacquant 2002). As the author of numerous classic works, he had become a necessary reference point in various "specialty" areas throughout the discipline (including education, culture, "theory," and the sociology of knowledge); he had also achieved canonical status in cultural anthropology as a result of his studies of the Kabyle in northern Algeria during the war for independence and its aftermath.[1] Nevertheless, Bourdieu's prominence increased exponentially during the 1990s, when he became a highly visible participant in political struggles against the neoliberal orthodoxy that was coming to dominate political discourse in Continental Europe (see Bourdieu 1998a; 2001a).[2]

Social class constitutes a fundamental analytic category in much of Bourdieu's research – so much so that he is routinely included in lists of leading contemporary class theorists. Yet despite its centrality, the particular understanding of this concept that animates his work remains murky in the secondary literature. There are, in fact, a number of reasons why it is unusually difficult to grasp:

- Neither Bourdieu's understanding of class nor his more general conceptual apparatus can be identified with a single "father figure" – whether this be Marx, Weber, Durkheim, or some lesser-known luminary – or with a research tradition descending from such a figure. To the contrary, on the question of class, as on most other questions, Bourdieu borrowed as needed from the sociological canon.
- Bourdieu was deeply opposed to the separation of theory and research – to such an extent that nearly all of his conceptual innovations were developed only in the context of concrete empirical analyses. This creates numerous difficulties for any discussion charged with providing a

---

[1] For a general introduction to Bourdieu's work, see Bourdieu and Wacquant (1992), as well as Swartz (1997), Brubaker (1985), and the essays collected in Calhoun, LiPuma, and Postone (1993).

[2] Political involvement, however, was not new to Bourdieu (see 2002).

"foundational" account of his approach to class or any other sociological object.[3] Analytic propositions must be extracted from instances of their application with as little distortion as possible. Furthermore, it is necessary, particularly when undertaking such an account in a place or time different from that in which Bourdieu wrote, to untangle the substance of these propositions from the peculiarities of the context to which they were applied.

- Bourdieu eschewed the "positivistic" methodological orientations that have become entrenched in much English-language class analysis: within an *œuvre* that spans thousands of pages, one will find almost no reliance on standard multivariate techniques. At the same time, however, he did not simply advocate "qualitative" methods. Instead, his research draws on an amalgamation of quantitative and qualitative data. Because the explanatory logic underlying this use of data is neither familiar nor obvious, his argumentation can be difficult to follow.
- In contrast to various prominent schools of contemporary class analysis, Bourdieu did not make use of rational action theory. Indeed, his account of social class is distinguished from these schools on two grounds. First, his theory of action revolved around the concept of "habitus," defined as a socially constituted system of dispositions that orient "thoughts, perceptions, expressions, and actions" (Bourdieu 1990a [1980], p. 55). In Bourdieu's sociology, action generated by the habitus can certainly approximate that specified by rational action theory, but only when situated within a social context sufficiently similar to that in which the habitus was formed. Rationality, in other words, is "*socially* bounded" in his view (Bourdieu and Wacquant 1992, p. 126; Bourdieu 1990a [1980], pp. 63–4). Secondly, however, Bourdieu's approach to social class also reserved an essential place for the analysis of symbolic systems – an element which typically finds little or no place in models predicated on the assumption of rational action.

Given these obstacles, an elaboration of Bourdieu's approach to social class cannot be reduced to the presentation of a list of axiomatic propositions. To the contrary, such an elaboration must, first and foremost, take as its point of departure a concrete exercise in class analysis. In Bourdieu's case, this implies a focus on the now-classic study, *Distinction: A Social Critique of the Judgment of Taste* (1984; originally published in 1979). It is in the context of an examination of this study (supplemented, to be sure,

---

[3] Bourdieu was generally skeptical of attempts to work out the theoretical logic underlying his works in isolation from their empirical deployment (referring derisively to such attempts as "scholasticism"). Nevertheless, he did undertake, albeit tentatively, the theoretical clarification of various concepts. On the question of social class, these include Bourdieu 1987; 1990b, pp. 122–39; 1991, pp. 229–51; 1998b [1994], 1–18.

by a consideration of relevant earlier and later works) that we can confront Bourdieu's unique conceptual apparatus and his uncharacteristic methods for handling data.

Preliminary themes

Based on data collected in France in the 1960s and 1970s, *Distinction* takes as its object the relation between social classes and status groups – with the latter understood, following Weber, in the sense of collectivities defined by a uniformity of lifestyle.[4] Before proceeding to a discussion of the text, however, two basic concerns can be specified that motivate many of the unique features of Bourdieu's approach to class. These relate to (1) the significance and role of the analysis of *symbolic systems* in class analysis, and (2) the question of *boundaries* between classes.

In an early article that sketched many of the arguments which later appeared in *Distinction*, Bourdieu explicitly takes up Weber's well-known account of "class" and "status group":

> everything seems to indicate that Weber opposes class and status group as two types of *real* unities which would come together more or less frequently according to the type of society . . . ; [however,] to give Weberian analyses all of their force and impact, it is necessary to see them instead as *nominal* unities . . . which are always the result of a choice to accent the economic aspect or the symbolic aspect – aspects which always coexist in the same reality . . . (Bourdieu 1966, pp. 212–13; my addition; emphases modified)

Bourdieu thus interprets Weber's contrast between class and status in terms of a distinction between the material (or "economic") and the symbolic. He maintains, moreover, that these should not be viewed as alternative types of stratification giving rise to different types of social collectivities. To the contrary, the distinction between class and status group must be seen purely as an analytical convenience – one which Bourdieu, moreover, is inclined to disallow. The upshot of this is an insistence that class analysis can not be reduced to the analysis of economic relations; rather, it *simultaneously* entails an analysis of symbolic relations, roughly along the lines of the status differentiation referred to by Weber.

In addition to asserting that class analysis has both an economic and a symbolic dimension, Bourdieu also rejects one of the most fundamental aspects of class theory: the perceived obligation to demarcate classes from

---

[4] As Weber put it, "status honor is normally expressed by the fact that above all else a specific *style of life* can be expected from those who wish to belong to the circle" (1958, p. 187).

one another *a priori*. The reasons behind this rejection are apparent in remarks such as the following:

[n]umerous studies of "social classes"... merely elaborate the practical questions which are forced on those who hold political power. Political leaders are continually faced with the... practical imperatives which arise from the logic of the struggle within the political field, such as... the need to mobilize the greatest possible number of votes while at the same time asserting the irreducibility of their project to those of other leaders. Thus they are condemned to raise the problem of the social world in the typically substantialist logic of the boundaries between groups and the size of the mobilizable group... (Bourdieu 1991, p. 246)

Bourdieu was led to disassociate the sociology of class from the project of theoretically specifying boundaries between classes for a number of reasons. In the first place, argumentation over the boundary separating one social collectivity from another is a fundamental form of political conflict, and Bourdieu adhered throughout his career to a vision of social science which repudiated the amalgamation of political and scientific interest (on this point, see also Donnelly 1997).[5] Secondly, he contends that by drawing boundaries ahead of time, sociologists also run the risk (in their research practice, and possibly even their theory) of treating classes as "self-subsistent entities... which come 'preformed,' and only then... [enter into] dynamic flows... " (Emirbayer 1997, p. 283) – or in other words, according to a "substantialist" logic. Both of these objections stem, in part, from Bourdieu's antipathy towards arguments (frequent during the 1960s and 1970s) over the "real" lines of division separating classes – above all, those separating the "middle class" from the proletariat – and the political implications of the location of these lines. Against the fundamental premises of such arguments, Bourdieu insists vehemently that "the question with which all sociology ought to begin" is "that of the existence... and mode of existence of collectives" (Bourdieu 1991, p. 250). As will be seen, the implication of this question is that boundaries must be understood in terms of *social practices* rather than *theoretical conjecture*.

Having identified these fundamental concerns, we may turn to a discussion of *Distinction*. The following section (II) will provide an initial sketch of Bourdieu's understanding of class, one that, of necessity, abstracts from its full complexity. This will serve to bring into focus the dogged manner in which he pursues the question of "the existence... and mode of existence of collectives." In doing so, it will also necessarily introduce

---

[5] Thus, in *Distinction*, Bourdieu declares that "many of the words which sociology uses to designate the classes it constructs are borrowed from ordinary usage, where they serve to express the (generally polemical) view that one group has of another" (Bourdieu 1984 [1979], p. 169).

elements from Bourdieu's formidable conceptual arsenal – including the central notions of capital, habitus, and field. The subsequent section (III) will return to issues that were initially left aside in order to provide a more comprehensive view. In particular, it will take up the subject of how different forms of social domination are related to one another in Bourdieu's work, and how his views evolved over the course of his career.

An outline of Bourdieu's theory of class

Bourdieu describes *Distinction* as "an endeavor to rethink Max Weber's opposition between class and *Stand*" (1984 [1979], p. xii). As we have seen, this endeavor had occupied him since the 1960s, in particular because it raised the question of the relation between the economic and the symbolic. In Bourdieu's view, differences of status (that is, of lifestyle) may be seen as manifestations of social class differences. To evaluate this proposition, he devises an explanatory argument which postulates, first, a causal connection between class location and "habitus"; and, secondly, a relation of "expression" between habitus and a variety of practices situated in different domains of consumption – practices which cohere symbolically to form a whole (a "style of life"). Thirdly, however, Bourdieu further asserts that these practices serve to constitute social collectivities – that is, "status groups" – by establishing symbolic boundaries between individuals occupying different locations in the class structure. The process through which this occurs is a contentious one, taking the form of what he calls a "classificatory struggle." And, finally, Bourdieu demonstrates that this struggle amounts to only one of the many modalities through which "symbolic power" is exercised.

Class structure

To start with, it must be recognized that for Bourdieu, the notion of a class structure encompasses the entirety of the occupational division of labor. This implies that he grants the notion a considerably wider purview than do Marxian theories, which restrict its scope to a system of positions defined in terms of ownership of and/or control over the means of production. Consequently, Bourdieu is not confronted by the problem upon which so many Marxian theories have foundered – namely, that of determining how to cope with all those positions in the division of labor which cannot be characterized in terms of the canonical division between "owners" and "workers" (or which cannot be characterized "adequately" or "satisfactorily" in these terms). Thus, his model effectively encompasses not only the "middle-class" occupations that have been the source of so much grief in the Marxian tradition, but also those which have hovered at the fringes of most class analytical schemes, including positions in public administration and the state "apparatus," the so-called "professions," and – not least of all – intellectuals, artists, and other "cultural producers."

In Bourdieu's understanding, the occupational division of labor forms a *system*. This implies that locations in the division of labor are differentiated from – and thus related to – one another in terms of theoretically meaningful factors. For Bourdieu, these factors derive from the distributions of "capital." Bourdieu regards as capital "the set of actually usable resources and powers" (1984, p. 114). He insists, moreover, that there exist multiple *species* of capital which cannot be subsumed under a single generic concept. In the present context, the most important of these are economic and cultural capital (see Bourdieu 1986; Bourdieu and Wacquant 1992, pp. 117–20).[6] Whereas Bourdieu tended to treat the meaning of the former concept as more or less self-evident throughout the course his career, the latter was the object of extensive elaboration (and has given rise to extensive debate). Put simply, the notion of cultural capital merely refers to a culturally specific "competence," albeit one which is unequally distributed and which is efficacious – as a "resource" or a "power" – in a particular social setting (see Lareau and Weininger 2003). In highly differentiated societies, two social agencies are primarily responsible for "inculcating" cultural capital: the family and the school. Its most fundamental feature lies in the fact that, because it is embodied, its acquisition requires an investment of time (Bourdieu 1986, p. 244–6).[7]

Bourdieu thus develops his model of the class structure by means of an analysis of survey data which includes a wide variety of indicators of the economic and cultural capital possessed by individuals located in positions throughout the occupational system. The model may be

---

[6] Bourdieu is well known for also having identified a third form of capital: "social capital" (see Bourdieu 1986). This form of capital is of secondary importance in the analysis of capitalist societies for Bourdieu; it took on a more central role, however, in his occasional discussions of state socialist societies (see Bourdieu 1998b [1994], pp. 14–18).

[7] Cultural capital may also exist in an "objectified" form – that is, in the form of material objects whose production or consumption presupposes a quantum of embodied cultural capital. And, it may occur in an "institutionalized" form, meaning as an embodied competence which has been certified by an official agency possessing the authority to legally "warrant" its existence – that is, in the form of educational credentials (Bourdieu 1986). One of the foremost characteristics of cultural capital, for Bourdieu, is hereditability; as such, it can make a substantial contribution to the intergenerational reproduction of the distribution of individuals across class locations, since "the social conditions of its transmission and acquisition are more disguised than those of economic capital" (Bourdieu 1986, p. 245).

understood as a factorial space constituted by three orthogonal axes.[8]
The first (and most important) axis differentiates locations in the occupational system according to the total *volume* of capital (economic and
cultural) possessed by incumbents. For Bourdieu, class location is a function of position on this axis. Thus, his data indicate that members of
occupational categories such as industrialists, private sector executives,
and college professors occupy overlapping positions at the upper end of
the axis, and hence share the same class location; Bourdieu thus refers
to these categories collectively as the "dominant class" (or sometimes
the "bourgeoisie"). Similarly, manual workers and farm laborers occupy
overlapping positions at the other end of the axis, indicating that they
share a class location opposed to the occupations making up the dominant class; these categories are collectively designated the "working class"
(or "*les classes populaires*"). In between, we find overlapping occupational
categories such as small business owners, technicians, secretaries, and
primary school teachers, which are collectively termed the "petty bourgeoisie" (see Bourdieu 1984 [1979], pp. 128–9).

The second axis in the factorial space differentiates positions within
class locations. Bourdieu refers to opposed positions along this axis with
the Marxian vocabulary of "class fractions." This terminology, however,
should not be interpreted according to Marxian theories, as the meaning
he attributes to it falls well outside the scope of Marxism. For Bourdieu,
classes are divided internally according to the *composition* of the capital
possessed by incumbents – that is, the relative preponderance of economic or cultural capitals within "the set of actually usable resources
and powers." Thus, occupational categories within the dominant class
are differentiated from one another such that professors and "artistic
producers" – the occupations whose incumbents hold the greatest cultural capital and the least economic capital – are opposed to industrialists
and commercial employers – the occupations whose incumbents hold a
preponderance of economic capital but relatively little cultural capital.
Located in between these two polar extremes are the professions, whose
incumbents exhibit a relatively symmetrical asset structure. In a similar manner, the petty bourgeoisie is differentiated along the second axis
between the small business owners, endowed primarily with economic

---

[8] Bourdieu's preferred statistical technique is Multiple Correspondence Analysis (MCA), a
technique similar to factor analysis, but used with categorical variables. One characteristic
of MCA which is of particular interest to him is the fact that individual cases retain
their categorical "identities" within the factorial space. This makes it possible to plot
the dispersion of the members of each occupational category within the space (see the
summary results of such an analysis provided in Bourdieu 1984 [1979], pp. 128–9, and
for "full" models, pp. 262, 340). For an interesting discussion of Bourdieu's use of MCA,
see Rouanet, Ackermann, and Le Roux (2000).

capital, and primary school teachers, endowed primarily with cultural capital. Intermediate between them are categories such as technicians, office workers, and secretaries.[9]

The occupational division of labor is differentiated along a third axis, one which amounts to a quasi-structural treatment of time. Generated primarily from indicators of the economic and cultural capital of the family of origin, this axis differentiates positions according to the *trajectories* followed by their incumbents – or in other words, according to the change or stability they have experienced over time in the volume and composition of their capital. Here Bourdieu's data reveal, for example, that members of the professions are more likely than any other members of the bourgeoisie to have been born into this class. His approach, it can be noted, opens up an intriguing area for the study of mobility: in addition to vertical movements (along the first axis), mobility may also entail "horizontal" or "transverse" movements (along the second axis) – that is, an individual's class location and his or her fraction location are simultaneously variable over time. Bourdieu refers to the latter type of movement, in which a preponderance of one type of asset gives way to a preponderance of the other, as a "conversion" of capitals.[10]

The model that Bourdieu constructs of occupational division of labor in this manner is intended to be understood as a structure of objective positions – that is, as locations which are "occupied" by individuals, but which exist as a "quasi reality" (Bourdieu and Wacquant 1992, p. 27) independently of them. As such, Bourdieu terms it the *social space* of the social formation under analysis. It is meant to represent a single system of objective relations between the various possible combinations of the most important "powers and resources" in the social formation, and their evolution over time. As such, it stands at considerable distance from those developed by the more familiar traditions of class analysis. In particular, Bourdieu's social space is separated from them by the fact that the three axes which constitute it – volume, composition, and trajectory – are viewed as *continuous* dimensions, from both a methodological and a theoretical vantage point (Bourdieu 1990a [1980], p. 140). This implies that the model does not postulate any inherent lines of cleavage specifying the structural threshold where one class gives way to another, and

---

[9] Bourdieu is incapable of differentiating fractions within the working class on the basis of his available data; he remains strongly convinced, however, that better data would enable him to draw such a contrast (Bourdieu 1984 [1979], p. 115).

[10] Mobility along the "horizontal" axis of the structure is governed by what Bourdieu calls the prevailing "conversion rate" between the different capitals (for example, the prevailing economic costs and returns associated with education). This rate is historically variable, being the product of conflicts between those who hold a preponderance of one or the other species of capital.

hence, that within "this universe of continuity" the identification of discrete class (and fraction) locations amounts to no more than a heuristic convenience (see Bourdieu 1984 [1979], pp. 258–9, 339). Correlatively, although the fact that Bourdieu conceptualizes social space in gradational terms appears to echo those "stratification" models in which the occupational order is understood as a continuous scale of positions (differentiated, for example, in terms of the rewards they carry), it nevertheless stands far apart from them by virtue of its *multidimensional* configuration (see Bourdieu 1984 [1979], pp. 124–5; also 1991, pp. 244–5). As noted, this opens the way to an analysis of forms of mobility ("conversion" of capital) that such models ignore; and, as will be demonstrated, it also opens the way to an analysis of forms of conflict that such models are incapable of acknowledging.[11]

Class habitus

Bourdieu establishes an *indirect* causal link between positions in social space and practices by means of the concept of habitus, which in his explanatory scheme provides an essential mediation: "social class, understood as a system of objective determinations, must be brought into relation not with the individual or with the 'class' as a population, i.e. as an aggregate of . . . individuals, but with the *class habitus*" (Bourdieu 1977 [1972], p. 85, emphases altered). This concept, more than any other in Bourdieu's repertoire, has given rise to perpetual meta-theoretical debate. In the present context, such debates can be safely ignored, and we can broach the subject of the habitus from a perspective suited to the question of *Distinction* and the class analysis undertaken there.

Bourdieu describes the fundamental purpose of the concept as that of "escaping both the objectivism of action understood as a mechanical reaction 'without an agent' and the subjectivism which portrays action as the deliberate pursuit of a conscious intention . . . " (Bourdieu and Wacquant

---

[11] As they themselves suggest, Bourdieu's conception of social space does resemble the "disaggregative" orientation to class analysis developed by Grusky and Sørensen (1998), at least insofar as both center on the occupational system. Nevertheless, substantial differences must be recognized. In particular, although Grusky and Sørensen wish to argue that occupational locations share many of the properties traditionally attributed to classes, it is difficult to see how, within their framework, one could speak of an occupational *structure* – on analogy to the traditional notion of a *class structure*. This is because they are unwilling to specify a principle (or principles) of variation or of differentiation which could establish theoretically meaningful relations between the total set of locations within the occupational system. Put simply, their approach lacks an analogue to Bourdieu's identification of volume, composition, and trajectory as the constitutive dimensions of social space. Thus, one might question the general appropriateness of their use of the class idiom.

1992, p. 121).[12] Above all, the notion of habitus designates a socially constituted system of *dispositions*. As such, it implies a view according to which actions are generated neither by explicit consideration of norms (that is, via the conscious subsumption of the action situation under a morally binding "rule") nor by rational calculation (that is, via calculation of the relative risks and rewards likely to accrue to different possible courses of action). Rather, in keeping with pragmatist philosophies, a dispositional understanding implies that under "typical" circumstances, action can proceed on a *pre-reflexive* basis – in other words, without recourse to conscious reflection on rules or estimations of results. Nevertheless, the notion of habitus is not to be conflated with that of "habit" (in the ordinary sense), according to which action would only be able to forego reflection to the extent that it was routinized and repetitive. To the contrary, dispositions may generate actions – or, as Bourdieu prefers to say, practices – that are highly spontaneous and inventive. His preferred illustrative examples are taken from music and sports: an accomplished musician is able to improvise within the context of a given harmonic structure without having to mentally rehearse alternative variations prior to actually playing them; similarly, an accomplished tennis player will charge the net in order to win a point without having to weigh the expected consequences of this strategy against others prior to actually engaging it (see Bourdieu 1990b, p. 11; 1990a [1980], pp. 52–65; Bourdieu and Wacquant 1992, pp. 19–22). To be sure, neither rational calculation nor intentional reference to rules are proscribed in Bourdieu's meta-theory; nevertheless, they are considered to be "derivative" sources of practice, in the sense that they are most likely to occur when the habitus finds itself compelled to cope with an unfamiliar environment (for example, the classically trained musician who agrees to perform with a jazz ensemble).

The habitus, according to Bourdieu, is differentially formed according to each actor's position in social space; as such, it is empirically variable and class specific (in Bourdieu's sense of the term). In elaborating this point, we must begin by acknowledging that, for Bourdieu, the process through which the habitus is constituted is not situated – or at least not primarily situated – at the "point of production." In other words, although the occupational system comprises the institutional core of the "class structure" for Bourdieu, it is neither the labor market nor the shop floor (or office cubicle) which functions as the site in which the causal processes giving rise to a class-specific habitus unfold. Rather, according

---

[12] See also Bourdieu and Wacquant (1992, p. 136): "[t]he notion of habitus accounts for the fact that social agents are neither particles of matter determined by external causes, nor little monads guided solely by internal reasons, executing a sort of perfectly rational internal program of action."

to Bourdieu, each location in social space – that is, each combination of volume and composition of capital – corresponds to a particular set of life conditions, which he terms the "class condition."[13] As such, it is intended to specify the particular conditions within which the habitus was formed, and in particular, the experience of material necessity.[14] According to Bourdieu, experience of the particular class condition that characterizes a given location in social space imprints a particular set of dispositions upon the individual.

These dispositions amount to what Bourdieu sometimes calls a "generative formula." He defines them as "an acquired system of generative schemes... [that] makes possible the... production of... thoughts, perceptions and actions" (Bourdieu 1990a [1980], p. 55). These schemes enable actors to apprehend their specific situation and its elements as meaningful, and to pursue – typically without reflection or calculation – a course of action which is "appropriate" to it. (This is why, Bourdieu argues, the regularities of action observed by social scientists often appear to be the result of adherence to norms or rational decision.) This capacity, on the one hand, is *limited*: the more the action situation departs from the conditions in which the habitus was constituted, the more likely it is that the habitus will be rendered ineffective (a kind of individual anomie). On the other hand, however, the "schemes" comprising the habitus are *transposable*: within the limits constituted by the conditions of their formation, they are fully capable of operating across different domains of social life, and therefore of conferring a *unity* on practices that are "phenomenally different." One form in which this unity is realized – and the essential one in *Distinction* – is the phenomenon of *taste*.

Class practices

As we noted above, for Bourdieu, sociology's fundamental question is "that of the existence... and mode of existence of collectives." One of the assumptions underlying *Distinction* is the premise that social collectivities are, at present, formed primarily in the arena of consumption.

[13] See Sørensen (this volume) for the distinction between conceptions of class based on the notion of life conditions and those based on the notion of exploitation. In Sørensen's view, the former require grounding in the latter's notion of "objective" – but typically "latent" – antagonistic interests in order to account for processes of class formation (e.g. collective action by the members of a class). As will be demonstrated, Bourdieu takes an entirely different view of this process.

[14] Initial formation of the habitus occurs in the context of each individual's "earliest upbringing." It can subsequently be modified by new experiences; however, the earliest experiences carry a "disproportionate weight" (Bourdieu 1977 [1972], p. 78; 1990a [1980], pp. 54, 60).

Indeed, this assumption forms the background to Bourdieu's emphasis on the importance of lifestyle. The next step of the explanatory process thus entails analysis of a wide variety of data on consumption practices and preferences, including those having to do with "canonized" forms of culture (art, literature, music, theater, etc.) and those that belong to culture in the wider, anthropological sense of the term (food, sports, newspapers, clothing, interior decor, etc.). By performing a correspondence analysis on these data, Bourdieu is able to demonstrate that the various indicators of lifestyle exhibit a structure that is isomorphic with (or as he prefers to say, "homologous" to) that of social space. More specifically, he is able to demonstrate that different preferences and practices cluster in different sectors of social space (Bourdieu 1998b [1994], pp. 4–6).

Because the habitus, as a system of dispositional "schemes," cannot be directly observed, it must be apprehended interpretively. Much of *Distinction* is therefore devoted to a qualitative study of the various preferences and practices which cluster in each sector of social space – that is, within each class and fraction – in order to identify the particular "scheme" or "principle" that underlies them, and which orients the expenditure of economic and cultural capital in a manner that gives rise to the semantic coherence of a lifestyle.[15] Thus, Bourdieu demonstrates that among the members of the dominant class, a unitary lifestyle emerges around what he calls "the sense of distinction." This habitus is defined, above all, by its overriding aesthetic sensibility. The various moments of everyday life constitute so many occasions for an expression of this sensibility. In particular, each comprises an opportunity for the subordination of function to form:

[w]hile it is clear that art offers it the greatest scope, there is no area of practice in which the intention of purifying, refining and sublimating facile impulses and primary needs cannot assert itself, or in which the stylization of life, i.e. the primacy of form over function, which leads to the denial of function, does not produce the same effects. In language, it gives the opposition between the popular outspokenness and the highly censored language of the bourgeois . . . The same economy of means is found in body language: here too, agitation and haste, grimaces and gesticulation are opposed . . . to the restraint and impassivity which signify elevation. Even the field of primary tastes is organized according to the primary opposition, with the antithesis between quantity and quality, belly and palate, matter and manners, substance and form. (Bourdieu 1984 [1979], pp. 175–6)

As this remark indicates, Bourdieu discerns a working class habitus that is "antithetical" to that of the dominant class: the "taste for necessity"

---

[15] Bourdieu's facility at teasing out the semantic coherence that obtains across the minutiae of everyday life give rise to an analytic richness which, unfortunately, cannot be evoked here.

which characterizes the lifestyle of members of this class inclines them to assign an absolute priority to function over form, to insist that art carry a moral message, and to demand choices that evidence a conformity with the class as a whole (which are viewed as an implicit demonstration of solidarity). For its part, the petty bourgeois exhibits a lifestyle born of the combination of an aspiration to the bourgeois lifestyle, on the one hand, and insufficient economic or (especially) cultural capital to attain it, on the other. Its members are therefore inclined to a "cultural goodwill": lacking "culture" (in the bourgeois sense) they tend to embrace "popularized" aesthetic forms (e.g. "light" opera) and to commit themselves to activities intended to achieve cultural self-betterment.

Furthermore, Bourdieu demonstrates substantial differences within both the dominant class and the petty bourgeoisie according to variations in the asset structures associated with the corresponding positions (that is, according to the composition of capital).[16] Thus, within the dominant class, those endowed primarily with economic capital – the commercial and industrial employers – express their "sense of distinction" through the pursuit of luxury goods and a carefully crafted opulence, whereas their counterparts – the "artistic producers" and university professors – express this impulse by practicing a cultural "asceticism" geared towards the intellectually most demanding (and least expensive) forms of culture. Bourdieu summarizes this opposition of habitus and lifestyles as follows:

[o]n one side, reading, and reading poetry, philosophical and political works, *Le Monde*, and the (generally leftish) literary or artistic magazines; on the other, hunting or betting, and when there is reading, reading *France-Soir* or... *Auto-Journal*... On one side, classic or avant-garde theater..., museums, classical music,... the Flea Market, camping, mountaineering or walking; on the other, business trips and expense account lunches, boulevard theater... and music-hall, variety shows on TV,... the auction room and "boutiques," luxury cars and a boat, three-star hotels and spas. (Bourdieu 1984 [1979], p. 283)

Situated in between these two poles of the dominant class are the professionals and (especially) the senior executives, who, eschewing both the overt luxury of the employers and the "asceticism" of the intellectuals, exhibit a lifestyle built around aesthetic commitments to "modernism," "dynamism," and "cosmopolitanism": embracing new technology and open to foreign culture, they view themselves as "liberated" and espouse a "laid back" way of life (Bourdieu 1984 [1979], pp. 295–315). Bourdieu goes on to chart analogous oppositions within the petty bourgeoisie, where variations in the ratio of economic to cultural capital correspond

---

[16] Recall (note 9, above) that Bourdieu is unable to clearly identify class fractions in the working class, but insists that this is a shortcoming of his data.

to different "modalities" of its members' signature "cultural goodwill." He also adduces numerous qualifications of his characterization of each class's and fraction's lifestyle as a result of internal differences in trajectory.

The lifestyles that Bourdieu documents so extensively in *Distinction* pertain to a specific place and time, and thus need not be extensively recounted here (for a discussion that provides some of the historical context, see Lane 2000, pp. 140–65). Instead, we may simply note that Bourdieu is able to provide a compendium of data establishing both that an isomorphism obtains between the structure of social space and the distribution of consumption practices, and that this correspondence is mediated by a subjective system of dispositions whose "expression" across multiple domains of consumption confers a semantic unity on the practices that warrants reference to coherent "lifestyles." Thus, in keeping with the claims of his early remarks concerning Weber, he is able to establish a necessary relation between class and status. Nevertheless, as elaborated here, the analysis remains incomplete. Above all, this is because the presentation has been essentially static, freezing the practices being studied into a kind of snapshot. Hence,

one must move beyond this provisional objectivism, which, in "treating social facts as things," reifies what it describes. The social positions which present themselves to the observer as places juxtaposed in a static order of discrete compartments ... are also strategic emplacements, fortresses to be defended and captured in a field of struggles. (Bourdieu 1984 [1979], p. 244)

Differences of lifestyle are, for Bourdieu, profoundly implicated in conflicts over individuals' location in social space and the structure of that space itself. This implies that conflicts between classes and between class fractions have an ineluctably symbolic component. It is in this proposition that the full significance of Bourdieu's attempt to yoke together "class" and "status" becomes apparent.

Classificatory conflicts and symbolic violence

Following "capital" and "habitus," the third general concept of Bourdieu's sociology that must be introduced is that of field, a notion intended to condense his understanding of social structure. As we have already seen, Bourdieu views the class structure of a social formation as an objective network of positions which are systematically related to one another in terms of the distribution of cultural and economic capital across occupational locations. The concept of field is intended to foreclose an overly structuralist interpretation of social space – that is, one in which the individuals who "occupy" the various positions are reduced to the role of mere "bearers" of the structural relations that are encapsulated in them (see Bourdieu and Wacquant 1992, pp. 94–115). In this context, the term is meant to recall a battlefield or a playing field, and more specifically, the fact that the individuals who confront one another will enter into conflict or competition with one another, each from a more or less advantageous position (Bourdieu and Wacquant 1992, pp. 16–18). On this basis, Bourdieu's social space can equally be termed a "field of social classes" (e.g. Bourdieu 1984 [1979], p. 345; 1991, p. 41). In the context of *Distinction*, this means that lifestyles are caught up in social struggles.

Aspects of a lifestyle such as haute cuisine or an antique collection, on the one hand, are not simply distinct from "hearty" foods and mass-produced decorations, on the other. To the contrary, the different forms of the same lifestyle element (furniture, food, etc.) stand in a hierarchical relation to one another, and as a result of this, lifestyles themselves are socially ranked. According to Bourdieu, the hierarchical "status" of a lifestyle is a function of its proximity to or distance from the "legitimate culture." The latter refers to those elements of culture universally recognized as "worthy," "canonical," or in some other way "distinguished." As such, the composition of the legitimate culture is permanently in play: it is the object of a perpetual struggle. Thus, for example, when apprehended in relation to the underlying habitus that generated them, the characteristic minutiae of the bourgeois style of eating and the working-class style of eating amount to nothing less than "two antagonistic world views, . . . two representations of human excellence" (Bourdieu 1984 [1979], p. 199).

Bourdieu identifies at least two modalities according to which conflicts over the "legitimate culture" proceed. The first follows the well-established sociological model of the "trickle-down effect." According to his interpretation of this model, a perpetual competition exists over the appropriation of the most "distinguished" objects or practices. Initially seized upon by those with the greatest economic and/or cultural capital – that is, by the dominant class or one of its fractions – such objects or practices diffuse downward through social space over time; however, precisely to the extent that they become progressively "popularized," each earlier group of devotees tends to abandon them in favor of new objects and practices that will enable them to reassert the exclusivity of their taste. In this form of competition, which is quasi-imitative, the dominant class or one of its fractions invariably takes the leading role and acts as "taste-maker" (Bourdieu 1984 [1979], pp. 247–56). According to Bourdieu, the working class, generally incapable of asserting itself in such competitions as a result of both its lack of capital and its antithetical disposition, tends to stand aloof from them, and thus involuntarily acts as a negative reference point or "foil" against which the petty bourgeoisie and the dominant class can attempt to affirm their cultural distinction. Indeed, in Bourdieu's view, the working class's incapacity to participate in the race to claim those forms of culture whose legitimacy its members nonetheless acknowledge (at least implicitly) is so severe that they may be said to be "imbued with a sense of their cultural unworthiness" (Bourdieu 1984 [1979], p. 251).[17]

Conflicts over the legitimate culture more or less inevitably take a "trickle-down" form when the particular form of culture at issue is one for which the "consecration" that confers legitimacy is reserved to an institutionally sanctioned, highly closed group of "experts" or "professionals" (Bourdieu 1990a [1980], p. 138).[18] Fine art, with its highly circumscribed institutional spaces (university departments, museums, galleries, auction houses, etc.), communicative venues (journals, lectures, etc.), and interpersonal networks (artists' or journalists' cliques) represents a paradigmatic case. Although quite uncommon in Bourdieu's account of the working class's relation to culture, in the less rigidly circumscribed domains of culture he appears to detect glimmers of an alternative cultural conflict. In these cases, legitimacy itself is contested:

[t]he art of eating and drinking remains one of the few areas in which the working classes explicitly challenge the legitimate art of living. In the face of the new ethic of sobriety..., which is most recognized at the highest levels of the hierarchy, peasants and especially industrial workers maintain an ethic of convivial indulgence. A bon vivant is not just someone who enjoys eating and drinking; he is someone capable of entering in the generous and the familiar – that is, both simple and free – relationship that is encouraged and symbolized by eating and drinking together... (Bourdieu 1984 [1979], p. 179)

---

[17] Bourdieu would have perhaps had to modify his undeniably harsh depiction of working-class cultural dispossession and passivity had he been able to identify the distinct fractions within this class that his theory postulates, since he would then have been compelled to analyze its internecine conflicts. Nevertheless, however one judges this aspect of *Distinction*, it must be remembered that the premise of a hierarchy of lifestyles cannot be falsified simply by pointing to the canonization of "popular" (or once "popular") forms of culture. Bourdieu is fully aware of such phenomena, but argues that the consecration of working-class cultural forms inevitably occurs by way of intellectuals or artists; endowed with different habitus, these cultural forms carry an entirely different meaning for them (see Bourdieu 1984 [1979], pp. 47–8, 88, 372–4).

[18] The "consecration" of cultural objects and practices that is generated in these (relatively) closed and autonomous worlds is not unanimous; to the contrary, for Bourdieu it is the subject of sharp internal conflicts. This leads to a complex sets of relations between the various actors within such worlds and the various "publics" constituted by the different classes and fractions (although the working class remains almost completely outside such dynamics). Bourdieu's guiding hypothesis is that the divisions within these worlds are homologous to those characterizing the potential publics – that is, they are roughly isomorphic with social space. See Bourdieu 1984 [1979], pp. 230–44.

[T]he only area of working-class practice in which style in itself achieves stylization is that of language, with argot, . . . which implicitly affirms a counter-legitimacy with, for example, the intention of deriding and desacralizing the "values" of the dominant morality and aesthetic. (Bourdieu 1984 [1979], p. 395; see also p. 34; 1991, pp. 90–102)

If contestation of cultural hierarchies on the part of the working class remains rare, it is more frequent in the conflicts over the legitimate style of life that are waged within the petty bourgeoisie and the dominant class by their respective fractions. In the latter case, in particular, conflicts over the content and meaning of the legitimate culture are the norm, with each fraction seeking to elicit recognition from the others of the superiority of its own way of living and way of being.[19]

The practices and objects constitutive of a lifestyle, Bourdieu insists, do not merely "express" the schemes which comprise the habitus. To appreciate a certain type of music is, implicitly or explicitly, to spurn other available forms of music; to find some types of cuisine particularly appetizing is to find others unappealing; and to find certain schools of painting inspiring is to find others dull. In each of these cases, the rejected practices or objects carry an association with the social actors who engage in or possess them. For Bourdieu, in other words, the aesthetic sensibility that orients actors' everyday choices in matters of food, clothing, sports, art, and music – and which extends to things as seemingly trivial as their bodily posture – serves as a vehicle through which they *symbolize* their *social similarity* with and their *social difference* from one another. Through the minutiae of everyday consumption, in other words, each individual

---

[19] Bourdieu is routinely chastised for emphasizing the absolute primacy of a *belle lettriste* or "highbrow" form of culture which is now obsolete in France and which was never applicable to the United States and to various other countries. In fact, however, as Lane (2000, pp. 148–57) cogently reminds us, the analysis of the dominant class in *Distinction* clearly charts the eclipse (albeit in its early stages) of the paragon status attributed to "classical highbrow" culture, in favor not of the literary culture of the intellectuals, but the modernist one of the executives and managers.

It may be noted that studies of cultural consumption carried out in the US over the last few decades indicate the emergence of a new type of cultural hierarchy – what Peterson and Kern (1996) designate as the ideal of the "cultural omnivore." Under this ideal, rather than standing in a hierarchical relation, the different forms of each cultural practice or object – for example, the various cuisines, musical traditions, or literary genres – are understood to all have their own meritorious exemplars, as determined by evaluative criteria which are indigenous to their particular "cultural milieux," and therefore mutually irreducible. The resulting social imperative amounts to a kind of cultural "cosmopolitanism," hinging on facility with the immanent meaning and unique virtues of a wide range of objects and practices. What needs to be pointed out with regard to this cosmopolitanism is that it is perfectly capable of functioning as a status vehicle, and it strongly presupposes an asymmetrically distributed competence – both of which are demonstrated by Bryson (1996), who thus goes on to coin the term "multicultural capital."

continuously *classifies* him- or herself and, simultaneously, all others as alike or different. Acknowledgment of this symbolic function of everyday consumption behavior opens the way to the analysis of "classification struggles," in which Bourdieu (1984 [1979], p. 483) sees "a forgotten dimension of the class struggle."

As was established, Bourdieu conceptualizes social space as a factorial space. Thus, to make a rather obvious point, a space constituted by continuous axes is one that is *devoid of inherent boundaries*. Consequently, it is only through these constant, reciprocal acts of social classification that social *collectivities* are born: bounded social groups are the result of practices that seek to symbolically delimit "regions" of social space (Bourdieu 1984 [1979], pp. 174–75, 476; see also 1991, p. 120; 1990a [1980], p. 140). As such, they arise from the perception of social space through quasi-*categorical* symbolizations of affinity and incompatibility (which Bourdieu sometimes refers to as "categoremes" [1984 [1979], p. 475], in order to indicate that they tend to function at a pre-reflexive level). Indeed, for Bourdieu, the symbolic is a "separative power, ... *diacrisis*, *discretio*, drawing discrete units out of indivisible continuities, difference out of the undifferentiated" (Bourdieu 1984 [1979], p. 479). This implies that any social collectivity is the result of the combined symbolic acts of self-classification and classification by others that are applied to its members (and, therefore, also, to those who are excluded). However, the various actors do not contribute equally to this process of mutual categorization and classification. To the contrary, the capacity to establish the divisions which structure the perception of social space is not evenly dispersed across this space, since much of the symbolic *force* accruing to objects or practices that fulfil a classificatory function derives from their relative proximity to or distance from the legitimate culture (see Bourdieu 1991, p. 242; 1990a [1980], p. 139; 1987, p. 11; 1990b, p. 135).

For Bourdieu, the practices through which these processes of mutual classification unfold are guided by principles of taste that are lodged in the habitus, and thus situated below the threshold of reflexive consciousness. Nevertheless, they conform to a strategic logic (as with the example of the tennis player who charges the net). As a result, sociologists are compelled to attend closely to the seemingly trivial "games" of culture and the routine consumption choices of everyday life.

Every real inquiry into the divisions of the social world has to analyze the interests associated with membership or non-membership. As is shown by the attention devoted to strategic, "frontier" groups such as the "labor aristocracy," which hesitates between class compromise and class collaboration, ... the laying down of boundaries between the classes is inspired by the strategic aim of "counting in" or "being counted in," "cataloguing" or "annexing." (Bourdieu 1984 [1979], p. 476)

The full importance of the classificatory struggles that are waged through the medium of lifestyle becomes clear as soon as we recognize that before there can be any kind of "class conflict" (in the familiar sense of the term), symbolic processes must first transpire in which the relevant collectivities are demarcated from one another – that is, in which each identifies itself and its opponent(s) – along with the interests that can form the object of conflict (Bourdieu 1990b, p. 138).[20]

Nevertheless, given that the actors who are the objects of classificatory practices occupy particular positions in social space, and that the degree of similarity or difference between their habitus is a function of their location in this space, it follows that not all classificatory schemes have an equal likelihood of attaining social recognition. In other words, irrespective of the symbolic force that accrues to the particular agent who puts forth a classificatory scheme, the structure of social space – as the thoroughly *real referent* of all such schemes – necessarily conditions its feasibility (Bourdieu 1990b, p. 138).[21] Thus, for example, attempts to symbolically establish a belief in the categorical unity of the "cultural" fraction of the petty bourgeoisie, on the one hand, and the "economic" fraction of the dominant class, on the other, suffer from an inherent implausibility, since the actors in question, separated by wide intervening swaths of social space, possess highly divergent habitus. Simply put, the probability of any two actors' membership in the same social category is inversely proportional to the distance that separates them in social space

[20] In the Marxian tradition, the position which most closely approximates that of Bourdieu was developed by Przeworski (1985). See Weininger (2002, pp. 91–3) for a discussion of the differences between the two.

[21] The literature on cultural cosmopolitanism (note 19, above) is enough to cast doubt on those versions of "postmodernism" that assert the complete extirpation of culture from any social-structural mooring. For these theories, the efficacy of symbolic systems, understood as the medium through which the "social construction of reality" occurs, is no longer a function of their correspondence or non-correspondence to the real (or indeed to *any* "real," other than themselves). The "liberatory" variants typically make the further assumption that symbolic systems are more malleable and plastic than (now enervated) social systems, implying, among other things, that identity is the result of a reflexive self-fashioning that is altogether unconstrained by "birth or fortune." Here again, Lane (2000, pp. 157–9) provides a useful reminder, pointing out that numerous aspects of this "postmodern" worldview were already encapsulated in certain sections of *Distinction*. Making sly reference to some of the French philosophers of the day, Bourdieu traced the contours of a lifestyle which postulated self-realization through consumption and a "refusal to be pinned down in a particular site in social space." This pretension to unclassifiability – "a sort of dream of social flying, a desperate effort to defy the gravity of the social field" – was characteristic of the "new cultural intermediaries," that is, the fraction of the petty bourgeoisie employed in producing commercial symbolic products, and especially those members of the fraction who, originating in the dominant class, had experienced an unforeseen downward mobility (Bourdieu 1984 [1979], p. 370, see pp. 152–4, 365–71).

(Bourdieu 1991, p. 232). This said, however, it also remains true that the social space itself is free of any intrinsic boundaries. And given this continuous structure, it becomes clear that (contrary to the frequent charges of hyper-determinism leveled against Bourdieu) the introduction of symbolic "partitions" or boundaries into this space, and the consequent formation of social collectivities, amounts to a causally *irreducible* aspect of actors' practices. This has important consequences. Most significantly, it implies that the contours of the "social classes" which emerge through these practices are in no way pre-established: the "partitioning" of social space may occur in a highly aggregative or highly disaggregative manner along *each* of its constitutive axes, yielding an infinite number of possible configurations (Bourdieu 1987, p. 10). Hence, in certain situations it may be that "objective differences...reproduce themselves in the subjective experience of difference" (Bourdieu 1987, p. 5); in others, however, it may well be that "social neighborhood...has every chance of...being the point of greatest tension" (Bourdieu 1990a [1980], p. 137).

Arising from practices that are thematically oriented to altogether different ends (that is, to food, art, fashion, etc.), the boundaries that are established through lifestyles can have no precision. To the contrary, these boundaries are necessarily indeterminate and fuzzy (Bourdieu 1991, p. 234). For the same reason, they have no permanence, existing only in the flux of ongoing practices (Bourdieu 1990a [1980], p. 141). Hence, they are undeniably porous. Nevertheless, as "symbolic transformations of de facto differences" (Bourdieu 1991, p. 238), they are crucial to the maintenance or transformation of the underlying class structure. We must recall that the "practical taxonomies" which agents establish via the symbolic effects of their practices are not merely empty "grids" superimposed on the social space. The various practices, and through them the different lifestyles, all stand in a hierarchical relation to the legitimate culture – is, (schematically) to the canonized culture. As a consequence, social classification is simultaneously a social allocation of *honor*, in Weber's sense. And it is Bourdieu's fundamental thesis that, precisely because individuals perceive one another primarily through the "status" which attaches to their practices – or in other words, through the symbolic veil of honor – they misperceive the real basis of these practices: the economic and cultural capital that both underlies the different habitus and enables their realization. When differences of economic and cultural capital are misperceived as differences of honor, they function as what Bourdieu calls symbolic capital (see Bourdieu 1991, p. 238). This function can be understood as a "legitimizing theatricalization which always accompanies the exercise of power," and which "extends to all practices and in particular consumption." Consequently, according to Bourdieu, "[t]he very lifestyle of the holders of power contributes to the power that makes it possible, because its true conditions of possibility remain unrecognized ... " (1990a [1980], p. 139). Insofar as this is the case, the misperception of social space – which characterizes both the dominant and the dominated, but to the advantage of the latter – is also "symbolic violence."

From the practical state to the objective state: modalities of symbolic power

For Bourdieu, the indeterminate, porous boundaries that arise from the free play of (implicitly) antagonistic consumption practices amount to what might be called powers of "primitive classification" (see Durkheim and Mauss 1963; Bourdieu and Wacquant 1992, pp. 12–15). These powers are only a particular modality – albeit a fundamental one – in which the institution of boundaries may occur. Indeed, whenever classification is no longer left exclusively to the pre-reflexive "play" of the habitus, social boundaries – and therefore the collectivities that they constitute – are subject to *codification*. According to Bourdieu, "[t]o codify means to banish the effect of vagueness and indeterminacy, boundaries which are badly drawn and divisions which are only approximate, by producing clear classes and making clear cuts, establishing firm frontiers ... " (1990b, p. 82). This implies *formalization*: the criteria according to which cases are differentiated may be specified, and the resulting categories scrutinized according to logical considerations (for example, does membership in one preclude the possibility of membership in another, as with debates about the existence of "cross-class families"?). In contrast to the situational elasticity of social categorizations generated exclusively through consumption practices, boundaries which undergo codification enjoy a definite precision, and in some cases, a permanence and a force. Codification thus amounts to an "objectification" or "crystallization" of divisions that could otherwise only be generated spontaneously. Thus, by beginning from a dispositional level, Bourdieu's analysis of the formation of collectivities opens up a diverse set of phenomena for analysis, those concerning the processes through which differences existing in the "practical state" become transformed into objectified "frontiers." Moreover, because codification implies a transformation in the way boundaries operate, it also implies a transformation of the symbolic power that stands behind them. Indeed,

[t]he capacity for bringing into existence in an explicit state, ... of making public (i.e. objectified, visible, sayable, and even official) that which, not yet having

attained objective and collective existence, remained in a state of individual or serial existence . . . represents a formidable social power, that of bringing into existence groups by establishing . . . the explicit consensus of the whole group. (Bourdieu 1991, p. 236)

It is in the course of an analysis of the different modalities of symbolic power that the *politics* of classification fully emerge.

We may note, first of all, that an elementary codification occurs as soon as any collectivity – and thus, tacitly or explicitly, the boundary that separates it from other(s) – accedes to the level of discourse. As Bourdieu likes to point out, "any predicative statement with 'the working class' as its subject conceals an existential statement (*there is* a working class)" (1991, p. 250). The linguistic designation of the collective, the *name* (or social *label*), makes it possible for its boundaries to become an object of thematic concern, since it implies, at least potentially, a finite set of individuals whose limits can be traced, and a principle of inclusion which can be applied to particular cases (see Bourdieu 1984 [1979], p. 480). The implicit feelings of affinity or incompatibility engendered by similarities or differences of lifestyle – a relatively "serial" state of existence – can now be articulated; verbal designation of the collective enables an explicit recognition of the membership status of oneself and others ("He's not middle-class; he's a lawyer!"), and thereby confers an explicitly collective dimension on individuals' sense of personal identity. Furthermore, it is only with a discursive identity that is known and recognized by the members of the class (or fraction) that they become capable of acting in concert for a specified purpose – that is, of *mobilizing*. Hence, "social classes," as they are typically envisioned in social theory – namely, as groups entering into conflict for the sake of "class interests" – are profoundly discursive entities; and insofar as the preservation or transformation of the underlying distributions of economic and cultural capital in fact hinges on collective action, discourse contributes to the shaping and reshaping of social space itself. The linguistic designation of collectivities, in other words, must be credited with a power of "social construction," since it can bring into being a collective entity with an explicitly acknowledged existence and a capacity for collective action. Nevertheless, it is by no means wholly independent of lifestyle differences: part of the effectiveness of the linguistic designation of collectivities derives from its capacity to render overt social cleavages that were already given to pre-verbal experience, and thus, "familiar." Moreover, like these cleavages, discourse is constrained by the structure of social space, which forms its ultimate substrate (Bourdieu 1990b, p. 138).

As with the establishment of differences through lifestyle practices, discursive categorization of individuals can meet with resistance, since each individual is simultaneously classifier and classified. Furthermore, in this register too, individuals are unequally endowed with the capacity to impose their classifications. This inequality has particularly significant consequences in the realm of politics (for reasons that will be clarified shortly). Indeed, for Bourdieu, the working class's lack of cultural capital is so severe that its members are, to a certain extent, incapable of offering – and frequently do not consider themselves entitled to offer – "deliberative" judgments for circulation in the public sphere (see Bourdieu 1984 [1979], pp. 397–465). Consequently, authority to speak for the class – to articulate its history, political opinions, needs, and demands – must be *delegated* to a group of professional spokespersons, who are themselves supported by an organization (the party or the union) dedicated to the work of *representing* the collective. The class thus attains a particular ("metonymic") form of "objectified" existence in which the maintenance of its boundaries and the mobilization of its members is continuously *managed* by a corps of "specialists": "[t]he 'working class' exists in and through the body of representatives who give it an audible voice and a visible presence, and in and through the belief in its existence which this body of plenipotentiaries succeeds in imposing . . . " (Bourdieu 1991, p. 251; see also pp. 173–4).

Well beyond the elementary codification that discourse brings about, social institutions may possess the power to instate and regulate class- or fraction-constitutive boundaries characterized by a high degree of solidity and permanence, and may do so in independence from the classificatory schemes of the actors who are subject to categorization by them. Educational institutions, with the power to issue credentials, are Bourdieu's preferred example. Insofar as they carry a more or less universally recognized value in the labor market, credentials establish an objective frontier between holders and non-holders. At the same time, however, credentialization also exerts a symbolic effect, since it entails the introduction of a *qualitative discontinuity* into the continuum of cultural competences: the difference between the person with highest failing score on an examination and the person with the lowest passing score, Bourdieu (1990a [1980], pp. 137–8) points out, becomes a difference in *kind*. Social categories such as "professionals" and "skilled manual workers," for example, are largely circumscribed by the educational system's exclusive authority to confer credentials and to differentiate between types of credential ("technical certificates" versus "degrees").

The frontiers demarcating collectivities from one another attain their highest level of objectification when they are inscribed into *law* (Bourdieu

1987, p. 13). Here we encounter a fully codified symbolic system: law is interpreted, applied, and typically produced by a body of specially trained experts, and these processes are restricted to an institutional arena in which issues of coherence and consistency are paramount. It thus attains the fully formalized status of a *code* (Bourdieu 1990b, pp. 79–80), and exhibits a maximum of precision. Furthermore, legal boundaries are *enforceable*, with transgressions subject to sanction by an "official" agency – that is, a branch of the state.

The state itself stands at the apex of the progression we have been tracing. Appropriating Weber's formula, Bourdieu defines the state in terms of "the monopoly of the legitimate use of physical and *symbolic* violence over a definite territory" (Bourdieu 1998b [1994], p. 40). This means, above all, that the state, and it alone, retains the legitimate right to impose classificatory principles which enjoy a *compulsory* validity, or (as in the case of schools and the credentials they issue) to at least *adjudicate* the validity of all such principles (see Bourdieu 1990b, pp. 136–7). In addition to its power to craft and enforce law, the state also engages in various forms of social categorization via agencies dedicated to the enumeration of its population and the regulation of various activities (for example, in the economic sphere, with the development of occupational taxonomies or the regulation of working conditions). This power has discrepant consequences for the classificatory struggles that transpire at lower levels of codification (for example, through mobilizing discourses). On the one hand, the state can inscribe a set of categorizations into the social order that, as a result of their obligatory character, restrict the room for maneuver open to social actors. On the other hand, however, the state's authority can itself become an object in such struggles, via the mobilized collective's petition of agencies and bureaus: "[a] group's presence or absence in the official classification depends on its capacity to get itself recognized, to get itself noticed and admitted, and so to win a place in the social order" (Bourdieu 1984 [1979], pp. 480–1). Recognition by the state provides "an official definition of one's social identity," and thus "saves its bearers from the symbolic struggle of all against all" (Bourdieu 1991, p. 240). Beyond this, however, we must again recall that the collectivities which are born through (or whose existence is ratified by) the classificatory actions of the state cannot be viewed in terms of an empty "grid" superimposed on the social space. Rather, in establishing boundaries, the state also allocates "advantages and obligations" (Bourdieu 1984 [1979], pp. 476–7; see also 1991, pp. 180–1). Thus, for example, within the context of production, a successful petition of the state can result in the credential requirements, licensing exams, and other formal entry criteria that comprise the occupational barriers resulting in closure and generating "rents."[22] (However, it must be reiterated that, for Bourdieu, production – as opposed to consumption – is of secondary importance as a site in which the formation of solidaristic ties and collective mobilization are likely to occur in the contemporary period.)[23]

Our discussion has proceeded, in a sequential manner, from the diffuse, fluctuating boundaries that are generated through the play of consumption practices to the rigid, obligatory ones authorized by the state. However, neither social actors nor the sociologists who study them ever encounter a world that is symbolically undifferentiated. This is to say that the discussion has relied on an abstraction, one in which all objectified symbolic barriers were initially bracketed, so as to trace the progressive constitution of classifications from the uncodified state (lifestyles) through processes of discursive identification, collective mobilization, and finally, "officialization" by the state (see Bourdieu 1990a [1980], pp. 122–34). What emerges from an account developed in this manner is a point of fundamental importance to Bourdieu: all social collectivities are "historical artifacts" (Bourdieu 1987, pp. 8–9), and to fully grasp them, sociology has no choice but to "reconstruct the *historical labor* which has produced [the] social divisions" through which they were constituted (Bourdieu 1991, p. 248).

This being said, however, once we remove the brackets that were initially placed around objectified symbolic structures in order to trace their

---

[22] In order to maintain their "realist" conception of the occupational order, Grusky and Sørensen (1998, p. 1,195) are compelled to characterize the occupational classifications constructed by the state as mere "nominalist" exercises which can claim a grounding in reality only insofar as incumbents in the various occupations have already mobilized themselves and successfully petitioned the state to erect entry barriers. In doing so, Grusky and Sørensen fail to recognize that the substantial autonomy which state agencies usually enjoy (vis-à-vis those being classified) means that the construction of their classificatory systems are just as likely to be driven by the interests of the state bureaucrats themselves, as various historical studies have demonstrated (see Donnelly 1997, and the citations therein). Moreover, acknowledgment of this by no means entails a slide into epistemological nominalism, as they appear to assume. Precisely to the extent that *bureaucratic imposition* of a classificatory designation is able to elicit *recognition*, both from the incumbents and from those excluded, it is characterized by "that magical reality which (with Durkheim and Mauss) defines institutions as social fictions" (Bourdieu 1991, p. 251). The relevant question, as Donnelly (1997, p. 115) puts it, is "[w]hat consequences might official classifications have for the consciousness and action of social subjects?" In sum, it is necessary to recognize that, above and beyond ratifying "jurisdictional settlements," the state makes an independent contribution to the structuring of the occupational order – and that acknowledgment of its role need not jeopardize a commitment to epistemological "realism."

[23] For a historical study which, drawing closely on Bourdieu's conceptual repertoire, charts the emergence of a new occupational category via mobilization at the point of production and petition of the state, see Boltanski's (1987 [1982]) study of the formation of the *cadres*, as well as Wacquant's (1991) discussion of it.

genesis, it becomes clear that the social world, as it is actually encountered, is "always already" riven by innumerable symbolic cleavages, ranging from the diffuse to the fully codified. Consequently, the actors who engage in mutual classification – whether through consumption practices, discourse, or any other symbolic medium – have spent their lives immersed in an already classified world. Thus, their experience of the social world has always been an experience of distinctions. And as a result of immersion (especially during primary socialization) in a world that was previously divided, the existing structures of social classification were necessarily impressed upon their habitus. In other words, the habitus also incorporates "principles of vision and division" (Bourdieu 1998b [1994], p. 46) – meaning a general tendency to classify the things and people of the world in a determinate manner – that have been absorbed from the social environment in which it was formed: "[s]ocial divisions become principles of division, organizing the image of the social world" (Bourdieu 1984 [1979], p. 471). This lends the habitus a certain tendency toward *inertia* – that is, toward the reproduction in its own practice of classificatory structures encountered in early experience (see Bourdieu and Wacquant 1992, p. 133). This propensity is all the more prevalent the more the boundaries between classes (and fractions) are written into law, and therefore have an official status (Bourdieu 1990a [1980], pp. 138–9). Nevertheless, classificatory structures are unlikely to be perpetuated, ad infinitum, without modification or alteration. This is because, in the first place, events such as economic transformations may alter the distribution of capitals. In the second place, however, the fact that social space is so highly differentiated ensures the existence of multiple systems of classification, competing with one another in perpetuity; and it is precisely such competition which generates symbolic *invention*. In Bourdieu's estimation, "[i]t is in the intermediate positions of social space, especially in the United States, that the indeterminacy and objective uncertainty of relations between practices and positions is at a maximum, and also, consequently, the intensity of symbolic strategies" (1990b, p. 133).

Domination multiplied

As we have seen, Bourdieu's understanding of class has a number of features that set it apart from other treatments of the subject. These include its conceptualization of the class structure as a multidimensional social space; its emphasis on consumption, viewed as an arena of social life in which the possession of economic and cultural capital can be "theatrically" displayed; and its relentless focus on the symbolic dimension of practices, identified as the indispensable bridge between *structural proximity*, on the one hand, and *co-membership* in a social class (or fraction), on the other. At the same time, however, in developing this account of Bourdieu's class theory and class analysis, we have necessarily simplified, insofar as the social world it delineates is one in which all other forms of domination were left to the side. In what follows, we will therefore introduce elements such as region and, in particular, gender to the account. Because Bourdieu's thinking developed on these questions in the years following *Distinction*, we will first detail the assumptions that animate that work; subsequently, we will elaborate the revisions that can be found in later writings, and especially *Masculine Domination* (2001b [1998]), examining their implications for the earlier understanding of class.

Complex causes

Distinction is by no means concerned only with the impact of differences of economic and cultural capital on practices. To the contrary, various other "stratifying" factors – including gender, age, region, and (to a lesser extent) ethnicity – receive frequent discussion. However, whereas sociology conventionally considers these factors as distinct bases of domination or stratification – bases which, given a particular outcome, might (or might not) be effective in addition to class – Bourdieu takes a radically different approach. In order to clarify this approach, we must reconsider the causal link connecting occupancy of a particular position in social space to the formation of the habitus, and through it, to particular practices. Bourdieu's stance becomes apparent in a description of the manner in which the different aspects of one's location in social space (that is, volume of capital, composition of capital, and trajectory) are related to a variety of demographic characteristics (gender, age, ethnicity, etc.), and the manner in which, together, these different elements affect the habitus:

> [t]o account for the infinite diversity of practices in a way that is both unitary and specific, one has to break with *linear thinking*, which only recognizes simply ordered structures of direct determination, and endeavor to reconstruct the *networks* of intertwined relationships which are present in each of the factors. The *structural causality of a network of factors* is quite irreducible to the cumulated effects of... [a] set of linear relations...; through each of the factors is exerted the efficacy of all of the others.... (Bourdieu 1984 [1979], p. 107; translation modified)

The "structural causality" Bourdieu refers to can be understood in terms of a system of *causally interactive* factors (Weininger 2002, pp. 68–71). As noted, this system includes effects deriving both from one's location in social space and from the demographic characteristics. In asserting that causal relations are wholly interactive, Bourdieu implies that the impact of each of these factors on the formation of the habitus (and through it, on particular practices) varies according to an individual's "value" on each of the other factors. This amounts to a rejection of what Abbott (2001) refers to as the "main effects assumption" in causal logic – that is, the presupposition that causal factors operate independently of one another, unless the converse can be demonstrated empirically.[24]

However, Bourdieu also places an important substantive restriction on the manner in which the system of interactive factors is to be conceptualized. This restriction concerns the interpretation of the interactive relations. It is apparent in the terminology he chooses: the factors deriving from location in social space are identified as "primary," while the demographic characteristics are designated "secondary" factors (see Bourdieu 1984 [1979], pp. 101ff.). This indicates that, for Bourdieu, interactive relations are to be understood in terms of alterations that are induced in the effects attributable to demographic characteristics as location in social space changes. More concretely, it means that, on Bourdieu's interpretation, the impact of a factor such as gender on the habitus varies according to location in social space, and not vice-versa. Bourdieu's stance is apparent in remarks such as the following:

the whole set of socially constituted differences between the sexes tends to weaken as one moves up the social hierarchy and especially towards the . . . ["intellectual" pole] of the dominant class, where women tend to share the most typically male prerogatives such as the reading of "serious" newspapers and interest in politics, while the men do not hesitate to express interests and dispositions, in matters of taste, for example, which elsewhere would be regarded as "effeminate." (Bourdieu 1984 [1979], pp. 382–3; my addition)

The habitus is always "gendered"; however, the consequences of this (with respect to the practices that it produces) vary according to position in social space. Thus, volume of capital, composition of capital, and trajectory enjoy a certain primacy: the meaning ascribed to the "secondary" factors is a function of location in social space; the impact of location, by contrast, does not vary systematically as a function of the "secondary" factors. It is precisely this primacy which Bourdieu announces when he declares that "volume and composition of capital give specific form and value to the determination which the other factors (age, sex, place of residence, etc.) impose on practices" (Bourdieu 1984 [1979], p. 107).

[24] This aspect of Bourdieu's sociology has generally gone unnoticed in the English-language reception of his work. It has been recognized, however, in the French literature (e.g. Accardo 1997, pp. 191–211).

The corollary of this rather opaque account of causality is significant. In asserting the primacy of the factors related to location in social space in the formation of the habitus, Bourdieu is ascribing – on purely meta-theoretical grounds – a greater importance to them in the explanation of practices. Furthermore, he is *also* declaring them to be the primary lines along which social conflicts will erupt: "groups mobilized on the basis of a secondary criterion (such as sex or age) are likely to be bound together less permanently and less deeply than those mobilized on the basis the fundamental determinants of their condition" (Bourdieu 1984 [1979], p. 107) – that is, on the basis of volume, composition, and trajectory. In other words, in the "symbolic struggle of all against all," schemata based on gender, age, or ethnic categorizations have inherently less capacity to elicit recognition than those schemata which (like social class) remain consistent with the structural contours of social space.

Crosscutting classifications

In later work, Bourdieu jettisoned the assumption that the "life conditions" associated with a location in social space are the fundamental determinants of the habitus, eclipsing the role of "secondary" factors such as gender. This amounted to a revocation of the causal primacy attributed to volume of capital, composition of capital, and trajectory. In its place, we find the sketch of a sociology which is considerably more attuned to the historical specificities of the different bases of social domination. This is most apparent in his writings on gender.

A short book that charts a very wide terrain, Bourdieu's *Masculine Domination* aims to provide "an archeological history of the unconsciousness which, having no doubt been constructed in a very ancient and very archaic state of our societies, inhabits each of us, whether man or woman" (Bourdieu 2001b [1998], p. 54). The analytic strategy Bourdieu pursues is unusual: returning to data from earlier anthropological studies of the pre-modern people of Kabylia (located in northeastern Algeria), he attempts to explicate the "andocentric cosmology" which impresses itself upon habitus, and through them, comes to organize all institutions and practices. Proceeding on the supposition that gender domination is relatively transparent in this universe, he subsequently attempts to identify the "transhistorically constant" features with which it appears throughout the Mediterranean region by means of a comparison with contemporary societies.

In contrast to *Distinction*, Bourdieu's later work takes gender domination to be "the paradigmatic form of symbolic violence" (Bourdieu and Wacquant 1992, p. 170). Like all forms of collective identity, gender is the result of a social classification – in this case, one resting on the "mystic boundaries" that categorize male and female bodies (Bourdieu 2001b [1998], p. 2; the phrase is taken from Virginia Woolf). This classificatory principle originated, Bourdieu argues, in kinship systems in which marriage served as the mechanism through which alliances could be formed and prestige allocated between families. Women, in this system, functioned as objects of exchange rather than subjects, and hence their worth rested on their ability to conform to the "androcentric" ideal of femininity (Bourdieu 2001b [1998], pp. 42–9; Bourdieu and Wacquant 1992, pp. 173–4). (Virility is identified as the corresponding ideal applied to men.) As a particular symbolic scheme that is incorporated into the habitus, gender is highly distinct from class: built around a dualist opposition, it has attained a rigidity and a permanence unmatched by any other classificatory principle. This is largely because gender amounts to a symbolic system that has rooted itself in "certain indisputable natural properties," and therefore "naturalized" itself more effectively than any other – that is, legitimated itself via the constitution of a seemingly natural ground (Bourdieu 2001b [1998], pp. 13, 23). In the present context, it is impossible to fully analyze this work and its place in Bourdieu's corpus; instead, I would merely like to indicate some of the (generally implicit) revisions of his account of the relation between class and gender.

To be sure, *Masculine Domination* does contain remarks, reminiscent of the causal argument from *Distinction*, in which the gendered character of social actions is contingent on class location: "bodily properties are apprehended through schemes of perception whose use in acts of evaluation depends on the position occupied in social space" (Bourdieu 2001b [1998], p. 64). Nevertheless, these remarks are complemented by others in which the relation between class and gender shifts. Thus, for example, in describing the analytic transition from the study of a pre-modern society to a modern one, we find Bourdieu declaring:

[i]t is indeed astonishing to observe the extraordinary autonomy of sexual structures relative to economic structures, of modes of reproduction relative to modes of production. The same system of classificatory schemes is found, in its essential features, through the centuries and across economic and social differences. (Bourdieu 2001b [1998], p. 81; see also Bourdieu and Wacquant 1992, p. 174)

In recognizing the dramatic continuity of gender structures across historical time, Bourdieu is compelled to attribute a pronounced autonomy to them vis-à-vis economic structures. In doing so, he breaks sharply from his earlier treatment of gender (that is, from its specification as a "secondary" factor). This leads Bourdieu to outline a research agenda centered on specifying "the history of the agents and institutions which...contribute to the maintenance" of the permanence of gender structures (Bourdieu 2001b [1998], p. 83; italics removed). Among the institutions implicated in this process are the church, the state, and the educational system, as well as the family (Bourdieu 2001b [1998], pp. 82–8). Of fundamental interest are the highly variable ways in which each of these institutions has *codified the distinction between the sexes* over the course of history.

Bourdieu argues that although recent and contemporary feminist political movements have thrown gender asymmetries in visible relief, "some of the mechanisms which underlie this domination continue to function" (Bourdieu 2001b [1998], p. 56; see also pp. 88ff.). It is in his discussion of these mechanisms that we find the clearest revisions of the relation between class and gender:

whatever their position in social space, women have in common the fact that they are *separated from men by a negative symbolic coefficient* which, like skin color for blacks, or any other sign of membership in a stigmatized group, negatively affects everything that they are and do, and which is the source of a systematic set of homologous differences: despite the vast distance between them, there is something in common between a woman managing director...and the woman production line worker. (Bourdieu 2001b [1998], p. 93)

Statements such as this clearly indicate that, in keeping with the "autonomy" attributed to sexual structures across history, Bourdieu views gender divisions as an *independent* force structuring practices. At the same time, he also points to numerous "interactive" relations, but now seen as fully "symmetrical" – that is, gender and class location are each taken to moderate the effect that the other exercises on practices. Thus, in contrast to the causal logic at work in *Distinction*, we find remarks such as the following:

[s]ocial positions themselves are sexually characterized, and characterizing, and...in defending their jobs against feminization, men are trying to protect their most deep-rooted idea of themselves as men, especially in the case of social categories such as manual workers or occupations such as those of the army, which owe much, if not all of their value, even in their own eyes, to their image of manliness. (Bourdieu 2001b [1998], p. 96)

The point here, of course, is not simply that Bourdieu's later work embraces a conception of causality that more closely resembles standard "multivariate" logic. What emerges from these revisions is a somewhat different view of "the existence...and mode of existence of collectives." Whereas Bourdieu always acknowledged that social class, as a symbolic principle of "vision and division," had to compete with other such principles (including gender) in the classificatory struggle through which collectivities are constituted (see, for example, Bourdieu 1987, p. 12), as we saw, he nevertheless granted it a meta-theoretical primacy in *Distinction*. Once that primacy is revoked, class must compete on an equal footing, and the symbolic arena becomes exponentially more cacophonous, as it were, especially given the rigid and durable codification attained by principles of division such as gender and race in certain societies. This is all the more true since the complex *combinations* of domination generated by the intersection of different classificatory principles can no longer be automatically interpreted in predominantly class terms.[25] One implication of this is that the fate of social classes, understood as collectivities constituted through practices of social classification, becomes more contingent than ever on the historical vicissitudes of the *discourse* of social class.

Conclusion

For Bourdieu, "the existence . . . and mode of existence of collectives" is "the question with which all sociology ought to begin." This question remained at the center of his sociological vision to the end of his career. Indeed, the modifications that can be identified in his later work are fully consistent with this general focus, and in fact, only serve to deepen it. Bourdieu always assumed that class relations are qualified by other forms of domination; and by revoking the privilege previously accorded to class in his later writings, he fully opened himself to the idea of a complicated "intertwining" of forms of domination through history. Consequently, whereas his class theory – with its multidimensional conception of social space – had always stood aloof from the traditional idea (most prominent in certain versions of Marxism) of a social world reduced to two polarized blocs, in texts such as *Masculine Domination* it becomes clear that social classes amount only to facets of a complex classificatory prism.[26] Thus, even if the priority granted to social class was revoked, Bourdieu's work remains thoroughly coherent in its relentless focus on the various forms of *social classification*, understood as the *principia potestas* – the fundamental power – animating acts of symbolic violence.

In order to develop the implications of Bourdieu's question of "the existence of and mode of existence of collectives" for class analysis, we

---

[25] Wacquant's (2002) account of the simultaneous constitution and maintenance of class and racial divisions in the US by a historical series of four "peculiar institutions" can be read through the same explanatory lens.

[26] The traditional Marxian notion of a bifurcated social world, condensed to a single, antagonistic opposition between classes and unalloyed with other forms of social classification, remains one empirical possibility among others, albeit a highly unlikely one.

might turn to Marx's well-known tract "The Eighteenth Brumaire." In Marx's account of the coup of 1851, the French peasantry is famously described as a "sack of potatoes." Individual peasant families, each tied to a small parcel of land, are largely self-sufficient; they have little sustained social contact with one another and lack access to effective "means of communication." As a result, they are incapable of organizing themselves in order to mobilize and pursue their interests, instead remaining in what later commentators would term a "serial" state of existence. Marx thus acknowledges that before we can ask whether the peasantry (in this case) has "allied" itself with the bourgeoisie, the proletariat, or any other class, we must inquire whether it has the capacity to organize itself. True though this may be, Bourdieu reminds us that neither communication nor sustained social interaction between a set of individuals sharing the same life conditions are sufficient to generate a social collectivity, much less a mobilized one. Interests, no matter how putatively "objective" they may be, can never trigger collective social action on their own, and *pace* Marx, it is not merely technical impediments to organization that stand in the way. Indeed, without wanting to minimize the significance of technical constraints, it must be emphasized that between interests and collective actions there exists a chasm that can only be bridged by an immense amount of labor – a labor that is carried out, above all, in the *symbolic* register. The actors who organize and mobilize on behalf of "their" class must first recognize themselves as members of the same social collectivity, with the same interests and the same adversaries. This means that they must recognize themselves (and their counterparts in other classes) as sharing at least a minimal class identity.

In fact, the symbolic work that can be the precursor to mobilization is carried on continuously, by everyone. This makes it difficult to grasp sociologically. Indeed, it may be suggested that the only form of class analysis adequate to the task would be one which is able to fuse structural analysis with a phenomenological account of the innumerable acts of reciprocal classification that pervade social interaction. It is precisely this fusion, however, which traditional schools of class analysis have been unable to develop. This is most apparent in the case of Marxism. It is not difficult to identify a split in this tradition. On the one hand, for historians (e.g. Thompson 1966 [1963]) and ethnographers (e.g. Fantasia 1989), "class" is something that must be *made* in a definite historical time and place. Such studies can excel at sifting through the minutiae of daily activities or through the historical record in order to identify the constitution of classes through processes of collocation and demarcation that result in more or less bounded social groups. At the same time, however, these processes tend to be localized affairs which cannot be systematically connected to a broad underlying class structure.[27] More concretely, such studies cannot examine the possibility that classificatory orientations vary systematically with structural location, or that the strategies through which these orientations are pursued vary with the resources at hand; and this limitation becomes all the more serious the more one acknowledges that the class structure itself is highly differentiated and multidimensional. On the other hand, however, analysts who grant conceptual priority to the class structure (e.g. Wright 1997) are able to slot individuals into detailed "maps" of this structure. Nevertheless, having classified social actors in this manner, they are ill positioned to grasp processes of "classmaking." Such studies are characteristically content to examine whether (or to what degree) individuals' opinions and practices accord with those that would be predicted on the basis of their structural location. Nevertheless, lost from view is precisely what might be termed the *constructivist* dimension of social class. As Bourdieu suggests:

by assuming that actions and interactions could somehow be deduced from the structure, one dispenses with the question of the *movement from the theoretical group to the practical group*, that is to say, the question of the politics and of the political work required to impose a principle of vision and division of the social world, even when this principle is well-founded in reality. (Bourdieu 1987, p. 8; see also 1991, pp. 233–4)

(And it could be added that reliance on rational action theory, insofar as it reduces or eliminates the place of the symbolic in accounts of collective identity and collective action on meta-theoretical grounds, only exacerbates this myopia.) Bourdieu's entire approach to class, it might be suggested, is intended to methodically integrate the insights stemming from accounts which prioritize the structuralist and the constructivist dimensions, respectively, in a coherent program of empirical research (see 1984 [1979], p. 483).

The upshot of Bourdieu's approach is that the endless debate between proponents of nominalist and realist views of class is shown to be

---

[27] Some forty years ago, Thompson prefaced his study of working-class formation in late eighteenth- and early nineteenth-century England as follows:

[t]here is today an ever-present temptation to suppose that class is a thing. This was not Marx's meaning, in his own historical writing, yet the error vitiates much latter-day "Marxist" writing. "It," the working class, is assumed to have a real existence, which can be defined almost mathematically – so many men who stand in a certain relation to the means of production. Once this is assumed it becomes possible to deduce the class-consciousness which "it" ought to have (but seldom does have) if "it" was properly aware of its own position and real interests. (Thompson 1966 [1963], p. 10)

And he continued, "[c]lass is defined by men as they live their own history, and, in the end, this is its only definition" (Thompson 1966 [1963], p. 11).

misguided. The opposition between these views must not be understood as an epistemological alternative that confronts the class analyst. To the contrary, nominalism and realism amount to what might be described as distinct moments of the social process (Bourdieu 1990b, pp. 128–9; 1991, p. 234; see also 1984 [1979], pp. 169ff.). Social actors, it must be insisted, are distributed across an *objective structure* of positions which conditions the probability that any particular set of individuals will share the same lifestyle, the same collective name, or an organizational membership.[28] Nevertheless, the differential probabilities that this structure generates can only give rise to social collectivities if individuals are able to construct adequate *representations* of it, and in particular, of the boundaries which simultaneously divide and unify them – whether these be the diffuse, porous frontiers arising through consumption or rigid, precise ones inscribed into state policy and law (see Bourdieu 1984 [1979], pp. 169ff.).[29] Social classes, we might say, can only arise through the conjunction of two *partially* independent forces: the objective probabilities resulting from the structure of social space and the subjective "belief" in the existence of classes. As Wacquant states, "[c]lass lies neither in structures nor in agency alone but in their relationship as it is historically produced, reproduced, and transformed" (1991, p. 51). It is precisely this which Bourdieu (1990a [1980], p. 135) asserts when he declares that a class is defined simultaneously by its "being" and its "being-perceived."

Bourdieu always eschewed the grand historical narrative according to which class conflict is *the* "motor of history." And, as we have seen, in his later work class is stripped of any meta-theoretical privileges it may have enjoyed in his general sociological orientation. As a result, this orientation is able to provide the tools needed to address the phenomena that are usually referred to (rather indiscriminately) in terms of the "decomposition" of the working class. Thus, *The Weight of the World* (Bourdieu *et al.* 1999), an ethnographic account of socially induced suffering in France that Bourdieu and a team of colleagues published in 1993, contains abundant evidence and analysis of ethnic antagonisms in the working class that have emerged in the wake of immigration, transformations of the

---

[28] As Portes (2000) points out apropos of Grusky and Sørensen's (1998) theory, an approach that recognizes the "existence" of classes only where some type of economic (in their case, occupational) self-organization can be discerned leads to the awkward implication that some individuals – perhaps a majority – are "class-less." It follows that such an approach can provide little or no insight into the lifestyles, discourses, and associational patterns (etc.) of these individuals.

[29] Needless to say, the criteria by which the "adequacy" of a representation is to be assessed with respect to its social function of unifying and mobilizing are not the same criteria that would (or should) be used to assess its adequacy as an analytic construct produced for the purpose of sociological study (see Bourdieu 1984 [1979], p. 473).

industrial economy, and changes in the relation between credentials and jobs. And, drawing heavily on Bourdieu, Charlesworth's (2000) ethnography of Rotherham, a town in northern England, documents a community in which de-industrialization has triggered the "decay" of an entire way of life. Unable to find their situation reflected in political speech and disconnected from union-centered traditions (which are themselves dissolving), the younger members of the working class – despite sharing similar life conditions and a similar lifestyle – exhibit a collective identity that has slipped altogether below the threshold of discursive articulation. Under these conditions, their symbolic existence is reduced to what Bourdieu (1984 [1979], p. 178) calls a "lifestyle 'in-itself' " – that is, its characteristic practices and objects function primarily as signs of deprivation, and thus, as stigmata (see Charlesworth 2000, esp. pp. 150–202).

Among class theorists, Bourdieu stands out for having conferred a centrality on symbolic practices of social classification. For reasons we have examined, this centrality points beyond questions of social class, ultimately encompassing all forms of social categorization (gender, race, nation, etc.). The symbolic, in Bourdieu's view, is a formidable but highly elusive type of power, one that effects a "mysterious alchemy" (1991, p. 233). Classification, as the application of symbolic schemes, is essentially a two-sided process. On the one hand, it categorizes, divides, and separates individuals, and through this, constructs social collectivities: "social magic always manages to produce discontinuity out of continuity" (Bourdieu 1991, p. 120). In doing so, it constitutes the collective identities through which social actors come to know themselves and others. On the other hand, classification also entails the "theatricalizing display" of underlying powers, resources, and privileges – whether these take the form of economic capital, cultural capital, male prerogatives, etc. In this capacity, it functions as a medium through which claims for social honor are expressed and recognized (or rejected). By means of these two functions, it contributes to maintenance or transformation of the social order.

When classificatory schemes are simultaneously sedimented into dispositions and inscribed into the order of things (i.e. into discourse, institutions, and law), a "complicity" can develop between habitus and world which is profoundly recalcitrant to change. In particular, mere denunciation and "symbolic provocation" are rarely adequate to fracture this deep-seated agreement between the subjective and the objective. Nevertheless, Bourdieu resolutely insisted that intellectuals, and especially social scientists, as holders of an immense cultural capital, have a crucial role to play in struggles opposing forms of subordination that rest, at least in part, on symbolic power. Capable of speaking with a certain authority about the social world, and thus of intervening in its representation, intellectuals have the capacity to bring to light mechanisms of domination which were otherwise unnoticed and experiences of subjection which might otherwise have persisted beyond the limits of verbalization (see Bourdieu *et al.* 1999).[30] With this capacity, however, come certain perils. In particular, social scientists jeopardize their ability to explore the connection between different classificatory strategies, on the one hand, and location in social space, on the other, when they allow their discourse to be hijacked by a particular classificatory viewpoint – one upon which they seek to confer the authority (and aura) of "science." This is the case, for example, with crude assertions about the "death" or "life" of social class, which often amount to thinly euphemized expressions of the representational strategy of a particular group or fraction (Bourdieu 1987, pp. 2–3; 1990b, pp. 179–80).

Bourdieu always maintained that intellectuals, by virtue of the cultural capital they hold, comprise a fraction of the dominant class. This implied that they are far from being "free-floating," and hence that their classificatory propensities – often hinging on a distribution of honor or prestige that prioritizes things cultural over things material – are open to sociological investigation just like those of any other class or fraction. Bourdieu (1988 [1984]; Bourdieu and Wacquant 1992, pp. 62–74; see also Bourdieu 1990b, pp. 177–98) undertook this project with enthusiasm, conceiving of it as an opportunity to use sociology to reflexively generate an awareness of (and a measure of control over) the characteristic ways of viewing the social world that are peculiar to those who contemplate it for a living. At the same time, by acknowledging that intellectuals occupy their own determinate corner of social space, Bourdieu also refused the temptation to declare them the "organic" representatives of the dominated. And it remains a testament to his sociological lucidity that he insisted on this proposition throughout his career, willingly accepting all the ambiguities it implied for his political practice.

---

[30] It is precisely for this reason that Bourdieu always considered sociology a *critical* discipline:

> if there is no science but of the hidden, then the science of society is, per se, critical, without the scientist who chooses science ever having to choose to make a critique: the hidden is, in this case, a secret, and a well-kept one, even when no one is commissioned to keep it, because it contributes to the reproduction of a "social order" based on concealment of the most efficacious mechanisms of its reproduction and thereby serves the interests of those who have a vested interest in the conservation of that order. (Bourdieu and Passeron 1990 [1970], p. 218, n. 34)

5   Foundations of a rent-based class analysis

Aage B. Sørensen

Introduction

There is an enormous literature on the concept of class that consists mostly of debates about which properties should be included in the concept. The result is a variety of class schemes and arguments that center around which class scheme is most appropriate for capturing the class structure of modern society. Dahrendorf (1959) argues that classes should be identified with authority relations. Ossowski (1963 [1958]), and later Wright (1979), produce class schemes by cross-classifying property and authority or dominance relations. The class scheme identified with John Goldthorpe is based on property, employment, and authority relations (Goldthorpe 1987; Erikson and Goldthorpe 1992). Parkin (1979) and Murphy (1988) emphasize relationships of closure, and Giddens (1973), the degree of "structuration."

The purpose of the original proposal for the concept of class, by Marx, is to explain inequality, social movements, social conflict, and political processes – to construct a theory of history. The mechanism that produces this extraordinary explanatory power is *exploitation* of the working class by the capitalist class, which produces *antagonistic interests*. Interests may be said to be antagonistic when the gain of one actor, or a set of actors, excludes others from gaining the same advantage. The incumbents of classes realize, through a process usually referred to as *class formation*, that they have these interests and form collective actors that engage in conflicts that eventually change the class structure and society.

This paper was originally published as "Toward a Sounder Basis for Class Analysis," *American Journal of Sociology*, volume 105, number 6 (May 2000): 1,523–58. Earlier versions were presented at the ECSR conference, Rational Action Theory in Social Analysis: Applications and New Developments, Långholmen, Stockholm, October 16–20, 1997, and at lectures at the University of Oxford (November 1996) and Northwestern University (May 1997). I am indebted to the audiences at these lectures for helpful comments and to Hannah Brückner, John Goldthorpe, John Myles, Douglas Hibbs, Rolf Hoijer, Christopher Jencks, Michèle Ollivier, John Scott, Annemette Sørensen, Ruy Teixeira, Erik O. Wright, and the *AJS* reviewers for comments, criticisms, and helpful suggestions.

Exploitation, for Marx and in this discussion, means that there is a causal connection between the advantage and the disadvantage of two classes. This causal connection creates latent antagonistic interests that, when acted upon as a result of the development of class consciousness, create class conflict. The causal connection also implies that the distribution of advantages or disadvantages can only be changed by changing the class structure.

The theory of exploitation as the cause of advantages and disadvantages among classes is a theory of inequality. It is a "structural" theory of inequality because the source of inequality resides in the relation between classes and not in the efforts and skills of the incumbents of these classes. In that sense classes are "empty places" as neo-Marxists like to say, using a formulation proposed by Simmel (1908), and the theory is a genuine sociological theory that can be contrasted to standard economic theory of how people obtain unequal returns on their skills, abilities, and physical assets in the market.

For most of this century, there has been agreement that the original conception of exploitation proposed by Marx is untenable. It is based on a labor theory of value abandoned long ago, even by Marxist economists. Since the labor theory of value is a point of departure for the whole theory, one should have expected that the formulation of a more adequate structural theory of inequality would have been a major concern for the revisions of the class concept. Nevertheless, the problem with the original exploitation theory has received very little attention, the main exception being the analysis of the exploitation concept proposed by the economist Roemer (1982). However, Roemer's very general conception of exploitation will not necessarily generate antagonistic interests that produce class struggles and revolutions.

The neglect of specifying an adequate theory of exploitation means to some that everybody has become Weberian (Murphy 1988). But Weber's class concept proposes no structural theory of inequality that helps identify when class becomes relevant for social and political action. An essential ingredient of the original class concept as developed by Marx has therefore disappeared. This elision, of course, does not prevent the usefulness of class concepts used in empirical research to account for a variety of behavior and attitudes or social mobility, such as the concept proposed by Goldthorpe, or used to account for class-formation processes, such as those proposed by the neo-Weberians.

The main contrast is not between a neo-Marxist and a neo-Weberian concept of class. A more useful distinction is between class as conflict groups where conflict originates in *exploitation*, and class as a determinant of individual actions and mentalities where these consequences originate in the *life conditions* associated with different classes. Both class concepts have properties that reflect the extent and type of resources or assets possessed by incumbents of class positions. My proposal sees class as based in property rights, as did Marx's, but the concept of property used here is broader than the legal property rights definition usually employed. It is a concept of economic property rights defined as the ability to receive the return on an asset, directly or indirectly through exchange (Barzel 1997). Some of these rights may be supported by the state, and they are then legal rights, but people also obtain advantages from rights that are not legally enforceable. Property rights define a person's wealth, and I suggest that the *class as life conditions* concept reflects a person's total wealth. Part of this wealth may be in assets that generate returns or payments that are *rents*. Rents are returns on assets that are in fixed supply because single owners of the asset to the market control the supply of those assets so that the supply will not respond to an increase in price. I propose to define *exploitation class* as structural locations that provide rights to rent-producing assets. Exploitation classes defined by the presence and absence of rent-producing assets have antagonistic interests because rents create advantages to owners of rent-producing assets, and these advantages are obtained at the expense of nonowners. Class locations defined by class as life conditions do not necessarily have antagonistic interests, because rent-producing assets may not be part of the wealth a person controls.

In the next section of the article, I briefly review the most important class concepts with an emphasis on the theories of inequality associated with these concepts. Next, I develop the two class concepts based on wealth. The last part of the article discusses the proposed class concepts' ability to account for recent developments.

Theories of inequality and class concepts

Discussions of class concepts are often confusing because of the varieties of meaning of the term *class*. To clarify the discussion, it is useful to order class concepts according to their level of theoretical ambition. At the bottom, so to speak, are purely *nominal classifications* of a population according to a dimension of stratification: for example, income, occupational prestige, or socioeconomic status. These concepts make no claim to the empirical existence of classes, identified with class boundaries, nor do they suggest why the dimensions of inequality, on which the classifications are based, come to exist. These concepts are nevertheless useful, despite what neo-Marxists sometimes argue, for describing differentials in all kinds of attitudes and behaviors.

At the next level of theoretical ambition, we find class concepts that make claims about the empirical existence of observable groupings with identifiable boundaries. I will refer to these concepts as *class as life conditions*. They may be detected by identifying different lifestyles associated with different living conditions in community studies (e.g., Warner, Meeker, and Bells 1949), or they can be approximated by a variety of class indicators such as occupation, education, income, sources of income, and residence, providing measures of the living conditions of different classes. These concepts are prominent in empirical research on classes and their consequences.

In recent research, the most prominent class scheme of this type probably is the class scheme proposed by Goldthorpe (1987) and elaborated in Erikson and Goldthorpe (1992). It has been widely used and found very useful in empirical research. Goldthorpe (1987) emphasizes that for a class to form, that is for collective class action, members of a class should at least have similar reactions to their class situation. This is partly a question of how similar the class situations are. Thus, a main task is to identify homogeneous class categories using occupational categories. The scheme is used to identify mobility patterns, and has also been used to analyze inequality of educational opportunity (e.g., Erikson and Jönsson 1996) and differentials in attitudes and behaviors (Marshall et al. 1988). It is often claimed to be a Weberian scheme, but Goldthorpe rejects this attribution. Grusky and Sørensen (1998) extend the approach of identifying homogeneous groupings to its ultimate conclusion, arguing that unit occupations form the appropriate classificatory scheme. Indeed, if the concern is for identifying homogenous groupings to provide a useful site categorization for a variety of research purposes, this is a convincing argument.

Socialization and inoculation mechanisms are not specific to classes. The same mechanism would account for differences in attitudes and behaviors among persons raised in different local and national societies, or in different historical periods. Class as life conditions, therefore, is fundamentally a concept conveying the geography of social structure. These class schemes are descriptive of important differences between structural locations, but they are not meant to predict revolutions. As with nominal concepts, this does not prevent them from being useful in investigations of differences in lifestyles which they are meant to capture. Recent formulation of class concepts has emphasized such cultural differences by sites (e.g., Bell 1987) and argued for new cleavages in postmodernist accounts (e.g., Eyerman 1994). A thorough review of these approaches is provided by Grusky and Sørensen (1998).

These class concepts do not propose or assume an explicit theory of inequality or how inequality produces interests, but presumably assume that the inequalities creating the different life conditions are created by the market or by some other mechanism. While Goldthorpe identifies market, employment relations, and authority as the bases for the scheme, the precise link between these defining relationships and the actual scheme is not specified.[1]

In theoretical discussions of the class concept, Weber is usually listed alongside Marx as the other main original contributor.[2] Weber goes beyond descriptive concepts of class by explicitly locating class in the economic organization of society. "Class situation is ultimately market situation" (Weber 1968 [1946], p. 182). The need to realize and to preserve the full value of one's assets gives rise to *economic interests* around which classes in conflict sometimes may form. Weber assumes standard economic theory of how people obtain unequal returns on their assets and resources. However, this theory does not identify under what circumstances economic interests will be antagonistic, resulting in conflict. It is perfectly possible that Weberian classes do not have antagonistic interests because one class obtains an advantage at the expense of another class. In perfectly competitive markets, with no transaction costs, there are no permanent advantages, or above-market returns, to be obtained at the expense of somebody else.[3] Thus, class location is irrelevant. For economic interests to be in conflict, there must be advantages available that are not transitory.[4]

Weber does not emphasize this distinction between transitory and more enduring advantages that produce antagonistic interests. He provides two cues to what differentiates economic interests. One is the identification of

---

[1] Goldthorpe (2000: pp. 206–9) has recently begun this task, relying heavily on transaction cost economics.

[2] The importance of the Weberian class concept in the literature on class analysis is a bit curious. In *Economy and Society*, Weber (1978 [1922]) deals with class in two places, but both are very short fragments. While Marx can be said to never have given a single explicit development of the class concept, he certainly has class as the central concern of analysis in all of his writings. For Weber, there is neither a discussion nor an extensive analysis. Class simply seems not to have been an important concept for Weber. This is not for lack of alternative definitions and discussions of the concept proposed by Marx in Germany at the time when Weber wrote the fragments compiled in *Economy and Society*. Geiger (1932) lists sixteen definitions, all by German-language scholars. Except for Marx's definition, most are from the first decades of the twentieth century. Since only Marx and Weber have been translated into English, Weber has become the main justification for developing class concepts that are alternative to Marx's, despite the fragmentary nature of Weber's writings about this and the lack of importance of class concepts in his writings.

[3] This is the standard result of neoclassical economics' perfectly competitive Walrasian model, where all profits and rents will be eliminated in equilibrium. Weber, of course, cannot be blamed for ignoring this idealized conception of the economy, but the failure of Weberians to identify structural locations providing significant advantages results in a weaker theory than Marx's class concept.

[4] As pointed out by Hayek (1948), it is one of the ironies of a perfectly competitive market that there is no incentive for competition.

economic interests with the goods and services persons sell in the market of the economic opportunities they face. The second cue can be inferred from the statement:

It is the most elementary fact that the way in which the disposition over material property is distributed . . . in itself creates specific life chances. According to the law of marginal utility this mode of distribution excludes the non-owners from competing for highly valued goods . . . It monopolizes opportunities for profitable deals for all those who, provided with the goods, do not necessarily have to exchange them. (Weber 1946, p. 181)

I will argue below that the idea of the importance of monopoly is relevant for class analysis,[5] but for more specific reasons than the one suggested by Weber. The so-called neo-Weberians focus much attention on restrictions of access to classes, or closure, by conflating Weber's idea of status groups with class. The idea of class closure, emphasized by Giddens (1973), Parkin (1979), Murphy (1988), and others, suggests that classes have something to protect and want, but except for a general statement about property and credentials, there is no cue to when and if property and credentials give rise to antagonistic class interests forming a basis for class action.

At the highest level of theoretical ambition, we have the Marxist class concept, which provides a structural theory of inequality in the meaning I described above. The core process defining class relation, in Marx's class concept, is exploitation; that is, the process by which one class obtains an economic advantage at the expense of another class. In feudalism, the exploitation is transparent – the lords of the manor appropriate some of the product of the peasant, or even more transparently, force the peasant to work for the estate for part of the work week without a wage. In capitalism, the exploitation is hidden, as the worker presumably voluntarily agrees to work for a wage. However, the wage does not reflect the value of the worker's product, which equals the labor power embodied in the product – an abstract quantity not necessarily equal to the amount of labor embodied. The wage equals the exchange value or the price of labor that will reflect the cost of production of labor, as do other prices. The difference between the wage and the value produced is the source of the capitalist's surplus that generates profits, the end-all of all capitalist activity. The surplus belongs to the worker, and the capitalist therefore becomes rich at the expense of the worker. Clearly, the two classes should have antagonistic interests.

---

[5] This point will be illustrated through the idea of monopoly rents discussed in the next section.

Marx's explanation of inequality and oppression is a very attractive one, as the history of Marxism shows. It is surely an alluring idea that the misery of the working class is caused by workers' spending part of their work on enriching the capitalist through the property arrangement of capitalism. It not only provides an explanation for inequality, it also points to an effective remedy: one must change the class relations that create exploitation. However, the worker's right to the surplus is a normative claim originated by Marx and developed in Volume 1 of *Capital*. Surplus has no implications for observable economic quantities like prices. Marx realized this in Volume 3 and argued that the sum of surpluses in labor values and the sum of prices will be the same. However, "as a general rule, profit and surplus value are really two different magnitudes . . . The difference between profit value and surplus value . . . completely conceals the origin and the real nature of profit – not only for the capitalist, but also from the laborer" (Marx 1959b, p. 58). This hidden nature of the source of exploitation makes it impossible to use empirically the theory and is the source of the difficulties the labor theory of values encounters.

Exploitation is the appropriation of labor by the capitalist, just as labor was appropriated by the lord under feudalism. The distinction between the wage and the surplus value implies that the capitalist gains more the more surplus value he can get from the worker in a period of time. The *means of exploitation* available to the capitalist therefore are of paramount importance. Marx's class concept therefore acquires a dual dimension of legal ownership and domination, or power, that is seen as an essential element in the Marxist class concept in discussions and reformulation of the concept.[6] Neo-Marxists usually distinguish a proper Marxist class concept from Weberian formulations by emphasizing the lack of attention to the means of exploitation in Weberian formulations. The preferred formulation is that class is defined at the *point of production*.[7] Neo-Marxists are right about Weber, but have focused on the wrong dimension of the Marxist concept, *domination*, to avoid the difficulties of the labor theory of value.

Two much-cited proposals for a reformulation of the Marxist class concept rely on the means of exploitation as a main element of the concept of class (Dahrendorf 1959; Wright 1979). Dahrendorf (1959) presents the most radical formulation of the Marxist class concept by

---

[6] In addition to domination in employment, ideological and political structures also can be included, and we obtain the elaborate class concept developed by Poulantzas (1975).

[7] The main exception is the class concept proposed by Roemer (1982) to be discussed below. For a critique that emphasizes exactly the need for a Marxist concept to have classes defined "at the point of production," see Wright (1982). Wright later revised his position (e.g., Wright 1997).

eliminating the basis of exploitation, that is, legal property rights, from the class concept and keeping only dominance or authority.

The theoretical problem with Dahrendorf's reformulation is that he never details why authority relations should create antagonistic interests, the very root of class formation. Employment contracts are voluntary and represent an exchange of pay for the subordination to authority. In competitive labor markets, the possible discomfort and alienation felt by the subordination should be compensated by higher wages, as pointed out by Simon (1957) in his analysis of the employment contract. Therefore, there should be no antagonistic interests formed. Unless the labor theory of value is invoked, no exploitation is necessarily created by authority or domination.

Wright (1979, 1985) obtains class categories by cross-classifying ownership with authority in the manner also proposed by Ossowski (1963 [1958]), with unusually clear justifications. Since most of the population has little or no property, most of the class differentiation is by authority. Wright's concepts have been widely used in empirical research. Only Goldthorpe's class concept, discussed earlier, has been equally popular in empirical class analysis. Wright (1979) claims that his first class scheme is based on exploitation theory, but never presents or discusses this theory. Later Wright (1985) adopts the exploitation theory proposed by Roemer (1982) and reformulates the class scheme accordingly, maintaining authority (now called "control of organizational assets"; Wright 1985, p. 79) as a main dimension of class relations.

Research using Wright's class scheme finds an authority effect on earnings, but an effect of authority on earnings does not require a class interpretation. Authority is measured as number of subordinates, and this quantity will clearly correlate highly with job ladders established in promotion schemes used in internal labor markets. To establish that the effect is a genuine authority effect, a differentiation between staff and line positions is needed, and this has never been done. It is difficult to justify an economic rationale for an income effect of authority *per se* – see Sørensen (1991) for further development of this argument.

Marx introduced the means of exploitation, in particular authority, as an essential element of his class concept not to explain the incomes of managers and supervisors, but because the labor theory of value requires the dual dimensions of the class concept. If that theory is abandoned and replaced with neoclassical marginal productivity theory, the need for the means of exploitation disappears, for there is no distinction between exchange and surplus value in marginal productivity theory. In marginal productivity theory, the worker is paid what he contributes to the product: a lazy employee is paid less than a hard-working employee. Competition in the labor market guarantees that the capitalist pays no more and no less than the worker contributes to his production.

Marx did not employ marginal productivity theory, for he did not know about it. He certainly shared the belief in the competitive nature of labor markets under modern capitalism, and he may well have accepted the standard theory about these markets. As Roemer puts it, "The neoclassical model of the competitive economy is not a bad place for Marxists to start their study of idealized capitalism" (1982, p. 196).

Roemer attempts to formulate a theory of exploitation consistent with modern economic theory and Marx's original intent in developing his class concept, that is, that ownership of productive resources confers an advantage to the owner at the expense of the nonowner. Inequality in productive assets therefore creates exploitation: the value of what the poorer actor produces depends on the presence of the rich.[8] Roemer gives a game-theoretical illustration of the idea by defining exploitation as existing if the disadvantaged group is better off by withdrawing from the economy with their share of the productive assets.

This concept of exploitation as created by unequal assets in a market economy has peculiarities. Roemer (1986) shows that if we let actors have different time preferences, then it is possible that exploitation status and wealth will be inversely correlated. Roemer's solution to this property of his exploitation concept is to propose abandoning the concept altogether.[9] The possibility of formulating a satisfactory structural theory of inequality is therefore rejected.

The theoretically most ambitious concept, the concept of class as exploitation originating with Marx, does propose a mechanism of how antagonistic interests emerge and therefore how class conflict is generated. However, the theory rests on a labor theory of value that has been abandoned by economic theory. The various attempts to resurrect the concept by invoking authority are unsatisfactory because it is not clear that authority is a source of exploitation and antagonistic interests. The proposal to see exploitation as grounded in inequality in all assets also produces unsatisfactory results.

There is another solution. This is to maintain Marx's insistence on property rights as the source of exploitation, but to not see all wealth as a source of exploitation. I propose instead to restrict exploitation to inequality generated by ownership or possession of *rent-producing assets*.

---

[8] This is a generalization of what sometimes is called differential or Ricardian rents; see Sørensen (1996) for a discussion.

[9] According to Roemer, "exploitation theory is a domicile that we need no longer maintain: it has provided a home for raising a vigorous family, and now we must move on" (1986, p. 262).

Rent-producing assets or resources create inequalities where the advantage to the owner is obtained at the expense of nonowners. These nonowners would be better off if the rent-producing asset was redistributed or eliminated. A concept of *class as exploitation* based on the concept of rent is consistent with modern economic theory and therefore avoids the problems of the labor theory of value. It also avoids the anomalies discussed by Roemer.

Class and wealth

Marx thought that classes were based on rights to the payments on wealth, and Weber thought property to be very important for the emergence of economic classes. Exploitation is a question of economic advantage obtained at the expense of someone else. The right to the returns on wealth is indeed essential for the distribution of these returns, as I will show.

Rights to returns may reflect legal ownership. However, rights to the advantage provided by assets or resources need not be legal rights to be effective. Following Barzel (1997), economic property rights are properly seen as reflecting an individual's ability to consume a good or asset directly or consume through exchange, that is, to control the use of a good or an asset. Such economic rights may be enforceable by law and are then stronger, but they need not be supported by the state to be effective. Property rights are not absolute and constant, and they can be changed through individual or collective action to protect and enhance the rights. Such action incurs transaction costs that are the costs of transfer, capture, and protection of rights. Illustrations will be given below. When transaction costs are positive, rights are not perfectly delineated, and the transfer or protection of rights will be impeded or made impossible. Positive transaction costs may appear for a variety of reasons. Barzel (1997) emphasizes that some of the attributes of assets may be costly to measure and not fully known to actual or potential owners. These attributes are subject to capture by others who then obtain rights to the benefits from these attributes. Transfer of rights allowing an actor to realize the full value of his assets may be costly because mobility is costly or prevented by force. Collective action needed to rearrange property rights that create a monopoly is costly.[10]

---

[10] Barzel (1997) and others (see Eggertsson 1990 for a review) emphasizing a property rights approach to the analysis of economic institutions see transaction costs as resulting from lack of full information and foresight. This reflects the focus on voluntary exchange. I suggest that actors may be prevented from realizing the full value of their assets also because of force or costs of combining action of several actors in collective action and maintaining such action.

For example, in the modern corporation, stockholders do not own all of the assets of the organization but share it with other parties inside and outside the organization that have rights to gains from various attributes of the assets. Managers obtain some gains because stockholders cannot fully control their use of assets because of lack of information. Other employees may obtain advantages (to be discussed below), for example, by retaining control over their effort. That ownership is divided does not mean that the concept of property as the basis for exploitation should be abandoned, as Dahrendorf (1959)[11] proposes. For example, the absence of individual legal property rights to productive assets in socialist society does not mean that individuals do not gain from controlling the use of an asset in such a society. Only their property rights are more restricted in these societies, and it may be difficult to identify those who obtain the gains (Barzel 1997).

The broader concept of property rights proposed by Barzel implies that individuals – even slaves – usually have some property rights to assets under some circumstances (Barzel 1997, p. 105). This means that all individuals will have some wealth, even if it consists only of their ability to execute a task that can be exchanged for a wage.

A simple formalization may be helpful. Denote with v_j the value of resource or asset j, where value is given by the returns to j over the lifetime of the asset. These returns are usually monetary, but could also be social or psychological. Further, let c_{ij} be the right of actor i to asset j or the control i exercises over j. Then the total wealth possessed by i will be:

$$w_i = \sum_j c_{ij} w_j$$

where w_i is the wealth of actor i.[12]

Individuals maximize their wealth by maximizing the return on their assets, employing them in the production of goods and services. This usually means that they will need the use of other assets controlled by

---

[11] Dahrendorf (1959) rejects that property could be the basis for class formation. He bases the argument on the existence of inequality in state socialist society without private legal property rights to the means of production and on the emergence of the modern corporation with separation of legal ownership and control. Dahrendorf bases his argument on an overly restrictive concept of property, I hope to show.

[12] This formulation is similar to Coleman's definition of power in a market exchange system (Coleman 1990). Coleman sees this formulation as the equilibrium outcome of the exchange process where actors exchange control over resources to maximize their interest in a system with no externalities. No such equilibrium conception is invoked here. Further, Coleman focuses on the exchange of any resource. The main interest here is in productive resources. For wealth in assets or resources to be valuable, the assets must generate a return and hence be involved in the production of something.

other actors. Therefore, they need to transact with these other actors. A farmer needs land to maximize the return on the efforts and skills he may devote to farming; a worker needs an employer, machines, and raw materials, to realize the value of her main asset, that is, her labor power. These assets will often be controlled or owned by other actors – the landlord owns the land, the capitalist the machines. These assets can be bought by the actor needing them, or they can be rented. Rental here means transfer of use rights to the asset.[13] The laborer can rent out her labor power to the capitalist in return for a wage, or the laborer can rent the capitalist in return for a profit to him. Such rentals are especially important with durable assets or resources, and even when assets are bought and owned, good accounting practice suggests calculating the payment of a rental to the owner.

The total wealth controlled by actors defines their class situation with respect to *class* as *life conditions*. The assets controlled will determine their incomes and the variability of their incomes. Workers will obtain wages as a result of their effort and skills, and their particular employment opportunities will be important for the variation in their earnings. Assets will be relevant for the respect and prestige received from the community when knowledge of these assets permits a collective evaluation of the standing of actors. The assets controlled will shape opportunities for transactions with other actors and therefore preferences or economic interests in the meaning of interests suggested by Weber. By shaping welfare and well-being, as well as economic opportunities and the investments that maximize these opportunities, the total wealth and its composition create the behavioral dispositions that are accountable for the inoculation and socialization mechanisms associated with class as life conditions, which I will amplify further below.

When individuals need to transact with other actors to get access to assets they need to realize a return on their wealth, the actors may be able to control the supply of the needed asset. Costs of mobility or other costs may prevent access to alternative suppliers, the supply may be inherently limited by nature or the supplier of the needed access may have created a monopoly. This may allow actors controlling the needed asset to charge for use of the asset that is greater than the payment needed to cover the costs of the asset. For example, the owner of a mine in an isolated location may gain an advantage from lower wages because workers are not able to

---

[13] There is a possible confusion between rentals and rents. "Rental" refers to the transfer of use rights to an asset from one actor to another for a payment (a wage for labor, or interest for capital). These payments constitute returns to the holder of the benefit right to the asset. A component of this return may be an economic rent, to be discussed in detail below.

find alternative employment.[14] Workers are thus prevented from realizing the returns on their labor that they could have obtained elsewhere, and the mine owner has lower costs of production and therefore greater gains from production. The advantage thus gained from effectively being able to control the supply of assets is an economic rent.

Rents may also reflect lack of full information. Executives of organizations may obtain benefits far in excess of what is needed to secure their employment because they are able to control cash flows that stockholders are not able to monitor. Or the supply of the asset will be limited because its availability depends on the presence of specific other assets. In general, rents are advantages that prevent other actors from realizing the full return on their assets. Rents are crucial for the emergence of *exploitation classes* because those who benefit from rents have an interest in protecting their rights to the rent-producing assets, while those who are prevented from realizing the full return on their assets have an interest in eliminating the rents. Rents thus may create antagonistic interests and conflict.

To see how rents emerge, it is useful to consider the transactions involved in maximizing returns on productive assets more closely. The prices for the rentals of assets needed to maximize the returns on actor j's resources are costs to j for those assets he does not own and returns to j for those assets he does own. This means his wealth is crucially dependent on the prices of assets relevant for him. These prices depend in the usual manner on supply and demand in the market. If the supply of a certain asset, for which actor j pays a rental, increases, the price will fall and actor j's wealth increases since he has lower costs. Demand in a similar manner will influence the value of assets. This is the normal story.

Suppose now that actor k controls the supply of something j needs to employ her or his assets. Actor k may own land actor j needs access to in order for j to obtain a return on his labor and farming skills. They will negotiate a price for using the land and this price is a cost to j reducing the benefit he receives from his labor and skills. When negotiating the price, j and k will compare what other farmers pay for land. In the long run, competition will ensure that a price emerges that will ensure j a sufficient revenue to keep him alive and able to work the land and compensate the landlord for whatever costs he covers, for example, for fencing. Of course, j may try to buy the land instead of renting it, but for the eventual outcome this does not matter: the rental to the landowner is replaced by a rental of capital to finance the purchase, that is, of interest.

For the competitive equilibrium to occur it is important that the supply of land can vary in response to prices. It is also required that renters of land

---

[14] The mine owner then has a monopsony.

are mobile and thus able to take advantage of the rental offers provided by landowners. If these conditions are not met, if land is in fixed and limited supply or if renters of land – farmers or peasants – are prevented from being mobile by force or law, the owners of land can charge a rental price that is larger than the hypothetical competitive price that just covers their costs related to the ownership of land. The difference between the actual rental price and the competitive price is what is called an *economic rent*.

Rents are payments to assets that exceed the competitive price or the price sufficient to cover costs and therefore exceeding what is sufficient to bring about the employment of the asset. Thus, a rent on asset i can be defined as:

$$r_i = v_i^a = v_i^c$$

where v_i^a is the actual value of i and v_i^c is the value that would have emerged under competition and equal to the costs of making the asset available.[15] These values are given by the stream of income generated by the asset over time.

The existence of rents depends on the ability of the owner of the asset to control the supply. I have already alluded to the classic example: the tenancy contract associated with feudalism. Part of the benefit from the land goes to payment for the labor of the peasant,[16] and another part of the benefit goes to payment for capital expenditures on the land by the landlord. The rent benefit obtained from a tenancy arrangement is the remainder, that is, the payment not needed to employ the peasant and keep the land fertile. It is an advantage going to the landlord because of his rights to the returns on the asset that he controls.[17] But the rent benefit forces a disadvantage on the peasant, since he does not realize the full value of his labor and skill.

---

[15] Rent is a component of what we ordinarily call profit, but profit as usually calculated includes a payment to capital, or interest, earned as payment for past savings and a component of wage to the owner of the asset for his management of the asset. The latter components are not part of the rent received when interest and wages equal market rates of return.

[16] Classical economics saw land as the main source of rent, or ground rent to emphasize the dependency of the benefit on landownership (Marx, for example, uses this terminology). Rent is "that portion of the produce of the earth which is paid for the original and indestructible powers of the soil" (Ricardo 1951 [1821], p. 67).

[17] This is the typical arrangement. It can be argued that the benefit to the landlord is received in return for protection (North and Thomas 1973), but this can, at best, only account for the origin of the arrangement. Also Barzel (1997) argues that matters may be more complicated dependent on the type of contract that exists between the peasant and the landlord. For example, under certain arrangements, the peasant may obtain advantages at the expense of the landlord, by depleting nutrients from the ground.

The association of rents with land is not required. Rent will emerge on all productive assets that are in fixed supply and that actors need to maximize their wealth; or rent may be present as a result of transaction costs involved in getting access to needed assets. Alfred Marshall (1949 [1920]) devoted much attention to the concept of rent and generalized its applicability to benefits received from any productive resource or asset. He showed that rents also may appear as payments for the use of capital and labor in restricted supply; as payments for the use of unique combinations of capitals and labors, such as those created by certain technologies; and as payments for unusual and rare individual abilities that cannot be developed by training alone (musical talents, artistic creativity, athletic ability, etc.). Rents may be created in employment relationships when workers control their effort in an attempt to increase the advantage obtained by the wage because cost of monitoring prevents the employer from adjusting wages to effort. In general, the salient property is that a component of the payment obtained from the asset, or its return, is in excess of what is needed to bring out the supply of the asset.

The association of land with rent is not only an accident of history, it also reflects that tenancy arrangements usually are long-term and rents therefore are long-term. In a competitive economy, rents may emerge in industrial production as a result of an innovation or an import restriction. However, when others discover that there is an excess profit or rent available from owning a particular resource these others increase the supply of the resource if they can. This reduces the excess profit and eventually makes it disappear. Marshall (1949 [1920]) calls such temporary rents *quasi rents*. These temporary rents are the typical rents in capitalist production and will become important in our discussion below.

For our analysis it is extremely important that rents are advantages to the owner of assets that are not needed to bring about the use of these assets. If the competitive payment is enough to make the landlord willing to let the farmer use his land, then any excess is in a basic sense unnecessary. It is an advantage costing nothing. The farmer has a clear interest in reducing, and if possible eliminating, the rent. The landowner has an equally clear and opposite interest in preserving the advantage provided by the rent. Rents therefore create antagonistic interests. Certain rents are especially important for social structure and social change. These are enduring rents that, resulting from enduring property rights to rent producing assets, cause significant advantages and disadvantages. They are at the basis for class formation, as owners of such assets will protect their property rights to these assets, and nonowners will seek to eliminate these rights.

In summary, the individual's total wealth, as defined by her control of assets, will determine her life conditions and thus her class location in terms of class as life conditions. It will be argued below that the consequences of these conditions are not only dependent on the total wealth, but also on the overtime variability in the returns on that wealth (which define the variation in the value of the wealth). Part of the total wealth may generate benefits obtained at the expense of someone else, who would be better off with a different distribution of control or property rights to the various attributes of the assets. This *rent*-generating part defines class as exploitation. Below, I further develop these ideas, treating briefly first the idea of class as life conditions as total personal wealth and then treating in more detail the exploitation class concepts based on rights to returns from rent-producing wealth.

Wealth and class as life conditions

As noted above, there is an abundance of research that shows that class as life conditions indeed is a powerful determinant of all kinds of outcomes.[18] There is much less understanding of how these outcomes come about. We have, of course, a rich literature on socialization that demonstrates that class is associated with important socialization differences, we know about important value differences among different classes, and we also know about a host of lifestyle differences associated with different classes. However, this only moves the question one level back. What is it about the living conditions of different classes that accounts for these differences?

I propose that the answer is lifetime wealth and the expected variation in returns on that wealth for incumbents of different classes. There is abundant evidence that social class accounts for more outcomes the more homogeneous class categories are with respect to a variety of resources, or their wealth. It is important to consider not the cross-sectional distribution of income, but the long-term wealth profile that determines what economists call *permanent income and consumption patterns*. A person

---

[18] Also research using socioeconomic status as the independent variable provides abundant evidence. Socioeconomic status in the meaning of "goodness" (Goldthorpe and Hope 1974) seems to reflect people's belief about the living conditions associated with different occupations, and this is measured by the wealth of incumbents. There is no fundamental difference between what is measured by a class schema, such as Goldthorpe's schema (Goldthorpe 1987) and by socioeconomic status, except that the discrete class schema may capture nonvertical variation ignored by socioeconomic status measures. If socioeconomic status is grouped in discrete categories, we have a nominal concept of class as life conditions. There is some debate about whether discrete class schemes miss some socioeconomic effects (Hout and Hauser 1992).

who obtains a higher education will orient her lifestyle not to the level of income in her youth, but to the long-term expected living conditions corresponding to the wealth associated with her human capital.

Further, the variation in the returns on the wealth is important, particularly for the socialization patterns that emerge in different classes. An older literature found strong differences between social classes in what was called "the ability to defer gratification" (see, e.g., Schneider and Lysgaard 1953). This literature was largely dismissed in the seventies because it was seen as reflecting an attempt to "blame the victim" (see Ryan 1971). More recently, psychologists and economists have suggested a different formulation of the same phenomena (see Ainslie 1992). People discount future rewards, often at very high rates. In particular, there are strong differences among social classes or different socioeconomic levels in time orientation, with persons at low socioeconomic levels having a much shorter time horizon than others. Those with high discount rates invest less in their health and education, and in the health and education of their children.

These differences among classes in time orientation or deferred gratification patterns reflect the level of uncertainty in living conditions or the variability of returns. Such uncertainty is not the fault of the "victim," but is a rational reaction to the expected high uncertainty of returns.[19] Banks also charge a higher interest rate with uncertain investments, and banks presumably are acting rationally. The impact of uncertainty on people's investments in themselves, and their children, should be greater, the lower the overall level of resources. Fewer resources give less of a buffer.

A person's total wealth has two main components. One part is personal, human, and physical wealth that is acquired mostly outside of the labor market in and from families and schools, but some is acquired from on-the-job training. The other component is wealth acquired from employment relations.

The personal part of wealth that exists, independent of the actor's employment relationships, has several components. The amount of human capital obtained through investments in training and health is particularly important. There may also be skills and abilities that command rents.

Finally, the amount of wealth obviously depends on the endowments of physical capital provided by the family of origin and augmented by

---

[19] There is recent evidence from a population survey (Dominitz and Manski 1997) that people's feelings of insecurity vary among population groups exactly as one would predict from the distribution of wealth and variability of wealth returns.

the person through entrepreneurship and investment independently of his involvement with the labor market. This variation in endowments creates different incentives for investments in human capital and the like, and these differences explain the much emphasized nonvertical nature of the Goldthorpe class scheme, for example, the life conditions of farmers. This component of personal wealth is obviously of major importance for a full analysis of the class structure.

Individuals also obtain wealth from their employment relationships. They may have access to on-the-job training opportunities that increase their human capital. A component of the human capital acquired on the job may be specific to the job and the firm and give bargaining power to the worker. Because of specific human capital or collective action, the worker may gain above-market wages, increasing the value of his labor assets, and thus obtain a rent. The employment relationship will in these circumstances be closed in contrast to the open employment relationship characteristic of the competitive market. The resulting increase in the expected duration of employment relationships is crucially important for the variability of returns and therefore for the consequences of differences in wealth, because the shorter the employment relationships, the more variable will be the returns on wealth. The duration of the employment relation also is important for the amount of wealth obtained in the relationship. We should therefore expect persons in stable employment relationships to invest more in themselves and in their children. Professionals having large amounts of human capital and stable employment relationships should invest the most. Therefore, what Erikson and Goldthorpe (1992) call the "service class" should be especially successful securing their children's future. Though no specific test of the idea proposed here exists, an abundance of research on social mobility and inequality of educational opportunity demonstrates the ability of professionals and others with high levels of human capital and enduring employment relations to secure the success of their offspring.

Wealth, rents, and exploitation

The issue for the formulation of a theory of exploitation is to define a process by which some holder of an economic property right obtains an advantage at the expense of persons without these rights. As shown above, wealth transfers made possible by the acquisition of rights to assets generating economic rents satisfy this requirement.

Rents satisfy the requirements of the structural theory of inequality. Rents are created by social relationships of ownership of rent-producing assets (with the obvious exceptions of rents on natural abilities, to be treated later). Advantaged exploitation classes are positions in the social structure that allow individuals to gain control or economic property rights over assets or attributes of assets that generate rents, disadvantaged exploitation classes are defined by the absence of these rights.[20] Changing the property relations that generate rents will change the distribution of wealth and hence the class structure.

The holder of a rent-producing asset has an interest in securing the continued flow of benefits, and those denied the benefit, a clear interest in obtaining the benefit by acquiring it, or by destroying the social organizations that create the rents. When actors act on their interest, they create social organization and processes to protect or destroy rent benefits. These arrangements, well described by neo-Weberians, are processes of closure and usurpation (Parkin 1979) and the processes of moving from awareness of interests, through development of consciousness, to acting in pursuit of these interests (Giddens 1973). For the scenario to unfold, not only membership, but also interests must be enduring.

The distinction between temporary rents and enduring rents is very important for the analysis of class-formation processes. Class formation not only depends on stability of membership in structural locations providing antagonistic interests, as pointed out by Goldthorpe and Giddens. Class formation also depends on the rate of change in advantages or disadvantages provided by rents. This immediately suggests that structural conflict or class conflict should be more prevalent under feudalism than under capitalism, for rents are more permanent under feudalism. No revolution has occurred in an advanced capitalist society.

The importance of the distribution over time, of the advantages provided by rents is often ignored. A cross-sectional inequality does not necessarily imply a longer-term advantage provided by an enduring rent. For example, according to human capital theory, the higher incomes of the higher educated compensate for higher training costs and do not create a permanent advantage over the lifetime of the person. Thus, skills acquired according to the mechanism proposed by human capital theory do not create rents and therefore not classes. This is generally ignored in the so-called new class theory that sees classes emerge on the basis of skills

---

[20] Wright (1997) proposes a related definition of exploitation, though it is not formulated in terms of the concept of rent. In addition to the causal link between advantages and disadvantages of classes, Wright requires that the advantaged class depend on the fruits of the labor of the disadvantaged class for exploitation to exist. Thus when the European settlers displaced Native Americans they did not exploit by obtaining an advantage at the expense of the Native Americans, they engaged in "nonexploitative economic oppression" (Wright 1997, p. 11). The European settlers clearly created antagonistic interests that brought about conflict, so it is not clear what is added by the requirement of transfer of the fruits of labor power.

and education (Gouldner 1979; Konrad and Szélenyi 1979). Education can, of course, create rents, but a measure of educational attainment as used, for example, in Wright's class scheme cannot separate the rent from the human capital component. The role of education in class analysis will be discussed further below.

The types of social organization and processes that emerge around rent-producing assets differ according to which type of asset is being considered. Feudalism can be described as an elaborate organization for the distribution of rent benefits based in land and mercantilism as an extension of the arrangements to cover industrial production. In modern industrial society, there are three main types of rents to be considered, already identified by Marshall (1949 [1920]): (1) monopoly rents, based on monopolization of the supply of an asset, for example when a cable company gains a monopoly from a local government on distributing TV signals; (2) composite rents, formed by unique combinations of productive rents or asset specificity, for example when a worker has acquired skills only employable in a particular job; and (3) rents based on natural abilities and talents, for example the height and ball-catching ability to make a professional basketball team. I will consider some of the main properties of each of these types.

Monopoly rents

"Artificial" or social constraints on production create monopoly rents. The monopoly may have emerged "naturally" because of increasing returns to scale creating prohibitive costs of entering production for others, as in the production of automobiles. Often monopolies are created by governments as licenses or patents. Finally, social associations, such as trade unions or industry associations, who agree to regulate the production of something, create monopolies. In all these cases the supply of a product will not be sensitive to price, and rents will appear and persist unless the monopoly is broken.

For the sake of clarity, assume that the monopolist is working with production conditions that generate constant returns to scale so that average costs equal marginal costs. Nothing essential in the present argument depends on this assumption. Under perfect competition, output and price would be q_c and p_c and the price will correspond to the cost of the product. The monopolist is able to charge a price p_m above the price p_c that would prevail with perfect competition. This will cause an increase in revenue per unit produced that is an increase in the income of the producer over and above the amount needed to bring forth the production, that is, a rent. In addition to the creation of the rent and the corresponding increase in inequality, there will be a reduction in the wealth of society, for less is produced at the price p_m. This is the "deadweight loss" caused by monopoly rents and represents a welfare cost to society, which is a social waste of resources.

The increase in revenue to the monopolist is, of course, an advantage others might want. If others therefore successfully enter the market, the resulting competition might eventually erase the monopoly rent, lowering the price to p_c and increasing the quantity to q_c. When this happens, the temporary advantage to the initial producer is a quasi rent.

This scenario, of course, assumes that others can enter production. If there are prohibitive entry costs created by production technologies, governments or trade associations, competition will be about obtaining the monopoly. Such competition is the typical case of *rent seeking*, that is, zero-sum competition over rent-producing assets. The efforts and other costs involved in trying to acquire the rent-producing property or resource of course reduce the benefit of the monopoly. Indeed, those who wish to acquire the monopoly should be willing to pay the equivalent of benefits to obtain it, so that the rent benefit completely disappears. The costs of rent seeking do not increase the production of society and therefore represent wasted resources (Tullock 1980). This waste is in addition to the waste represented by the deadweight loss.

The nature of the rent seeking depends on whether the monopoly can be traded in the market or not. If it can be traded, the sale may create a large transfer of wealth to those who obtained the monopoly first, and subsequent owners will not realize a rent. For example, it is often argued that rents received by farmers, as agricultural subsidies, produce higher land values and therefore higher interest payments, eliminating the initial advantage. Once established, the rent creating monopoly is difficult to eliminate, even when the monopoly is fully capitalized and the rent has disappeared. Clearly the new owners are strongly interested in receiving the rents they have paid for, even though the advantage to them has disappeared. An example, described by Tullock (1980), is a taxi medallion system, similar to the one in New York City. The medallions are sold, producing large gains to the initial owners, but only normal rates of returns to subsequent owners. Their existence creates a welfare loss to consumers. This loss can be reduced only by removing the restriction on taxi driving, something that is almost impossible to do without forcing losses on the present owners of medallions.

A variety of monopoly rents emerge in the labor market. *Employment rents* emerge when employment and jobs are closed to outsiders by the collective action of unions, by government approved certification of professions, and by other occupational licenses.[21] Unions create rents when they close shops or ration employment through apprenticeship systems. Unions may also significantly alter the distribution of rents when they obtain egalitarian wage systems that will increase the wages to the least productive with the lowest market wages (for evidence see Freeman and Medoff 1984). Professional associations create rents when they obtain certification limiting employment to the properly certified or when they gain control over the recruitment to the profession through control over educational institutions; medical schools are a good example of this. In general, educational credentials, used as rationing devices for employment or for access to employment-specific education for professions, create monopoly rents to those holding the credentials. Credentials will be further discussed below.

Employment rents create rent seeking as zero-sum competition for positional goods (Hirsch 1976) in what I have called "vacancy competition" (Sørensen 1983). Employment rents are not only monopoly rents. Positions may also be closed without the assistance of outside agencies like unions or professional associations. In internal labor markets, closed positions can be created without collective agreements because of the existence of composite rents created by asset specificity, for example specific skills, to be discussed below.

The importance of monopoly rents is questioned by some. As noted, rents create a "deadweight" loss that is an externality reducing the welfare of society. There is an important objection to externalities in an idealized economic system, which is useful for the development of theory, presented by Coase (1960). Coase argues that given an allocation of property rights, there will be no externalities, including those created by monopoly rents, if there are no transaction costs. One of his examples of an externality is cattle trampling on land, destroying corn. The cattle's owner is usually said to be liable for the costs imposed on the farmer growing corn, but Coase argues that this treatment is asymmetrical. The issue is whether the costs of avoiding the trampling are greater than the costs of fencing or of moving the cattle elsewhere. Rational actors will compare these costs and bargain about the cost of fencing and eliminate the externality. Applied to rents, this means that the nonowners of the rent-producing asset should negotiate a deal with the owner, to compensate him for the elimination of the monopoly. Thus institutions that exist over longer periods in a competitive economy, including those

---

[21] Bowles and Gintis (1990) use the term employment rents to identify efficiency wages, i.e., above market wages created to induce effort, to be discussed below.

that appear to create monopoly rents, should be efficient and not rent creating, according to Coase.

The gains to monopolies usually are smaller than the costs they impose on others. Therefore, Coase bargaining would eliminate the welfare loss and with the abolition of the monopoly, output would increase to create the competitive situation. However, if rent-seeking costs have been incurred by the monopolist his losses may be substantial so that he also will need to receive compensation for these costs. This may be difficult to achieve, as noted above. Therefore, when rent-seeking costs have been substantial, monopoly rents may persist as has been pointed out by the rent-seeking literature (e.g., Tullock 1989).

Regardless of the problem with rent-seeking costs, there is a basic problem with the Coase argument when applied to larger categories of actors. The problem is argued by Dixit and Olson (1996). The individual rationality assumed by Coase, in formulating the idea of symmetric bargaining between two parties, does not necessarily create the collective rationality required when one of the parties, usually the disadvantaged party, is a larger group of actors. There are not only transaction costs involved with organization of a larger group to reduce free riding (Olson 1965). Dixit and Olson (1996) also show that even in the absence of transaction costs, the benefits of eliminating the externality per member of the larger group may be so small that no collective action will emerge. These organizational problems are what the class-formation literature is about, or rather what it should be about. There is rich literature on social movements that address the problem of when interests will effectively be translated into action, emphasizing resource mobilization, political processes and the collective action problem. This literature is curiously separated from the class-formation literature developed by the neo-Weberians.

Composite rents or rents on asset specificity

When two separate assets or resources are so specific to each other that payment to their joint use exceeds the payment to each resource in separate use, composite rents emerge. Marshall's prime example of composite rents is the joint advantage to owners and employees of an advantageous market position (Marshall 1949 [1920]). A specific example is the joint rent received when a mill is built on a water stream, to the owner of the mill and the owner of the stream. If there is only one site for the location of the mill, then the rents to the mill owner and to the owner of the water source cannot be separated: "There is nothing but 'higgling and bargaining' to settle how the excess of the value of the two together over that which the site has for other purposes shall go to the owner of the latter" (Marshall 1949 [1920], p. 520).

Composite rents emerge from what in the literature on transaction costs is called asset specificity. They emerge, for example, when workers have obtained specific on-the-job training and therefore are more productive in one firm than in another (Becker 1964). Also, monitoring and agency problems may create composite rents. The composite rent creates a joint advantage that would disappear if the match between the firm and the worker is dissolved, so that employment relations become closed. There are two types of solutions to these problems.

First, the composite rent could be eliminated by organizing production so that the transaction cost problems disappear and employment relations become open. With respect to specific skills, this would imply eliminating the use of such skills. Such deskilling by eliminating the need for specific skills differs from the original deskilling idea made prominent by Braverman (1974), which suggests that capitalism will try to eliminate the need for all skills in the labor market. A general trend toward deskilling has never been established, despite many attempts, nor does it make theoretical sense that employers inevitably stand to gain by reducing the general level of skills required. However, reducing composite rents due to specific on-the-job training would be a plausible strategy.

The second solution is to reduce the importance of composite rents, without destroying closed employment relations to outsiders, by using organizational devices that increase effort. A large organizational literature on internal labor markets may be seen as analyzing organizational solutions to the problem of increasing the firm's share of composite rents. A prominent solution is the creation of promotion schemes to elicit effort. Promotion schemes capitalize on the interdependence of effort created by zero-sum competition over the wage and earnings differential provided by promotion ladders that are positional goods.

Promotion ladders create cross-sectional inequality. It is this inequality that is attributed to class by the Wright class scheme as an effect of authority. However, promotion ladders may be designed to provide less than the market wage at the start of the career, legitimized by training, and higher than market wages at the end of the career, according to the deferred payment theory (Lazear 1995). This pattern ties the worker to the firm and preserves the composite rent: she receives positive and negative rents depending on her seniority in the system. This does not mean that workers will obtain an overall surplus over their lifetime. As with investments in education, the cross-sectional distribution does not inform about the long-term advantage obtained. If the promotion ladders work as intended, they elicit effort and capture composite rents for the employer, quite contrary to the usual interpretation of the authority effect.

The interpretation of promotion systems as rent-capturing systems also implies that employers have an incentive to default on the positive rents the worker is to receive at the end of the career by dismissing the worker when these positive rents emerge. This will create "reputational" problems for individual firms, but if many firms collude in the practice, the reputational effects are diminished.

Another device to elicit effort and capture a larger share of the composite rent is the incentive wage systems. By paying employees more than their market wage, firms increase effort since workers will be reluctant to shirk out of fear of losing their jobs.[22] Wright (1979) used such an efficiency wage explanation for the income advantage of "semi-autonomous" employers.[23] In his latest class scheme, Wright proposes a similar explanation for the wage advantage of managers, called a "loyalty rent." The efficiency wage explanation is used by Krueger and Summers (1987) to account for the persistent wage differentials across industries that cannot be attributed to unmeasured worker characteristics or compensating differentials.

Rents on natural and cultural endowments

Marshall (1949 [1920]) suggests that rents emerge on "free gifts of nature" in the form of genetic endowments that result in the ability to produce something in demand. The rents directly reflect genetic endowment, as when genes are responsible for certain physical attributes facilitating certain tasks; for example, height for basketball players. Or, the rents obtain indirectly when an individual endowment facilitates training for certain skills, as in academic achievement. In the latter case, the endowment need not be genetic. Cultural endowments are important for learning, but hard to learn for those not socialized into a given culture, or who lack the requisite cultural capital (Bourdieu and Passeron 1990 [1970]). Cultural capital thus may be seen as a source of rent similar to genetic endowment.

It may seem paradoxical to include rents on individual endowments as a source of structural inequality. However, these rents have important social

---

[22] Bowles and Gintis (1990) see the creation of efficiency wage as the outcome of the "contested exchange" that defines the unequal power relations created in capitalism by unequal assets.

[23] Efficiency wage theory provides an explanation for involuntary unemployment (Solow 1979). The wage advantage makes unemployment a disciplining device, because the worker will often only be able to obtain the competitive wage after the layoff. We should therefore expect that layoffs are particularly frequent in industries with high concentration, such as automobiles and steel, consistent with evidence.

consequences that connect to the class analysis literature.[24] In particular, rents on natural and cultural endowments have important consequences for the emergence of credentials.

General ability creates higher productivity and higher wages in many employments. Higher productivity may alternatively be obtained by training. The training costs needed by the less able create a surplus for the able, assuming that equally productive able and untrained workers receive the same wage as the less able and trained workers. With an expansion of demand for credentials – that is, an increasing demand for education – the rents become larger for the more able. They therefore seek even more education and higher and more expensive credentials. This self-stimulating demand is the main thesis of the credentialism literature (e.g., Collins 1979). The larger rents provide an incentive for institutions of higher education to increase tuition costs. They therefore share in the rents produced by credentials. Those rents then permit the hiring of prestigious faculty to train the easily trained, enhancing the reputation of these institutions and further increasing the rent on the credentials they confer.[25]

Those possessing high credentials wish to secure an advantage to their offspring. This is facilitated by making cultural capital relevant for training. However, the very existence of credentials also is important. The superior ability of one's offspring cannot be secured, but much can be done to secure a valuable credential for the offspring by facilitating access to institutions providing valuable credentials. In the absence of such credentials, less able offspring from high-status backgrounds might have to compete for valued employment with the more able from more humble origins. The monopoly on employment ensured by the credential protects the less able from high-status backgrounds from being outcompeted by the more able from lower-status backgrounds. Credentials thus increase the ability of high-status groups to confer their advantage to their less able offspring and increase the advantage to their more able offspring. There are strong incentives for high-status groups to create credentials and closure as emphasized by the neo-Weberians (Parkin 1979; Murphy 1988).

In general, the differential rents generated by individual endowments imply that increasing equality of educational opportunity through educational expansion should increase the rents on natural and cultural endowments. Such policies therefore should be strongly supported by those who

---

[24] For other social implications of rents on individual endowments, see Sørensen (1996).
[25] I am indebted to an anonymous reviewer for this observation.

already obtain considerable rents on their endowments, such as professors.[26]

Exploitation classes and collective action in modern capitalism

Rent-seeking activities create lobbies to influence the regulatory activities, subsidies and welfare policies of governments. Social movements lobby to improve the welfare of the disadvantaged by granting them rents. Major corporations lobby through campaign contributions designed to obtain the type of policies and regulations that increase the rents to these corporations. Rents divide owners of different productive assets – as when owners of land are in conflict with owners of industrial productive assets about corn tariffs – and they unite workers and capitalists to preserve import regulations and trade barriers that create rents to certain firms and industries.

That class action in modern capitalist society is about rent seeking and the protection of property rights to rent-producing assets clearly creates a different conception to what Marx had in mind when he analyzed capitalism in the late nineteenth century. Marx's conception, for example, does not require monopolies and asset specificities for the creation of advantage. The surplus created by labor will be a universal feature of capitalism, which will derive its nature from the relentless pursuits of ever-falling rates of profit. However, when the labor theory of value is abandoned, it is impossible to sustain the idea that there is a permanent "hidden" form for surplus in capitalist production in the manner conceived of by Karl Marx. The main class actions will be rent seeking, the protection of existing rents, and the destruction of rents.

It is an interesting question whether rent seeking, rent protection, and the destruction of rents might sustain Marx's grand scenario for the development of capitalism. Marx was certainly right about the dynamics of advanced capitalism. The engine of this dynamic is the pursuit of acquiring rent-producing assets through innovation and product development and by creating demand through advertising for profitable products. The relentless pursuit of advantages that exceed above-market returns – through the reorganization of firms and corporations, sometimes in the form of mergers and acquisitions, sometimes in the form of divestment – is also a pronounced feature of modern capitalism. These processes

---

[26] Working-class parties in the past were indeed skeptical about policies to equalize educational opportunity (for Scandinavia, see Erickson and Jönsson 1996).

result in quasi rents that are usually quickly eliminated by competition. Individual capitalists gain and lose, and some obtain great fortunes. Even though their fortunes result from quasi rents, they are not destroyed by the elimination of these quasi rents. The process expands markets and produces globalism. The story is well known and well described.

Enduring rents to individual owners of capital require some type of collective action. The main form of collective action among capitalists is the establishment of cartels. Cartels may, of course, be hindered by government antitrust regulations. They may be effective despite such obstacles by various types of network organization among boards of directors and the like, but the incentive to break an agreement is always present. A more effective strategy for obtaining enduring rents is to obtain help from the state to preserve an advantage: the granting of a license or some other form of protection from the entry of competitors. An army of lobbyists tries to obtain such advantages by informing legislators about the consequences and advantages of their actions. The rationale for state creation of monopoly rents is usually that some public benefit will be obtained by the regulation that otherwise will be lost: competent doctors, safe cars, and the family farm.

Can Marx's scenario for the class structure of advanced capitalism be sustained with the conception of rent-based classes as exploitation? Marx's emiseration prediction is usually taken as a main reason for revising his theory. Clearly the idea of increased absolute poverty of the working class, caused by increased exploitation, has been rejected by the economic growth that has occurred since Marx wrote. For a long period, also a decrease in relative inequality was observed in most societies. This decrease was replaced by an increase in inequality in the United States and many other advanced societies in the early 1980s, an increase that has continued since then. Nevertheless, it is not possible to sustain the idea that we find an increased polarization and homogenization of the working class. There is, however, substantial recent evidence that shows that capital has become very effective at eliminating the advantages of the working class in terms of rents obtained in the labor market. Eliminating these advantages has contributed to the increase in inequality.

Capital will gain by the destruction of monopoly rents in the labor market and by increasing its share of composite rents or destroying the source of these composite rents. The elimination of rents in the labor market benefits the capitalist when he benefits from the increased efficiency of production. He further benefits when his wealth is dependent on valuation of how efficiently he produces. The stock market provides this valuation. The stock market has, in the period where inequality has increased, very much increased the wealth of stockholders and rewarded rent elimination in the labor market. There are several main ways in which this has been achieved, and all have resulted in increased inequality: (1) eliminating rents created by collective action, in unions, (2) eliminating internal labor markets and composite rents, and (3) lowering the real value of the minimum wage.

Unions create rents in two ways. They may provide significant wage premium for workers covered by union contracts. Nonunion workers may also obtain benefits when employers try to avoid unions. These benefits tend to accrue to workers who are highly skilled. As shown by Freeman and Medoff (1984), though unions do provide benefits, the rents are quite modest. The main effect of unions is to reduce wage inequality. Unions are especially effective at decreasing the wage spread between more and less productive workers. Unions may create substantial rents to low-skilled or otherwise less productive workers.

A well-known major change in the labor market has been the reduction in union power. This is a reduction both in the number of workers that are union members and in the ability of unions to obtain wage increases and secure bargaining agreements. The reduction in membership has been from about one-third of the nonagricultural labor force to now 16 percent. The influence of the unions on the wage structure is far greater than its membership (Mitchell 1985). However, the decline in membership has also been accompanied by declining union power. The evidence is the increase in the number of concessions, the decline in the number of strikes, and the moderation of union demands (Mitchell 1985). For evidence on how these trends have contributed to the increase in inequality, see Fortin and Lemieux (1997). They also point to the importance of deregulation of highly concentrated industries, eliminating the composite rents obtained by workers and firms in these industries.

Closed employment and composite rents are widespread also in industries and firms without union presence, in internal labor markets, and for groups of workers traditionally not unionized, such as many white-collar groups. The composite rents obtained in these settings are eliminated by layoffs. Layoffs without recall reduce job security, but not necessarily employment. However, the loss of job security means also the loss of whatever rents the worker has obtained. With job security a worker can never do worse than his present job. If a better job comes along, he can move to this job, and the timing of this move need not have anything to do with increases in productivity. Therefore a system of closed employment, as in internal labor markets, produces career patterns that represent increases in rents only and not increases in productivity. These career structures are destroyed by downsizing.

Layoffs have increased overall over the last fifteen years from 1.2 to 1.4 million jobs lost in 1979 and 1980 to 3.4 million in 1993. Layoffs grew to 2.62 million in 1982 and never fell below 2 million in the 1980s. They again increased in the 1991 recession and seem to have remained stable since. The proportion of white-collar workers in the total number of layoffs has increased markedly to about 40 percent of the job eliminations (Bureau of Labor Statistics 1998). There appears to be a strong link between the occurrence of downsizing and the performance of company stocks, suggesting that the financial markets, in many cases, force downsizing on the firm (Love 1997).

Composite rents associated with internal labor markets can also be eliminated by job redesign and other changes in production technology. Or, they can be eliminated by removing asset specificity through outsourcing and subcontracting for labor. There is much talk about such changes, including how they could encourage the evolution of new types of employment relationships.

The elimination of employment rents through downsizing and job redesign often means that workers are forced to look for new jobs in the labor market without much choice of which job to accept. This should mean that the next job after the downsizing is likely to be a worse job. It also means that the match between the downsized worker's productivity and wage is likely to differ from previous employment. There should be a closer match between actual individual productivity and wage level as a result of the job displacement. There is some evidence that suggests a tighter relationship between wages and productivity in the 1980s than in the 1970s (Levy and Murnane 1992; Mitchell 1985). Holzer (1990) thus finds a better match than Medoff and Abraham (1981), but the two studies are not very comparable. Juhn, Murphy, and Pierce (1993) find the increase in inequality driven by increased returns to unmeasured skills.

Consistent with the idea of a stronger link between wages and personal endowments, we also observe a marked increase in within-occupation inequality. This is true for all occupations, but it is especially true for managers and sales personnel. In fact, for men the overall Gini coefficient rose from .315 to .332 between 1980 and 1989, but in the managerial and sales occupations combined, it increased from .322 to .353. For all other occupations, the Gini increases from .302 to .312 (Ryscavage and Henle 1990, p. 11). As inequality increased, structural locations seemed less relevant for explaining the variation in earnings.[27]

The increase in inequality is very much driven by an increase in wages and earnings of the highest-paid workers and stagnation or decline for

---

[27] There is substantial evidence for Canada for the declining importance of "structural" or job characteristics as wage inequality increased (Myles, Picot, and Wannell 1988).

others. The stagnation and decline follow from the rent destruction. The increases for the highest-paid result from rent sharing with capital and may be legitimized by arguments that top managers were underpaid in the 1970s and therefore did not have enough of an incentive for doing their very best; in particular, they may have been more tolerant of rents to other employees (see, e.g., Jensen and Murphy 1990).

Stock market valuation clearly has been important for changing this situation. Another mechanism to increase manager incentive has come about through leveraged buyouts that force managers to squeeze all slack out of the firm to meet debt obligations. Leveraged buyouts also make top managers much wealthier. Finally, the increased competitiveness may have increased the rents on the abilities that boards of directors believe are needed in tough managers.

The declining real value of the minimum wage, until quite recently, also reduces employment rents for those less productive workers paid more than their competitive wage because of the minimum wage. This brings more poverty, for nothing guarantees that a competitive wage moves a worker above the poverty line. The rent destruction in the labor markets, except perhaps for the highest-paid managers, leaves a labor market more flexible and more fluid, for fewer groups have anything to protect. The result is less structure, meaning less positional inequality, but more inequality overall. Thus, while greater homogenization overall may not have resulted from these recent trends, the destruction of rents in the labor market has created a labor market with fewer structural supports for the returns to labor. The idea of a homogenization of the working class can be sustained if it refers to the availability of structural advantages making earnings from work less dependent on individual endowments and more dependent on occupational choice and collective action.

Nothing guarantees that efficient labor markets create good lives. Rents are required in modern society to provide decent standards of living for the poorest part of the population. These rents are provided from the state in the form of income support and other welfare goods. The modern welfare state provides required support, but also creates an arena for rent seeking by all, including the middle strata with effective interest groups. It is beyond the scope of this discussion to deal with rent protection and rent seeking in the welfare state. Elsewhere (Sørensen 1998), I have provided a treatment of the breakdown of traditional norms around the provision of welfare goods and resulting increased rent seeking.

Conclusion

A sound basis for class concepts should be based on property rights to assets and resources that generate economic benefits. Property rights should be conceived of broadly. They are economic property rights defined as the ability to receive the return on an asset, directly or indirectly through exchange (Barzel 1997). Some of these rights may be supported by the state, and they are then legal rights, but people also obtain advantages from rights that are not legally enforceable. Property rights define an actor's wealth and I suggest that the *class as life conditions* reflects a person's total wealth. Part of this wealth may be in assets that generate returns or payments that are rents. Rent distribution creates *exploitation classes* that may engage in collective action.

Class as life condition is a very useful concept for analyses of how patterns of attitudes, behaviors, and socialization vary by location in social structure. A prominent example is the class concept proposed by Goldthorpe (1987; see also Erikson and Goldthorpe 1992). A major objective for constructing class schemes that account for different living conditions is to identify homogeneous groupings with respect to total wealth, type of wealth, and the variability of wealth over time. Such groupings will differ in the amount and type of investments they make in themselves and their children. We therefore obtain class schemes that include nonvertical dimensions reflecting the type of wealth possessed and its variability over time, as generated, for example, by the stability of employment relationships.

The present proposal overcomes the evident problem associated with Weberian and neo-Weberian class analysis where there is no proposal for why anyone should be upset about their position in society and engage in class formation. Enduring rents identify antagonistic interests. Those who do not own a rent-producing asset suffer a disadvantage as the result of the rent. It is in their interest to eliminate the rent, and in the interest of the rent receiver to protect the advantage. The proposal I present here provides new insights. The concept of quasi rents suggests that monopoly rents often are transitory and the associated interests therefore not enduring. Thus, not only will stability of membership in structural locations and closure be important for class formation, but variations over time in rent advantages are important for predicting class formation. Rents provide a new interpretation of credentialism as a device to preserve and transmit advantages from one generation to the next with uncertainty about the ability of offspring.

The rent-based concept of class as exploitation provides an explanation for the recent increase in earnings inequality and for the practice of downsizing to destroy rents in the labor market.

The main class action will be by actors to seek rents, to protect rent privileges, and to destroy rents in structural locations, such as internal labor markets. The argument here implies that it is to the advantage of the capitalist class to produce a labor market conforming to the assumption of neoclassical economics, and I have tried to show that capitalism in the last decades has been successful in eliminating rents to labor. Eliminating rents in the labor market creates more efficient labor markets – that is, labor markets with less structure and more fluidity. A rents-free labor market will be one where simple class schemes are increasingly less applicable. The destruction of rents also creates more inequality within the labor market and produces more wealth that accrues to some of those owning means of production – for example, capitalists – whether they are old families, new entrepreneurs, pension funds or graduate students with mutual funds. The resulting society conforms to Marx's predictions about the nature of advanced capitalism: "The bourgeoisie, whenever it has got the upper hand, has put an end to all feudal, patriarchal, idyllic relations . . . It has resolved personal worth into exchange value, and in place of the numberless indefeasible chartered freedoms, has set up a single, unconscionable freedom – Free Trade" (Marx 1959a [1848], p. 323).

Thus, the main prediction about the development of capitalism from rent-based class theory is that rents will disappear from structural locations in the labor market. This will result in a structureless society, without the nooks and crannies of social structure we have come to expect because feudalism is slow to disappear. The result is the transfer of wealth to those who have rights to rent-producing assets, even though these assets usually are quasi rents, for the wealth created by quasi rents is not destroyed when the rent is destroyed. As a result, we see increasing wealth inequality (Wolff 1995).

If Marx's grand scenario for advanced capitalism is interpreted as having to do with the distribution of rents, it is sustained. Rent seeking creates the dynamics of capitalism, and the destruction of rents in the labor market creates a structurally more homogenous working class, that is, a working class without structural supports for its welfare.

6   Foundations of a post-class analysis

Jan Pakulski

Contemporary class theories and analyses are grandchildren of Marxism. As noted by Wright in the Introduction, they share with their classic antecedent a broad explanatory aspiration. They aim at charting and explaining the structure of inequality, especially in economically defined life chances, by linking these inequalities with the patterns of property and employment relations. They also aim at identifying key conflict-generating economic cleavages, especially those that underlie transformative social struggles. In doing that, they combine and compete with a number of alternative – that is nonclass – analytic and theoretical constructs. The latter include concepts and propositions derived from the Tocquevillian, Durkheimian and Weberian theoretical heritage: occupational theories of stratification that focus on social division of labor and occupational closure; "status" theories of inequality identifying value-conventional sources of racial, gender and ethno-national inequality and conflict; and theories concentrating on political power, organizational hierarchies of authority and the accompanying social tensions and struggles. This competition is complicated by partial convergence between the competitors. As the preceding chapters show, the classic Marxist heritage has undergone a number of reformulations that blur the boundaries between the original analytic distinctions of class, occupation, status, and political power. Therefore any rendition of an analytic and theoretical confrontation between class and nonclass accounts of social inequality, division and conflict has to rely on some – often contested – definitional distinctions. It is assumed here that class is a fundamentally economic phenomenon, that it is reflected in patterns of social "groupness," that class location is reflected in social consciousness, identity, and antagonism, and that it generates forms of action in the economic and political fields that have a potential to transform capitalism.

Thus defined, class theory and analysis face two major problems: that of validity, that is, the degree of empirical confirmation of their key tenets, and that of relevance, that is, capacity to highlight the most salient features of contemporary social hierarchy, division, and conflict. On both counts, especially that of relevance, class theory and class analysis face criticism.[1] According to critics, their capacity to highlight the key aspects of social hierarchy, division, and conflict has been declining. This is because "class formation," especially the social and political articulation of working classes, is in decline. Other aspects of social inequality and antagonism come to the fore, reflecting the divisions of race and gender, the impact of citizenship, the distribution of political power, and the actions of elites.[2] Consequently, and in contrast with its classic predecessor, contemporary class analysis becomes an abstract academic pursuit that is insulated from political practices of social movements and parties.

The defenders of class analysis argue – in many ways convincingly – that the classic class models need updating and elaboration. The foundations of such updated class theory and analysis as proposed by Erik Wright, Richard Breen, David Grusky, and Aage Sørensen, show the great theoretical and analytic potential of class constructs. Yet, their authors also face a series of dilemmas. First, there is a dilemma of identity. The more valid and relevant the proposed class constructs, the more similar they become to their close competitors, especially to Weberian and Durkheimian analyses of occupational and status stratification. This analytic-theoretical morphing[3] raises a question whether a "class theory" stripped of its distinctive elements is still worth calling a theory of class. The second is a dilemma of explanatory trade-offs. The more fine-tuned the class theoretical and analytic claims, the less capably they highlight and explain the most salient features of contemporary social hierarchy and antagonism. Hence the frequent "juxtapositions" of updated class analyses with nonclass (gender, race, occupational, political, etc.) analyses that raise further questions of the relevance of class constructs. Class theory and analysis, it seems, face dangers of either morphing with their competitors or being improved into oblivion.

The strategy proposed here is quite different from that suggested by the advocates of class. Instead of reconstructing, updating and "developing" class theory and analysis, I suggest absorbing them into a more comprehensive, complex, and plural – but less deterministic – theoretical and historical vision of social ordering and change. The first step towards such absorption is a particularization of class as a historical-analytic concept.

---

[1] For example, Pakulski and Waters (1996a, b, c), Clark and Lipset (2001).

[2] The best test of relevance is the capacity of class analysis to shed light on such key developments of the last century as the formation of communist states, the rise and defeat of fascism, the extension of citizenship, the mobilization of "new" (civil rights, feminist, green, and minority rights) movements, the fall of European communism, the unification of Europe, and the mobilization of religious fundamentalisms.

[3] Identified, among others, by Waters (1991) and discussed in more detail in Pakulski and Waters (1996b).

This involves locating class within a historical-developmental sequence as a *particular* social configuration of inequality typical of the industrial era. In other words, it is proposed that the "classness" of social inequalities, and therefore the relevance of class analysis, vary historically. As argued in the concluding section, "classness" reached its peak in industrial society and has been declining while postindustrial and postmodern trends intensify. Contemporary advanced societies remain unequal, but in a classless way. These increasingly complex configurations of classless inequality and antagonism, it is argued here, call for more comprehensive theoretical and analytic constructs.[4]

Aspects of class

While in the popular discourse "class" is a synonym of social hierarchy and structured inequality in general, in social analysis and academic discourse it carries more specific meanings. These meanings – the semantic "halo" of the class concept – typically reflect the central tenets of the "classic template":

- the centrality of property and employment relations (the class structure) in shaping social inequality, that is, the distribution of societal power and economic life chances in general, and income in particular;
- the centrality of class structure in shaping other social relations and acting as the matrix for "social structuration." This implies "class formation," i.e. a correspondence between class structure on the one hand, and the pattern social "groupness" on the other; and
- the centrality of class structure in structuring social antagonism and overt conflict. This implies that class conflict and class struggle shape sociopolitical cleavages and remain key propellants of social change.

This characterization of class raises three questions: about the relative strength of class determination of access to key "power resources" and therefore the relationship between class and social hierarchy; about the relative strength of class formation and therefore the relationship between class and social division; and about the relative salience of class antagonism in shaping social conflicts. Consequently, debates about the relevance of the class concept for the analysis of contemporary advanced societies inevitably address not only the questions concerning the scope of "class inequality," that is, the inequality attributed to the operation of class structure (typically defined by property/employment relations), but also the issue of "class formation" and "class conflict." Classes are not only structural positions, but also real antagonistic collectivities.

---

[4] Such constructs are outlined in more details elsewhere – see Pakulski (2004). Below I sketch only the "foundational" backbone nonclass analysis.

How salient and important are class determinations of inequalities vis-à-vis other nonclass determinations? How strong are class divisions vis-à-vis nonclass – e.g., occupational, racial, ethno-national – social divisions? How strong and salient are class identities vis-à-vis nonclass – e.g., gender, regional, religious – identifications? What are the trends in their relative social and political salience? The advocates of updated class analysis, especially Wright, argue that while class is important, the degree of its social and political salience varies, and it can be modest. Yet, if this salience of class proves not only relatively low but also declining, it would undermine the very rationale of reconstructing and upgrading class theory and analysis. Intellectual investment in alternative accounts would promise better explanatory returns.

Among the most frequently discussed alternatives to class analysis are the "multidimensional" Weberian analyses of stratification, Durkheimian analyses of occupational differentiation, Tocquevillian approaches focusing on civil society, and studies of power stratification and elite formation. While some of them are discussed by Erik Wright, Richard Breen, David Grusky, and Elliott Weininger as springboards for updated class analysis, I will argue here that they are more usefully seen as theoretical foundations for *alternative* (to class) accounts of inequality and antagonism in advanced society.

Classic foundations of social (nonclass) analysis

Alexis de Tocqueville's (1945 [1862]) vision of social inequalities and their modern dynamics is in many ways a mirror image of the Marxist class vision. While Marx diagnosed class polarization, Tocqueville charted a progressive equalization of conditions, expansion of democratic practices and proliferation of egalitarian norms and manners. This progressive equalization, according to Tocqueville, reflected the cumulative impact of Christian values, expanding commerce and industry, growing affluence, the increasing strength of civil society (civic associations), and the progressive democratization of culture. Social interaction and mobility, he argued, were becoming frequent and open, ownership was becoming fluid, and property was more equally divided. The new ("democratic") social order was not only egalitarian but also individualistic. The individual, and not a corporate collectivity, became the center of initiatives. That fostered progressive individualization and massification of motives, tastes, concerns, and action. Equality and democracy, in other words, promoted "alikeness," and this quality gave further impetus to social leveling. Under the condition of triumphant republican democracy, predicted Tocqueville, the "passion for equality" would spread through all domains of life and all aspects of human relations, including political, work, and domestic spheres.

Contemporary students of social inequality pay special attention to Tocqueville's analysis of a new form of social hierarchy that grows under republican democracy. Five features of this hierarchy are particularly salient. First, it is flattened, because universal citizenship is reflected not only in mass enfranchisement, but also in the "democracy of manners." Modern citizens despise haughtiness and question all claims to superiority. Uniformity and informality of manners become habitual among all social strata. This promotes a high level of social mobility – a second feature of the democratic hierarchy. In republican democracy upward social mobility occurs predominantly through economic success, and is widely acclaimed. Success, and its most clear symptom, wealth, are objects of popular admiration. Such perceptions are further strengthened by the leveling of occupational statuses – which is the third feature of republican hierarchy. All professions become open, in a social sense, because most professionals become employees. Caste-like social divisions either weaken or completely disappear. While inequalities of wealth persist, they do not give rise to social distances and divisions. The new rich do not form a new socially elevated and insulated aristocracy, and they do not monopolize political privilege. Wealth and power are formally separated, though corrupt practices such as buying offices and appropriating political spoils are widespread. Fourth, the flattening of hierarchies and narrowing of social distances is reflected in the massification of education and the spread of public information. Schooling is open, education is seen as an important avenue of social advancement, and widespread literacy forms the social foundation for the popular press. This, in turn, fosters a condition of public opinion and informed civic participation. Finally, gender divisions are also affected by the democratic trends: paternalism crumbles, and women gain increasing independence, though matrimony still imposes on them "irrevocable bonds." This leads Tocqueville to a bold declaration: "I believe that the social changes that bring nearer to the same level the father and son, the master and servant, and, in general, superiors and inferiors will raise woman and make her more and more equal to men" (1945 [1862], II, p. 211).

Tocqueville adds two important qualifications to this vision of progressive "equality of condition" (which we may label "classless inequality"). First, he is quite skeptical as to the prospect for racial integration, even if, as he predicts, slavery is eliminated. What is more likely to occur is an informal segregation and antagonism fueled by the democratic aspirations of the black population. In an even more pessimistic tone, he predicts a persisting segregation of Native Americans combined with progressive destruction of their cultures – all done, as he sarcastically notes, with "respect for the laws of humanity." Second, he is also skeptical about the prospects for equalization of workmen and the business elite. However, while unequal, neither of them is likely to turn into a cohesive social class. The workers are too atomized to form cohesive collectivities; the business elite is too mobile, internally fragmented due to competition, and too socially heterogeneous to form a cohesive group.[5]

Marxist and Tocquevillian analyses reveal the two faces of modern social hierarchies and offer two paradigmatic views of modern trends. For Marxists, class divisions mark a new form of hierarchical oppression, exploitation and domination that hides behind a façade of "free labor contract," liberal ideology, and egalitarian manners. Marxists are credited with bringing to light these hidden aspects of modern social inequality, and with attributing class inequality to the core features of modern capitalism: private ownership of capital and commodification of labor. The Tocquevillian insights are equally central and profound: in modern society economic inequalities coincide with – and are overshadowed by – the leveling of manners and civic statuses. Republican democracy generates new hierarchies of wealth, but also bridges social gaps created by expanding industrial wealth. The main problem faced by modern society is not class division, but civic division between democratically elected political despots and politically impotent denizens preoccupied with material concerns.[6]

Emile Durkheim (1933) offers another alternative to a class analytic and theoretical template. Social inequalities are seen by Durkheim in the context of progressive social differentiation, itself a product of increasing social interactions or "moral density." The fact that new social functions that emerge in the process of differentiation are organized in a hierarchical manner is less important for Durkheim than the *mode* of this organization. While in traditional societies the social hierarchies are rigid and ideologically justified, in modern societies they are open, and normally enjoy functional legitimacy.

Durkheim made an important distinction between socially acceptable inequalities, namely those which were functional to the industrial order and reflected collective values and ideals, and those that were arbitrarily imposed. In the most general sense, the former reflected the distance

---

[5] "To tell the truth, though there are rich men, the class of rich men does not exist; for these rich individuals have no feelings and purposes, no traditions or hopes, in common; there are individuals, therefore, but no definite class . . . Their relative position is not a permanent one; they are constantly drawn together or separated by their interests" (1945 [1862], II, p. 160).
[6] Tocqueville analyzed this danger in his studies of "despotic democracy."

from the "sacred": the ideas, objects and formulas set out as special, forbidden, and awe-inspiring. These sacred realms were subsequently identified with central social values, the universally cherished standards. Social inequalities were socially legitimate if they reflected social values. In modern societies such value-foundation was reflected in references to "merit": investments, application, and efficiency. By contrast, the illegitimate inequalities – and Durkheim included here a broad range of discriminations condemned by socialists and liberals alike – either lacked value-backing or resulted from a "forced division of labor," a label applied to non-meritocratic hierarchy and privilege.

Social inequalities related to uneven distribution of property were seen by Durkheim as legitimate. Unlike Marx and Weber, Durkheim attributed to property a sacred/religious origin, and he saw the privileges of ownership as legitimated by the residues of property's sacred status. The legal exclusions that accompanied property rights revealed for Durkheim clear links with ancient taboos and rituals. In a similar way, Durkheim linked gender hierarchies with the sacred realm of ancient popular classifications and symbolic taxonomies that shaped social perceptions and distances, especially between "us" and "them." Durkheim's studies of these "primitive classifications" formed a theoretical foundation of the social anthropology of inequality subsequently evoked by Pierre Bourdieu.

In a similar way, Durkheim also argued that political inequalities, especially those related to the roles in the state, carry a strong residue of sacredness as well as functional legitimacy. State leaders carry the residues of sacred authority enjoyed by tribal chieftains and *patres familias*. At the same time, the special role of the state – as the "brain of society" – necessitates the authority and autonomy of state elites. Political hierarchy, in this view, is reinforced by its functional importance (social coordination) and by the links with the sacred realm. This is why recruitment to these authority positions has to be carried out in a ritualized manner. Incumbents have to prove their fitness for the job by displaying merit and following successfully a prescribed *cursus honorum*.

Durkheim's second major contribution to sociology of inequality concerns the form and the evolution of occupational hierarchies. Social differentiation (the celebrated "division of labor") is elevated by Durkheim to the status of the constitutive process of modernization. It results in the fragmentation of larger social units, such as estates, guilds, *and classes*. In contrast to Marx, Durkheim therefore predicts fragmentation and decomposition of hierarchical collectivities and a multiplication of occupational groups. He also predicts that relationships between occupational groups are likely to be harmonious rather than conflictual, because of increasing regulation of economic contest by occupational associations and the state.

Occupational groups become central elements of the new stratification system because they confer identity, status, and material rewards. They are aided by the state that becomes a major manager of social stability and cohesion.

Social hierarchy will also be shaped, according to Durkheim, by "value polymorphy" and progressive individualism, the latter reflected in the growing emphasis on individual rights. Nevertheless, he was worried by an apparent clustering of occupational groups into large-scale and potentially conflictual "interest associations." Such entities did not fit well with modern "organically solidary" societies, because they relied on "mechanical" bonds derived from ideologically constructed "shared interest." Thus, while recognizing the "unjust advantage" enjoyed by employers, Durkheim considered class formation and polarization as unlikely. The principle of class solidarity was incompatible with the principle of social differentiation, and the antagonistic ideology of class struggle clashed with the sense of complementarity engendered in organic bonds.[7] Instead of class formation and conflict, Durkheim predicted an ongoing and largely harmonious (though always threatened by anomie) occupational differentiation accompanied by state regulation.

David Grusky (2001, p. 18, and Chapter 3 above) follows closely in Durkheim's footsteps by proposing that we consider occupations as the basic units of modern social hierarchy. Large-scale class-like entities are nominal and, unlike occupations, they do not form real and meaningful groupings. Occupations are the product of spontaneous differentiation and "organic" social clustering. They form genuine "moral communities" (rather than mere associations) and engender strong identities. Occupations are also recognized and sponsored by the state and implicated in all forms of reward determinations. As well, they serve as conduits for career aspirations and promote similarity of lifestyles, tastes, and consumption. Even if they become temporarily aggregated into large-scale classes, such aggregates are fragile.

Grusky's argument becomes problematic when he suggests that occupations should be considered "real classes." It is not clear what is gained by conflating the two terms and concepts: those of class and occupational group. His attempt at formulating a Durkheimian theory of exploitation (through rent extraction) is even more problematic, because it flies in the face of Durkheimian functionalism that underlies the master

---

[7] If one class in society is obliged, in order to live, to take any price for its services, while another can abstain from such action thanks to resources at its disposal, which, however, are not necessarily due to any social superiority, the second has an unjust advantage over the first in law. In other words, there cannot be rich and poor at birth without there being unjust contracts (Durkheim 1933, p. 384).

vision of occupational differentiation. This move leads Grusky away from Durkheimian sociology of occupational differentiation and towards the Weberian theory of market closure. Like Parkin (1979) and Murphy (1988), he argues that occupational and professional groups become the main conduits for closure – which can be seen as both exploitative and defensive.

Now, there is a radical difference between functional differentiation and closure. The former is spontaneous conflict resolution (reducing competition); the latter implies conflict and imposition. Only when one considers occupational groups as conduits for closure do they appear as antagonistic class-like groups. Thus the theory of occupational closure and rent extraction can be formulated only by parting the way with the core tenets of Durkheimian theory. There is a theoretical cost of this departure. By abandoning the Durkheimian vision of functional differentiation Grusky weakens his ability to explain the *origins* of occupational clusters. Moreover, he faces the evidence of declining closure (state "deregulation") and waning industrial conflict in advanced societies. This seems to be more in line with the trends anticipated by Durkheim than with predictions derived from the theories of closure.

The main foundations for nonclass social analysis of inequality and conflict were laid by Max Weber, especially in his rich but unsystematic notes on *Economy and Society* (1978 [1922]). What is particularly striking in those notes – and often ignored by both the "left Weberians" and sympathetic Marxist critics – is their polemical tone. Weber rejects Marx's sweeping claims about universal centrality of class inequality, exploitation, division, and antagonism. He also formulates an alternative vision of social stratification in which societal power and life chances are shaped jointly by market endowments, established cultural conventions of honor, and organizational power, especially within the state. These different "generators" may operate solo, in which case social inequalities follow one predominant principle of distribution, or they may combine in producing complex gradations of societal power and life chances. Either way, market, status and power positions seldom form matrices for group formation. The latter implicate the cultural realm of meaning (Weber 1978 [1922]: pp. 306–7, 927–39).

Both Weber and his followers have argued convincingly for maintaining an analytic separation between the three "generators" and accompanying dimensions of social inequality – class, status and party – and for seeing social stratification and group formation as complex and contingent. These arguments have been typically directed against Marxist class analysts who try to subsume the three generators under the single concept of class, and who often assume an isomorphy between unequal positions and social structure.[8] Weberians also warn against assuming the correspondence between the structure of inequality, the patterns of group formation, and the regularities of social action. The three, Weber warns, seldom coincide. "Social classes," for example, reflect the barriers in social mobility and interaction and they often cut across class boundaries. Similarly, "status groups" form on the matrix of lifestyle and consumption patterns, and they typically ignore class distinctions.

Together with "classic" elite theorists (Vilfredo Pareto, Gaetano Mosca, and Robert Michels), Weber also highlights the centrality of political power as the key aspect of social inequalities in modern societies. Together, they argue that it is political power, especially the power of the modern state, that typically undergirds social privileges in modern society. Power comes not only from control of the means of production and from market endowments, but also, and increasingly, from organization, that is, from the control of the means of political domination. Therefore social organization inevitably gives rise to elites – cohesive and solidary oligarchies at the apex of large organizations. While the elite–mass gap is bound to remain wide, even in formally democratic societies, power hierarchies are likely to generate strong legitimacy by embracing formally democratic procedures. Classless egalitarianism may be an ideological dream, but open political hierarchy and responsible democratic elites are a possibility.

Weberian sociology of power forms a convenient springboard for both a critique of class theory and an alternative form of social analysis of inequality, division, and antagonism. The main "generative structures" of social inequality in Weberian sociology are market/property, communal, and authority relations. They reflect, respectively: property rights and market freedoms; the established values and conventions of honor distribution; and the strength of corporate bureaucracies (especially in the state). Together, they form socially and historically diverse matrices for the distribution of societal power and individual life chances. However, these matrices do not necessarily correspond with the ways in which social relations form, social clustering occurs, social divisions appear, and social antagonisms arise. These aspects of hierarchical social formation reflect the autonomous processes of social clustering and closure, identity and

---

[8] It is the relative prevalence, relative salience of generative spheres of relations, that is important in shaping the pattern of social inequality, mode of stratification and the overall type of society. "Depending on the prevailing mode of stratification," he observes, "we shall speak of a 'status society' or a 'class society'" (Weber 1978 [1922], p. 306). Most historical societies analysed by Weber – in fact, all societies other than the modern Western type – have been described as "status societies," that is societies in which other than class inequalities have been most salient.

solidarity formation, cultural distantiation, and political organization – all embedded in the dominant meaning systems. Social divisions may form along the class-market lines, as well as along ethnic, regional (national), party-ideological, racial or religious lines – the point stressed by contemporary neo-Weberians (e.g., Giddens 1973, Scott 1996) and theorists of social space and differential association (e.g., Laumann 1973, Stewart, Prandys, and Blackborn 1980).

Complex structures of inequality

Social inequality may vary in the degree of complexity – the interaction of different structural "generators" – and degree of social articulation, social group formation. Social stratification – the degree to which social inequality is structured into lasting hierarchies – is also variable. So is sociocultural articulation of hierarchical strata through patterns of shared identities and differential association. When sociocultural articulation is weak – that is, when strata boundaries are blurred, group identities and solidarities are weak, distances are crosscutting, and divisions are fickle – social inequalities may take a complex and unstratified form. Late modernity, it is argued here, marks a shift in this direction of complex inequality. This calls for an overhaul of our views of social inequality, division, and antagonism. The key steps in such an overhaul involve:

Recognizing the multiplicity of generative structures

As noted by most analysts of industrial modernization, Max Weber in particular, classes always coincided and competed with other aspects of inequality (1978 [1922], pp. 306–7, 927–39). While the key power resources can be translated into each other, they seldom cumulate and crystallize into consistent social hierarchies and divisions. This is because class, status, and party derive from different aspects of social relations and are accompanied by different formulae legitimizing the distribution of social resources. Class favors the formula "to everyone according to property and marketable skills." It is insensitive to traditional status claims, and therefore revolutionary in its social consequences. The party-authority hierarchies rely on the principle "to everyone according to rank," that is a hierarchical distance from the organizational power centers. Modern state bureaucracies are particularly effective generators of such rank orders, and they became backbones of stratification under state socialism. Finally, the status claims follow the formula "to everyone according to established social conventions." Such conventions of asymmetric status attribution are typically grounded in tradition (e.g., traditional interpretations of holy texts, established practice, etc.), but they also evolve with new forms of socially recognized "distinction."

Recognizing the impact of education and knowledge

When writing about status groups in early twentieth-century Europe, Weber mentioned, albeit briefly, new forms of educational "credentialism":

> The development of the diploma from the universities, and business and engineering colleges, and the universal clamour for the creation of educational certificates in all fields make for the formation of a privileged stratum in bureaus and offices. Such certificates support their holders' claim for intermarriages with notable families, claims to adhere to "codes of honour" ... claims for a "respectable" remuneration rather than remuneration for work well done, claims for assured advancement and old-age insurance and, above all, claims to monopolise social and economically advantageous positions. (Weber 1948, pp. 241–2)

Success in credentializing depends on securing the capacity to maintain, defend, and enforce the rights of credential-holders. As both Weber and his contemporary followers (especially Harold Perkin and Frank Parkin) stress, the claims of these categories, especially the professionals, evoke the status principle of distribution ("according to educational credentials"). Yet they also confront and question the old status claims based on tradition. Therefore the emergent educational status groups are highly ambivalent, if not outright hostile, towards the claims made on the basis of tradition and class. Thus while the professional closure often utilizes market monopolies, it also ignores the "naked property rights." Contemporary professions, intellectuals, and managers thus constitute status-type groupings, rather than classes.

Such contemporary status groupings operate in the secular and legal-rational context. They reflect the pervasive liberal ideology of equal opportunity cum merit. One may argue that this ideology sits uneasily with class principles. The latter have to adjust to status distinctions – the point made by sociocultural class theorists, such as Pierre Bourdieu, reputation stratificationists, such as Edward Shils, human capital theorists, such as Gary Becker, and students of postindustrialism, such as Daniel Bell. The special status of education (certified higher education in particular) derives from its privileged role as a convenient "index of merit," rather than the mere source of marketable skills. Higher education, in particular, turns into the key social articulator of the universalistic principle of achievement and merit. This critical role of education is inherent in, and reinforced by, the dominant liberal ideology that identifies education with merit.[9]

Recognizing the impact of citizenship and democracy

Tocqueville's analysis of progressive "equality of condition" formed a springboard for contemporary analyses of civic and political inequality. Paradoxically, as students of citizenship and democracy note, the extension of citizenship brings some social leveling, but also a new type of hierarchy and division. On this point, Tocqueville's intuitions converge with Weberian ideas, though Tocqueville links the new "despotic" tendencies with the weakness of civil society, while Weber attributes such tendencies to "plebiscitary" trends inherent in mass democratization and bureaucratic ascendancy. Both Tocquevillian and Weberian scholars see political stratification as crosscutting – and in some ways overshadowing – both the traditional status hierarchies and economic class divisions.

Tocqueville's analysis anticipates Weber's historical analyses of the egalitarian civic status emerging from the historical expansion of Western cities and nation-states. The expanding citizenship rights in Britain were analyzed by Marshall (1950) and subsequently generalized by Turner (1990). Citizenship grew in coverage and scope. The granting of basic civil liberties was followed by extension of rights into political and social domains. The social/welfare rights, in particular, pitched citizenship against the "power of property" and the "cash nexus" thus affecting the patterns of social inequality. While most social analysts see this expansion of citizenship as a source of egalitarian trends, some also point to hierarchical implications. The appearance of "noncitizens" – refugees, illegal migrants, asylum seekers, and widely tolerated but disenfranchised *Gastarbeiters* – heralds the formation of a new civic "underclass" and highlights a new dimension of stratification through civic-political exclusion.

The impact of gender and racial relations

The changing form of gender and ethno-racial inequality deserve a special comment. Both approximate "status inequalities" – they are derived from and engendered in traditional social conventions reinforced by ideology and coded into age-long discriminatory social practices, especially in the domestic-familial sphere. Gender inequalities have been reproduced

---

[9] Educational categories become not only important status positions but also potent matrices of social formation – a fact confirmed by the strength of educational homogamy, friendship networks, and political mobilization (see the studies of new social movements).

through traditional cultural norms and underlying values. This is why they are strongest in traditional (often pre-capitalist) societies, and why changes in class relations (e.g. those that followed the Russian and Chinese revolutions) did not alter them significantly. By contrast, the rapid de-traditionalization associated with spreading rationalism, individualism and secularism helps in reducing gender gaps.

Gender and ethno-racial inequalities continue to radiate into public spheres, and this results in "genderization" and "racialization" of occupations, market segments, and political roles. But they seldom produce gender or racial strata. Rather, the genderization of occupations and market segments illustrates the hybridization of social stratification that adds to the complexity of contemporary patterns of inequality. This hybridization involves an interpenetration of two stratifying mechanisms in a way that makes it difficult to disentangle their causal effects. Thus the expansion of the market mechanism transforms the market into a "quasi-cultural" domain. In turn, status conventions formed outside the market sphere become articulated as "market capacities" through widely accepted – and typically taken for granted – restrictions and facilitations in employment and working conditions. The operation of the market, in other words, reflects communal norms and relationships formed outside the sphere of employment. At the same time, these very norms and relations are legitimated and reinforced through the market idiom of efficiency, productivity, etc.

As these examples indicate, hybridization is not restricted to the interpenetration between the market and communal relations. A similar interpenetration occurs between the market command systems, and communal norms. The concentration of industrial production, for example, has accompanied the emergence of corporate managerial positions. The life chances of corporate managers are a function of marketable skills, hierarchical location, and the very size cum strategic location of the corporation. This is particularly important when private and state hierarchies combine in the process of corporatist fusions – as occurred in Western Europe in the mid-twentieth century.[10]

Stratification and social formation

Increasing hybridization heralds the decomposition of the industrial classes and the concomitant departure from class society. This is reflected

---

[10] The emergence of corporate elites and the subordinate operatives, the "white-collar" strata, has been analyzed by Ralf Dahrendorf (1959), C. Wright Mills (1951, 1956) and contemporary elite theorists.

in an increasingly complex pattern of hierarchical group formation – social stratification – to which we must now turn.

Social stratification refers to structured vertical patterning: social hierarchy plus social division. Clusters of unequal positions are linked by social proximity and separated by social distances. It also refers to *processes* of hierarchical social clustering and closure. Such processes are reversible; changing inequality patterns involve destratification and restratification along class and nonclass lines.

Social clustering and closure

In the process of stratification social inequalities acquire a shape of stable social hierarchies, patterned relations of superiority and inferiority, systematic inclusions and exclusions, social distances and proximities. While this is a matter of degree, "stratification proper" emerges only when there is a minimal social formation, that is, a relatively clear and stable vertical patterning through social clustering and closure. It makes little sense to talk about stratified society in the absence of such recognizable "social strata."

Clustering typically involves overlaps between different aspects of inequality in a way that facilitates social recognition; social closure involves the formation of persisting social distances and proximities. Thus class stratification, especially in late nineteenth-century Britain, involved what we may call "status usurpation" (and degradation) through increasing overlap and convergence of class and traditional status positions. A merger through intermarriages of industrial bourgeoisie and landed gentry was but one example of this convergence; status degradation of craftsmen and industrial workers was another.

Following the Weberian track, we can say that the distinctiveness of social strata depends on the degree of social closure, the capacity of strata members to restrict important social interactions, and sociodemographic closure, the capacity for reproduction across generations. The best markers of social closure have been intermarriages and intergenerational continuity of economic roles. Intermarriages within the sets of socially recognized strata (be they classes, status groups, or political ranks) reinforce strata reproduction. Such reproduction is also facilitated by a formation of sociocultural habitus through which social distinction and social stigma become meaningful and legitimate (though never unchallenged, as Bourdieu notes).

Attention of contemporary stratification sociologists focuses on "occupational classes," that is, vertical clusters of positions forming on the matrix of technical division of labor, as well as property and employment relations.[11] Occupational class formation has been well researched. Some critics note that the boundaries of "occupational classes" are porous and fickle. When they solidify, this typically follows credentialization. However, such credentialization, especially if it involves educational certification and meritocratic legitimation, tends to follow the logic of status group formation (as noted by Turner 1988). Similarly, racial and ethno-strata (e.g. blacks in the US, Chinese in East Asia, Aborigines in Australia) can be seen as examples of contemporary status-like strata. They merge with and crosscut sociopolitical hierarchies. Contemporary elites and "political classes" are examples of vertical social clusters in such hierarchies forming around positions of political influence.[12]

Students of occupational classes point to a proliferation of loosely structured and vertically organized social clusters. This proliferation reflects the progressive differentiation (the central tenets of Durkheimian sociology) that erodes the internal homogeneity of the large-scale occupational clusters, such as industrial workers or agricultural laborers. While in the past such clusters may have approximated classes, contemporary occupational divisions are too weak and fragmented to do so. Social formation seems to follow the pattern of progressive differentiation that is both technical and social in nature.

Communities and groups

Until now we have discussed the first aspect of social formation, namely clustering and closure. Both are matters of degree. They result in what Holton (1996) and Turner (1996) (following Toennies' classical distinction) call *gesellschaftlich* clusters and strata. *Gemeinschaftlich* groupings require stronger social formation involving sociocultural articulation: development of collective identities and solidarities. Such strong formation is typically accomplished through leadership and organization. When social categories attain such identities and solidarities – a rare and contingent development – they transform into communities and may also spawn organized collective actors, typically parties or movements.

Community and group formation lies at the center of the social stratification perspective. Seen from the Durkheimian perspective, stratification

---

[11] It must be remembered, though, that status elements also enter social class formation. What makes the resulting groupings social classes is the original matrix on which they grow or, to put it differently, the social bases of inclusion-exclusion, as well as (though more difficult to determine) the type of motivations and interests involved – in the case of social class, predominantly "class interest."

[12] Partocratic strata and the politically circumscribed *nomenklaturas* in communist societies are also good examples of such strata. See classical elite theorists and, in the context of class analysis, works of Wesolowski e.g. 1977.

involves the formation of in-out-group solidarities and distances, and the accompanying processes of social evaluations cum ranking in relation to the dominant values. This path of analysis points to three interrelated aspects of stratification process: social classification and boundary drawing, evaluation cum granting/claiming of social esteem which reflect the "distance from the sacred," internal identity-formation and cohesion building. The latter processes involve the formation of strong collective representations and internal normative regulation.

Durkheimian sociology of inequalities pays more attention to popular classification and boundary drawing than to vertical ranking, that is, the "stratification proper." This reflects the well-known Durkheim observation that especially those who consider themselves as socially disadvantaged always contest hierarchical orders. Communities and groups may, or may not, form "consensual" hierarchical orders. If they do, these orders – reflecting shared values (or the distance from the sacred) – are precarious. The interplay of social differentiation (horizontal group formation) and stratification (contested vertical ordering and ranking) is the favorite topic of students of social distances and solidarities.[13]

The neo-Weberian and elite perspectives highlight the formation of vertical communities within national power hierarchies. Both see them as contingent and complex, reflecting shared lifestyle, communication channels, common enemy, and effective leadership as key factors enhancing community. The main symptom of communal bonds is a shared identity backed by a popular label of recognition. Such identity – and easy self-identification – form the foundation for solidary action. Perhaps the best examples of communal power groupings are political elites. The minimum degree of internal cohesion and "groupness," in fact, is a definitional feature of elites.

Hierarchical communal groups are rare because their formation and social reproduction consume vast amounts of collective energy and resources. Social distances have to be cultivated through patterned

---

[13] See, for example, Bourdieu (1984 [1979]) and Bottero and Prandy (2003). As noted by Durkheim (eg. 1933, pp. 356–8) and his followers, the relentless division of labor generates *occupational* differentiation and stratification. This may result in "social class divisions" when differentiation combines with "pathological" (in Durkheim's view) social separation and isolation, when social "division becomes dispersion" and when normative regulation fails. Formation of "working classes" (in the plural) and industrial conflict with the employers are symptomatic of these divisions in large-scale industry. However, Durkheim also sees a tendency towards normatively regulated occupational differentiation and integration, especially in the climate of spreading the "cult of the individual" and highly differentiated "conscience collective" (pluralism of values). The resulting pattern of occupational stratification, as pointed out by Parsons, is highly fluid, complex and diverse. Strata formation follows societal and local "evaluative frameworks," hence operating according to status, rather than class, principle.

interaction and lifestyle distinction (Weber). Communities also rely on cultural reproduction of classifications and ritual reassertion of shared values (Durkheim). It is not surprising therefore that the best examples of such communal strata are typically historical status groups, such as "classic" Indian castes. The two contemporary examples of large-scale *gesellschaftlich* groupings – nations and professional associations – do not lend themselves well to stratification analysis. Attempts at identifying contemporary *gesellschaftlich* strata on a subnational level, especially in advanced societies, have seldom been successful.

This often leads to a highly problematic distinction between "objective" (structural) and "subjective" (meaningful) aspects of social hierarchy. Class structure, for example, is sometimes seen by its proponents as independent of actor/subject (often false) consciousness and only loosely related to social perceptions, norms, and the actual patterns of associations. It is also found among some sympathetic critics of class analysis, such as Beck (1992) and Eder (1993) who sees classes as "objective" material substrata on which various forms of highly individualized "subjective" identifications, cultural orientations, and lifestyles grow. The dangers of such an option is that – if the "mediating" links are not specified – it weakens the explanatory potential of stratification theory and invites supplementary accounts of identity formation, cultural orientations, and lifestyles. Some such "mediations" and supplementary accounts are suggested by Bourdieu (1984 [1979]), who insists that "class formation" is mediated through, first, the habitus and then the popular classifications.[14] The problem is that the mediating causal complexes may work both ways. It is not clear, therefore, whether and to what degree habitus and popular classifications shape the social space (the distribution of multiple capitals), or are shaped by it. While the more orthodox class theorists see the material-economic "substratum" as the ultimate determinant of meanings, some revisionists, like Bourdieu, suggest more complex causal complexes and admit sociocultural determinations.

Social actors

The key social actors are elites and organized political groups, including those representing social movements and lobbies. Occasionally, the status of collective actor is also attributed to stratified communities – be

---

[14] As Brubaker (1985, p. 761) points out,

> The conceptual space within which Bourdieu defines class is not that of production, but that of social relations in general. Class divisions are defined not by differing relations to the means of production, but by the differing conditions of existence, differing systems of dispositions produced by differential conditioning, and differing endowments of capital.

it class-occupational, ethnic, civic, or hybrid. They may use a class idiom of appeal – that is, mobilize interests and solidarities engendered in employment roles and market capacities – or a status idiom, or a power-political idiom, or a combination of different idiomatic appeals. Appeals to ethno-racial exclusion and discrimination, as in the case of the civil rights and minority movements, or appeals to shared religion and race, as in the case of anti-Western fundamentalist movements, illustrate such mixed mobilization strategies.

The emergence of collective actors heralds the deepening of socio-political cleavages. As Lipset and Rokkan (1967) remind us, the dominant sociopolitical cleavages in the West originated in the national and industrial revolutions. The industrial revolution generated strong class (owner–worker) as well as sectoral (agricultural–industrial) cleavages. The organizational formatting of these cleavages in Europe occurred at the beginning of the twentieth century, and it was accomplished by elites that effectively used a class idiom of appeal. These elites, and the organizations they headed, had "coupled" with and organized vertical clusters identified as class constituencies. The elites appealed to common "class interests" of these clusters, focused debates on issues of work and production, stressed the social implications of property rights and asymmetric power in employment contracts, and linked their programs with ideological packages that reflected the left–right polarity.[15] While this class formatting proved very successful in the past in generating "working-class" movements and parties (as well as some "middle-class" political movements), it has always competed with alternative formatting along national, regional, religious, civic, and ethnic lines. The latter have been dominant in the last decades of the twentieth century, as illustrated by the successful mobilization of "new" social movements that spawned new political parties and propelled to power new elite factions.

Diverse social formation

Thus structured inequalities, as seen here, vary in degree of complexity and social articulation. In a minimal sense, they involve loose social hierarchies forming around unevenly distributed resources. Structured forms of inequality – social stratification – imply a minimum vertical clustering. In a stronger sense, social stratification involves the emergence of stratified communal groupings – the processes associated with the formation of

---

[15] See Clark and Lipset's (2001) model. Sartori (1969), together with elite theorists, emphasizes a process of structuring from above.

distinct and strong collective identities. Communal strata may also spawn collective social actors. This is an ongoing and reversible process, as illustrated by the rise and decline of class-allied movements, parties, and elites. Overlapping inequalities and divisions may reinforce stratification, while complex and crosscutting inequalities, especially when combined with open mobility, result in destratification. Destratification and restratification typically coincide; old patterns and configurations give way to new ones.

The degree of social formation of hierarchical groupings tends to vary at different points of stratification systems. Typically, social formation is strongest at the top of social hierarchies, where elites form. In fact, strong social formation (consensus, cohesion, and interaction) has been seen as a definitional feature of elites. The upper strata also form social circles, establishments, clubs, and other status groups with various degrees of exclusiveness. The middle and lower ranks tend to be less socially structured and are often described as a fluid "middle mass" (e.g., Broom and Jones 1976).

Configurations of inequality – a typology

One can assume a minimum degree of social formation below which one talks about mere social inequality, rather than social stratification. While such boundary judgments are necessarily arbitrary, a typological distinction between inequality and stratification is extremely useful in charting social trends of destratification vs. restratification. Such trends have been discussed in the context of debate about the relevance of class by Stanislaw Ossowski (1963 [1958], pp. 89–118) and Dennis Wrong (1976 [1964], pp. 5–16). They coined the terms "nonegalitarian classlessness," "inequality without stratification," and "classless inequality." Social inequalities, they argued, may take an unstratified form, as well as stratified but nonclass forms. These configurations of inequality may result from ascendancy of status groups or political ranks, and/or from the decomposition of the old classes and social strata.

The waning of pre-modern estates ("social orders") in Europe was a good example of destratification, which was followed by restratification and industrial class formation. The latter was complicated by the fact that the waning estate hierarchies left behind residual aristocracies and nobilities, as well as specific "status strata" of urban "intelligentsia." Another example of destratification was the suppression of class orders following the political takeovers and revolutions in Soviet-type societies. It involved "elimination" of upper classes and strata, and was accompanied by a

Social formation

Generative structures	*High/Strong*	*Low/Weak*
Single/dominant "generator" and low complexity	dominant stratification (e.g., "class society")	dominant inequality
Multiple/hybridized "generators" and high complexity	complex/hybrid stratification	complex "classless" inequality

Figure 6.1 Configurations of inequality – a typology

rapid ascendancy of political rank stratification, especially the emergence of party-state officialdom and the *nomenklatura*.

The pattern of variation in configurations of inequality is summarized in figure 6.1. The proposed typology results from a crosscutting of the two dimensions: (i) the degree of complexity, the predominance of one type of "generator" and the concomitant dominant principle of resource allocation, and (ii) the strength/degree of hierarchical social formation which we dichotomized into strong versus weak. The crosscutting of these two results in four types: dominant stratification, dominant inequality, hybrid stratification, and complex inequality (figure 6.1).

This opens the way for more precise definitions of the key concepts. In class society property/market-generated inequalities are most salient, and the degree of class formation is high. Unequal life chances of individuals reflect principally their property status and market endowments; life chances of family/household members reflect the endowments of the head. Honor and influence follow class position; social divisions form around class boundaries and inequalities. When formation is strong, group awareness and identity are reflected in organization and solidary action (class politics). This type follows closely the model promoted by Marxist class analysts and – as acknowledged below – it was approximated by industrial West European societies in the late nineteenth century and the first half of the twentieth century.

Class inequality is characterized by a dominance of class generators of inequality accompanied by weak social formation, a weak social articulation of class. While societal power is distributed predominantly according to the principle "to everyone according to property and market endowments," there are no discernible class groupings, divisions, or conflicts. One may argue that this type of inequality characterizes periods of rapid social change and transition. Early nineteenth-century Western societies, Marx and Engels argued, approximated this type, at least as far as the articulation of the "major classes" was concerned. While status principles of distribution weakened and class inequalities started to overshadow the estate system, class formation was embryonic.

Complex social inequality and hybrid stratification refer to configurations in which no single system of inequality predominates. Instead, the life chances form around complex profiles combining class, status, and authority positions. Gendered occupational strata and market segments, as well as racial and ethno-specific "underclass" enclaves, are good examples of such hybrid configurations of inequality. If clustering is strong and social strata develop around the complex combinations of positions, we are dealing with complex/hybrid stratification. In order to label such strata with a degree of accuracy, one needs multiple descriptors, such as "unskilled migrant women," "white-collar urban blacks" or "the Catholic intelligentsia."

Like any general and ideal typology, this one offers only a partial help in resolving the class debate. It charts the analytic field, but does not help in operationalizing the boundaries. One may also object that such a typology is loaded, that it makes dominant stratification type (including "class society") less realistic, less likely to be identified than other types. After all, objectors may say, class inequalities and divisions have *always* coincided with divisions generated by communal and state-authoritarian relations, and therefore a configuration approximating this type may be rare. There are two answers to these objections. First, they miss the point. While the "boundary judgments" are not specified, class stratification and class inequality *are* admitted here as realistic possibilities – as realistic as any other configuration. In fact, it is argued below that configurations of inequality in Western Europe at the turn of the century approximated closely class society type. Such configurations persisted throughout the world wars and post-war decades, reproduced mainly through sociopolitical formatting in the context of corporatist deals. Second, the typology is to be utilized for charting *trends*, rather than pigeonholing *cases*. For this purpose, its generality and ideal-typical nature are less of a liability.

Perhaps the most controversial claim made below is that social inequalities in contemporary advanced societies increasingly approximate the fourth type in figure 6.1, that is complex ("classless") inequality. This means that social inequalities in such societies increasingly form on multiple and hybridized matrices, and that social formation is weak, thus resulting in multiple, continuous, and crosscutting hierarchies, and in weakly articulated, fickle groupings. Such a configuration has been analyzed elsewhere under a label of "status-conventional hierarchy" subject to *fragmentation* and *contingency* (Pakulski and Waters 1996c). A shift towards complex stratification has to be seen in a historical context of destratification and class decomposition, to which we now turn.

Modern trends – a short history of class

As noted by Weber, the processes of class formation in Western Europe, especially the formation of working-class communities, reflected rather unique coincidence of spatial concentration, good communication, clear visions of the "class enemy," and above all ideological and political leadership exercised by the political elite of socialist movements. Political leaders and activists of these movements successfully convinced large sections of manual (mainly industrial) workers that they shared economic and political interests and should embark on the proposed programs of social reconstruction. Working-class consciousness, solidarity, and identity were, to a large extent, political accomplishments. They reflected the relatively uniform working conditions in the factory system, territorial proximity and, above all, new opportunities opened by bureaucratization and democratization of nation-states in the context of war mobilizations. Even at the time when functional, occupational, and lifestyle differentiation eroded the underlying commonalities of working conditions and lifestyles, class unity and identity could be maintained through political organization and renewed ideological appeals. To paraphrase Pizzorno, it was the politically instilled class identity that enabled the leaders to define, and effectively appeal to, the shared class interest. This political and ideological foundation of class was recognized even by the most radical wing of the working-class movement, the Bolsheviks. For Vladimir Lenin and Georg Lukács it was the party – more precisely party leadership – that truly represented the working class and its interests.

Emile Durkheim anticipated fragmentation of "working classes." The internal cohesion (solidarity) of such classes was of a mechanical-ideological nature. The social articulation of class division and conflict reflected anomic conditions of early industrialization, rather than a "normal" trend. Progressive functional differentiation and individualism, predicted Durkheim, would erode the commonalities of work and interests, and the state would promote occupational and syndicalist aggregations. The processes of social change, combined with social engineering (normative regulation sponsored by the occupational groups, education, state activities and the spread of civic religions) would and should blur overarching class identities and divisions. Social citizenship and nationalism would become ideological contenders to class solidarity.

These predictions proved largely accurate. The processes of social differentiation, progressive individualization, and the gradual absorption of racial minorities and women into the labor force undermined class formation already in the second quarter of the twentieth century. So did the extension of citizenship rights, especially the social/welfare rights. The life of social classes was prolonged mainly through ideological and political organization: ideologies with class references, class-oriented party programs, and class-coupled elites. Persisting "class politics" formed a lifeline for class at the time of rapid differentiation of working conditions and lifestyles. Liberal corporatism facilitated this sociopolitical perpetuation of class identities by sponsoring class parties and class politics (the "democratic class struggle" and corporatist deals). Paradoxically, it also blunted class conflicts by insisting on their institutional regulation (Dahrendorf 1959). These conflicts transformed into legalized rituals of national collective negotiations and bargaining. Such etatized and politically organized classes survived until the wave of deregulation and new politics in the 1970s.

The view of classes as ideologically and politically organized entities may sound to any Marxist class theorist's ears like a heresy. Yet, such a view may help in explaining the sequential diagnoses of class decomposition (Dahrendorf), fragmentation (Lipset), and waning class politics (Clark). It allows us to see class formation as first weakened by occupational differentiation and market fragmentation, then undermined by the unraveling corporatist deals, and finally destroyed by the decomposition of class elites, organizations (parties and trade unions), and ideologies. The latter followed the withering away of corporatism and the advancement of globalization. These processes of historical decomposition of class society can be summarized in three stages:

  I. Early modern industrializing societies (liberal capitalism), where class divisions overlapped with estate divisions thus enhancing social class formation. Social and political formation is strongest at both ends of the social/power spectrum: manual working class and industrial bourgeoisie. Liberal ideology (emphasizing equality of opportunity) and political citizenship erode estate divisions. This marks a transition from estate to class stratification.

 II. Modern industrial societies (organized capitalism), where class divisions are strong and politically articulated (class parties, movements, ideologies, etc.). Bureaucratic and professional hierarchies combine and overlap with class divisions. Nationally organized inequalities are managed by the states in the context of corporatist deals. Industrial development and urbanization facilitate the social articulation of middle classes. However, progressive occupational differentiation and market segmentation lead to fragmentation of the major classes. This heralds a transition from class stratification to hybrid stratification.

III. Late/postmodern, postindustrial societies (disorganized capitalism) where industrial classes decompose. The collapsing corporatist deals, globalization, intense social differentiation and progressive individualism prompt further (ideological and political) class decomposition and destratification. Conventional status inequalities that emerge in the process of class decomposition are fickle, resembling a status bazaar. This heralds a transition from hybrid stratification to complex (classless) inequality.

Towards complex (classless) inequalities

The shift to the third stage marks a change in the configuration of social inequalities. If one adopts a geological analogy (which underlies the stratification imagery), postmodernization constitutes an earthquake destroying the formerly well-articulated, clustered, and layered class and status formations. The very notion of stratification has to be critically reviewed in order to adjust the imagery and concepts to the complex, yet less stratified and less nationally organized, social configuration of inequalities.

The late/postmodern shift is driven mainly by social differentiation, which is functional, social, and moral in its nature.[16] Differentiation involves not only the specialization of functions, appearance of new distinctions and formation of new boundaries, but also an increasing transparency of this process, increasing reflexivity and awareness of a conventional and social character of the boundary-forming processes. This transparency strips the process of social differentiation of its "naturalness." It also makes the centrally organized social reproduction of distinctions and social boundaries increasingly problematic. Consequently, such boundaries become localized and fickle, and their persistence depends on reinforcement through organization. Since the latter is expensive (in the economic and social sense), social formation is impeded. New status conventions generated in the process of differentiation lack permanency;

---

[16] The logic of these processes has been the centerpiece of social analysis from Emile Durkheim to Pierre Bourdieu. The novel elements include: 1) Flexible specialization that erodes consistency of occupational tasks and homogeneity of occupational categories. Proliferation of roles requiring flexibility and adaptability. Increasing scope of flexible employment. 2) Extending scope and diversity of market transactions due to the tendency to extend commodity status to new aspects of human products and activities (e.g., brands, software, genetic materials). Access to information, signs, and symbols become important aspect of life chances. 3) Proliferation of horizontal networks within and across the bureaucratic corporate hierarchies. Declining clarity of hierarchical relations. 4) Growing density of social relations facilitated by widening access to new communication and information technologies. 5) Increasing consumption, especially of symbols and services. Proliferation of lifestyles and social identities related to consumption styles and tastes.

norms are contested and boundaries are mobile and porous. As Pierre Bourdieu notes, the boundaries of what he calls "contemporary classes" are like flickering flames.

Continuous and intense differentiation undermines existing social formations. Fragmentation and specialization of tasks is accompanied by their reassembly, especially in the high-tech manufacturing and service sectors, in the form of "flexibly specialized" task groups (e.g., Piore and Sabel 1984). Another consequence of this flexible specialization is further blurring of functional roles, further fragmentation of occupational categories, and further erosion of careers. Discontinuous and lateral job moves experienced by an increasing proportion of service workers are also associated with differentiation of rewards and working conditions. Qualitative factors (work environment, flexible hours, ecological safety, exposure to stress, etc.) become important considerations, thus entering the increasingly complex – and themselves differentiated – criteria of status evaluation. With multiple market fragmentation, the notion of an over-arching social hierarchy becomes problematic. Social differentiation blurs social stratification.

In the most advanced societies, the effects of social differentiation are amplified by the centrality of consumption. The growing level of affluence means reduction in working time and increase in the time spent consuming. It also extends conspicuous consumption across the socioeconomic hierarchy. Moreover, as pointed out by Jean Baudrillard (1988), this consumption becomes increasingly symbolic, and increasingly implicated in the processes of social ordering. The classifications that encode behavior and form matrices of group formation are increasingly detached from production/employment relations, material needs and interests. Consumer objects, increasingly semantic in their nature, start to operate as autonomous social-structuring systems. Such structuring contributes to social differentiation rather than stratification – because sumptuary activities do not lend themselves easily to consensual evaluations – and results in weak and fickle formations.

The obverse of social differentiation is progressive individualism. As suggested by Durkheim and Simmel, it is both the cause and the effect of social differentiation. According to Durkheim, individualism accompanies the "organic" social cohesion and favors complementary difference over alikeness. When elevated by the liberal ideology to a status of social "meta-principle," individualism undermines further collectivistic projects, thus hindering social class formation. In the highly individualized culture weak and transient ties predominate over strong and lasting collective bonds. Achieving and cultivating group solidarities – other than short-term and defensive – becomes difficult. On the other hand, individualism promotes the formation of weak tie-based temporary associations, stylized quasi-groupings, typical of the fashion industry. These, however, are more aspects of social differentiation than stratification.

The combined processes of differentiation and individualization affect the patterns of communal relations by enhancing pluralism of values and lifestyles. Increased interpenetration of value systems accompanying the globalization process aids and reinforces this process even further. Status standards and the underlying value systems are increasingly complex and exposed to challenges – thus unable to sustain stable hierarchies. The old status groupings are either waning or fragmenting because closures and systematic exclusions are likely to be contested. If new status communities are formed, their position requires constant negotiated maintenance. Consequently, the status group formation is impeded. Weak, tentative, and localized formations predominate.

Further extensions of citizenship into social/welfare rights have been arrested. However, the proliferation of demands for rights has continued, mainly in the cultural/symbolic areas – as rights to dignified, non-stigmatizing representation in the popular media. That means, again, that the systems of social distances and discriminations that underlie status-group formation are increasingly difficult to legitimate and maintain. Racial, ethnic, age, gender, etc. forms of discrimination are challenged on the moral, political, and symbolic levels. They are questioned even as terminological distinctions – the phenomenon often criticized as "political correctness." They still structure relationships and social distances, but – when no longer upheld by religion, law, morality, popular ideology, and even politically correct linguistic conventions – in a hidden and localized way. Liberal citizenship, in other words, hinders status stratification, though status inequalities persist.

Mass democratization operates in a similar manner. As anticipated by Weber, it takes an increasingly plebiscitary or populist turn. The erosion of organized *Volksparteien*, including mass-class parties, and the burgeoning sphere of new politics, break the corporatist constraints on political articulation and organization. This further undermines social formation. As Clark and Lipset (2001) show, patterns of political association detach themselves from social cleavages, as well as from the old ideological packages of Left and Right which had developed in the context of the "democratic class struggle." The "new political culture" is conducive to political fragmentation and short-term alliances; it reflects "issue-politics" and responds to short-term protest-movement mobilizations, rather than organized and class-based cleavages and politics.

Conclusions

If the above diagnosis of postmodern trends is correct, class inequalities and divisions of the industrial era will continue to give way to complex inequality. With this shift, the relevance and class analysis is bound to diminish even further. Not because it is incorrect, but because it focuses on social configurations that are waning. More general forms of social analysis that acknowledge the changing configurations of inequality may provide more adequate analytic and theoretical tools for sociology. Such tools have been identified in the classical heritage of Tocquevillian, Durkheimian and Weberian sociology of inequality. Social analysis built on such analytic and theoretical foundations fits better than class analysis the "postmodern condition" characterized by growing social complexity. It particularizes the concept of class and waives the assumptions about the primacy of class structure as the backbone of the social structure and the matrix of social stratification.

Which strategy – the reconstruction and updating of class theory and analysis, as suggested by other contributors to this volume, or developing a broadly based social analysis of inequality and antagonism, as suggested here – is better, that is, more capable of highlighting and accounting for contemporary configurations of social inequality and antagonisms? On that question, one should stress, the jury is still out. And, considering the paradigmatic nature of the competing analytic and theoretical constructs, it may be out for a long while.[17] Ultimately, the adjudication of the debate is likely to come both from the academic community testing the validity of class theories against their nonclass competitors and from political practitioners embracing the most popular and appealing concepts and accounts.

[17] See a discussion of the competing paradigms in Pakulski (2001).

Conclusion: If "class" is the answer, what is the question?

Erik Olin Wright

The specific definitions and elaborations of the concept of class that have been explored in this book are shaped by the diverse kinds of questions class is thought to answer. A concept whose task is to help answer a question about broad historical variations in the social organization of inequality is likely to be defined quite differently from a concept used to answer a relatively narrow question about the subjective identity of individuals in contemporary society. These questions, in turn, are embedded in broad theoretical frameworks. This is one of the things which theoretical frameworks do: they help pose questions. Questions are not generated simply by curiosity and imagination encountering the empirical world; they are generated by curiosity and imagination, organized by theoretical assumptions and animated by normative concerns, encountering the empirical world. These assumptions and concerns are what give specific questions salience and demarcate the tasks that the concept of class is called upon to accomplish. One way of trying to sort out the various perspectives on class explored in this book is thus to map them onto the salient inventory questions posed within class analysis. This will be the task of this chapter.

Six questions are particularly important for which the word "class" often figures centrally in the answers:

1. *Distributional location:* "How are people objectively located in distributions of material inequality?"
2. *Subjectively salient groups:* "What explains how people, individually and collectively, subjectively locate themselves and others within a structure of inequality?"
3. *Life chances:* "What explains inequalities in life chances and material standards of living?"
4. *Antagonistic conflicts:* "What social cleavages systematically shape overt conflicts?"
5. *Historical variation:* "How should we characterize and explain the variations across history in the social organization of inequalities?"

6. *Emancipation:* "What sorts of transformations are needed to eliminate oppression and exploitation within capitalist societies?"

Of course, one could add to this list in various ways. For example, class is often used as part of the answer to questions like "Why do people vote for specific political parties?" or "What explains variations across people in consumption patterns, tastes, and lifestyles?" Such questions, however, are typically closely linked to one or more of those listed above. The voting question, for example, is closely connected to the problems of explaining life chances, subjective identity, and antagonistic conflicts, since an important reason why one might think class differences would be connected to voting is because of the opposing interests and identities of people in different classes. Similarly, the lifestyle question is closely linked to the questions about life chances and subjective identity. Since a menu of six questions already generates a fairly complex way of mapping the variations in frameworks of class analysis, for present purposes I will limit the discussion to this list.

The different approaches to class analysis discussed in this book build their concepts of class to help answer different clusters of these questions. Table 7.1 distinguishes three ways in which a particular question might be linked to an approach to class analysis. First, a question can constitute the *primary anchor* of a particular approach. These are the questions most fundamentally connected to the broader theoretical framework within which the tasks of class analysis are situated. Primary anchoring questions define the central criteria that the concept of class needs to fulfil in order to function within the agenda of the framework. If it could be shown that class as defined by a given approach was not a salient part of the answer to that approach's primary anchoring question, then this would indicate either that the definition of the concept of class within the approach needed significant modification or that some more fundamental transformation of the broader theoretical framework was needed. Second, some questions are part of the core theoretical agenda of an approach to class analysis, but are subordinated to the primary anchoring question. These *secondary anchoring* questions help to specify the explanatory and descriptive reach of the proposed concept of class, but do not generate the primary criteria for the definition of class. If class, as defined within an approach, were shown not to contribute to answering these questions this would narrow the theoretical ambition of the concept, but would not necessarily undermine its core purposes. Finally, some questions may play some role in the broad empirical agenda of class analysis but be of secondary importance for the theoretical structure.

Let us now look at each of these questions and see how they are linked to the different approaches to class analysis in this book. This task, of

Table 7.1 *Six primary questions of class analysis*

Approach to class analysis	Anchoring questions					
	1. Distributional location	2. Subjectively salient groups	3. Life chances	4. Antagonistic conflicts	5. Historical variation	6. Emancipation
Popular usage	***	*	**	*		
David Grusky (neo-Durkheimian)	**	***	**	*	*	
Jan Pakulski	**	***	**	**		
Pierre Bourdieu	**	**	***	*	**	
Richard Breen and John Goldthorpe (neo-Weberian)	**	*	***	*		
Aage Sorensen	**	*	**	***		
Max Weber	*	*	**	*	***	
Erik Olin Wright (neo-Marxian)	*	*	**	**	**	***

*** primary anchoring question for the concept of class

** secondary anchoring question (subordinated to primary anchor)

* additional questions relevant to the concept of class, but not central to anchoring the definition

The questions within which "class" figures in the answers:

1. *Distributional location:* "How are people objectively located in distributions of material inequality?"

2. *Subjectively salient groups:* "What explains how people, individually and collectively, subjectively locate themselves and others within a structure of inequality?"

3. *Life chances:* "What explains inequalities in economically grounded life chances and material standards of living?"

4. *Antagonistic conflicts:* "what economically based cleavages most systematically shape overt conflicts?"

5. *Historical variation:* "How should we characterize and explain the variations across history in the social organization of inequalities?"

6. *Emancipation:* "What sorts of transformations are needed to eliminate economic oppression and exploitation within capitalist societies?"

course, is not a simple one, for the theoretical approaches discussed in this book do not frame their agendas explicitly in terms of these precise questions, and all of them are anchored in more than one question. I therefore sent this chapter to each of the living contributors to this book, inviting them to comment on my evaluations, and I subsequently revised the chapter in light of comments I received. While this does not mean that the contributors necessarily agreed completely with my characterization of their arguments, there were no strong objections to the formulations presented here.[1]

Distributional location

Class is often central to the question "How are people *objectively located* in distributions of material inequality?" In this case, class is defined in terms of material standards of living, usually indexed by income or, possibly, wealth. Class, in this agenda, is a *gradational* concept; the standard image is of rungs on a ladder, and the names for locations are accordingly such things as upper class, upper middle class, middle class, lower middle class, lower class, underclass.[2] This is the concept of class that figures most prominently in popular discourse, at least in countries like the United States without a strong working-class political tradition. When American politicians call for "middle-class tax cuts" what they characteristically mean is tax cuts for people in the middle of the income distribution. Class, in this context, is contrasted with other ways that people are objectively located within social structures, for example, by their citizenship status, their power, or their subjection to institutionalized forms of ascriptive discrimination.

Subjectively salient groups

The word "class" sometimes figures in the answer to the question "What explains how people, individually and collectively, locate themselves and

---

[1] David Grusky raised a number of issues with an earlier draft of the conclusion. In particular, he felt that his approach to class analysis is really anchored in a very broad question about micro-level variations in individual outcomes, and accordingly proposed an additional anchoring question: "*Individual-level outcomes*: What explains individual-level differences in life chances, lifestyles, attitudes, political behavior, and other forms of institutional participation (e.g., marriage, union membership, religious affiliation, other voluntary organization memberships)?" I reformulated some of the discussion in this chapter to respond to this, but felt that the first three questions listed above sufficiently cover these micro-level concerns that it was not necessary to add an additional question to the list.

[2] For a discussion of the contrast between *gradational* and *relational* conceptions of class, see Ossowski (1963 [1958]) and Wright (1979, pp. 5–8).

others within a structure of inequality?" Class is one of the possible answers to this question. In this case the concept would be defined something like this: "Classes are social categories that generate subjectively salient experiences which shape the identities used by people to locate those categories within a system of economic stratification."[3] With this definition of class, the actual content of these evaluative attributes will vary considerably across time and place. In some contexts, class-as-subjective-classification will revolve around lifestyles, in others around detailed occupations, and in still others around income levels. Sometimes the economic content of the subjective classification system is quite direct – as in income levels or occupational categories; in other contexts, it is more indirect, as in expressions such as "upper class." The number of classes will also vary contextually depending upon how the actors in a social situation themselves experience and define the relevant distinctions and the salient groups. Class, in this sense of the word, would be contrasted to other forms of subjectively salient evaluation – religion, ethnicity, gender, etc. – which may have economic dimensions but which are not centrally defined in economic terms.

This question about the formation of subjective identity plays a particularly important role in three of the approaches to class discussed in this book. One of the core themes of Pierre Bourdieu's class analysis, as elaborated by Elliot Weininger, is the salience of symbolic classifications, particularly as these are implicated in lifestyle differences and collective identities. Symbolic classifications and struggles over those classifications do not all revolve around class, but to the extent that they are linked to class-based differences in life chances, then symbolic classifications and their associated identities become central to Bourdieu's class analysis.

Subjective identity is also pivotal in the approaches to class elaborated by both David Grusky and Jan Pakulski. Grusky identifies classes in terms of what he considers "real" groups rather than simply nominal classifications. What makes a group "real" is that the boundaries that define the group have real micro-level effects on the life chances and experiences of individuals within the group in ways that are salient for identity, solidarity and action. In his view, in contemporary developed market societies such as the United States, such real, subjectively salient boundaries correspond to relatively disaggregated occupational categories, not to the "big classes" postulated in traditional Marxist and Weberian approaches to

[3] There is no implication in this definition that class, so defined, would provide a complete explanation of subjective identity and classification. Class would be seen as an experience-generating process, but experiences also require cultural practices to be turned into identities. This cultural mediation of the relationship between class and identity is an especially salient theme in Bourdieu's work.

class. Disaggregated occupational categories are institutionalized in ways that systematically generate the kinds of salient experiences and opportunities for people that turn those categories into real groups, groups that are subjectively meaningful and consequential, not simply formal classifications. Pakulski also places the problem of subjective identity and group formation at the center of his approach to class analysis. There was a time in the nondistant past – from sometime in the nineteenth century until the middle decades of the twentieth – in which stable group identities were, in significant ways, formed around economic inequalities within markets and production. By the end of the twentieth century, however, these economically rooted group identities, he argues, had broken down – the boundaries became fuzzy, individual lives crossed the boundaries of these previous class categories in complex ways, and other identities became much more salient. Class, Pakulski thus argues, is no longer a relevant answer to the question "What explains how people, individually and collectively, locate themselves and others within a structure of inequality?"[4]

Life chances

Perhaps the most prominent question in contemporary sociological research for which class is offered as part of the answer is "What *explains* inequalities in life chances and material standards of living?" This question plays a role, in one way or another, in virtually all approaches to class analysis. It is a more complex and demanding question than the first question about distributional location, for here the issue is not simply descriptively locating people within some kind of system of stratification, but identifying causal mechanisms that help determine salient features of that system. When class is used to explain inequality, typically the concept is not defined primarily by subjectively salient attributes of a social location but rather by *the relationship of people to income-generating resources* or assets of various sorts. Class thus becomes a *relational*, rather than simply *gradational* concept. Class, in this usage, is contrasted to the many other determinants of a person's life chances – for example, geographical location, forms of discrimination anchored in ascriptive characteristics, or

---

[4] The difference between Grusky and Pakulski in terms of their analysis of these issues lies more in how they wish to use the *word* "class" than in their substantive arguments. Grusky uses the word class to identify highly disaggregated, subjectively salient occupational groups. Pakulski uses the word in a more conventional way, restricting the term to those categories Grusky refers to as "big classes." In any event, both Grusky and Pakulski argue that the kind of broad social categories that both Marxists and Weberians identify as "classes" no longer constitute subjectively operative identities of coherent groups with real boundaries.

Table 7.2 *The life chances question in Marx, Weber, and Bourdieu*

	Salient resources that shape life chances			Relative centrality of three class analysis questions		
	capital and labor	human capital	cultural capital	life chances	historical variation	emancipation
Marx	x			3	2	1
Weber	x	x		2	1	
Bourdieu	x	x	x	1		

genetic endowments. Geographical location, discrimination, and genetic endowments may, of course, still figure in the analysis of class – they may, for example, play an important role in explaining why different sorts of people end up in different classes – but the definition of class as such centers on how people are linked to those income-generating assets.

The problem of life chances is closely linked to the normative issue of equality of opportunity. A very broadly held view in liberal societies is that inequalities in material rewards and status are not, in and of themselves, generally morally objectionable so long as individuals have equal opportunity for achieving these rewards. This issue is especially salient in terms of intergenerational mobility – to what extent do children born into families of different economic standing have equal opportunities to succeed in life – but it also bears on issues of intra-generational opportunities. Equality of life chances, therefore, is a background normative idea in discussions of class as a determinant of life chances.

Explaining variations in life chances plays a role in all approaches to class analysis, but it is especially salient in the traditions of Marx, Weber, and Bourdieu. Writers in all three of these traditions use the concept of class to talk about how the ways in which people are linked to various kinds of resources profoundly shape their opportunities and strategies in life. The three traditions of class analysis differ, however, in the precise elaboration of the question and relative importance of this question to their overall agendas, as summarized in table 7.2.

The basic insight of a class analysis of life chances is captured by the formula "what you have determines what you get." This leaves open, however, what range of resources or assets is included under "what you have" and what kinds of outcomes are included in "what you get." Bourdieu clearly has the most expansive notion of resources and the broadest conception of life chances. In Bourdieu's class analysis, the relevant resources for answering the life-chances question include financial assets (capital in the ordinary sense), skills and knowledge (or what is often called human capital), and, most distinctively, what he calls cultural capital.[5] Bourdieu also has a quite expansive notion of the scope of life chances relevant to class analysis, for he includes not simply material standard of living in the narrow economic sense, but also chances for symbolic rewards crucial for inequalities in social status. For Bourdieu, then, life chances for both material goods and symbolic status are determined by the relationship to the three forms of capital. Marx, in contrast, adopts the narrowest inventory of resources relevant to the question. At least in his relatively systematic discussions of class, the only assets that really matter for defining class in capitalist society are capital and labor power. Weber's class analysis falls between these two for he, like Bourdieu, explicitly includes skills as a distinctive kind of resource that shapes market capacities and thus life chances in a market society. Neo-Weberians, like Breen and Goldthorpe, often add to these market capacities job-specific attributes – like authority and responsibility for technically complex tasks – which also impact on life chances for people in such jobs.[6]

A second way in which these three traditions differ with respect to the life-chances question is in the extent to which their overall agendas of class analysis are anchored in this specific question. One of the reasons why Marxists often adopt a relatively thin understanding of the resources relevant to answering the question about life chances is that their concept of class is more deeply anchored in the questions about social emancipation and historical variation than in the question about individual life chances as such. This may explain why, when neo-Marxists try to systematically engage the problem of life chances, they often incorporate Weberian ideas into class analysis.

[5] There is ambiguity in Bourdieu's writings about precisely how many conceptually distinct forms of capital should figure in the analysis of life chances. On the one hand, as Elliott Weininger argues (Lareau and Weininger 2003), it may not make sense to treat cultural capital and human capital as distinct "forms of capital." On the other hand, it could also be argued that "social capital," a fourth kind of capital discussed by Bourdieu (but not generally brought into alignment with the other forms of capital in explaining life chances), is relevant for understanding class differences in life chances. Social capital consists especially of social networks in which people are embedded and which, in a variety of ways, facilitate their pursuit of various goals (and thus "life chances"). In the present context it is not important to resolve these issues. The important point is that Bourdieu adopts a more expansive notion of the resources that figure in the class analysis of life chances than is typical of either neo-Weberian or neo-Marxist class analysis.

[6] Authority and technically complex tasks in a job are not exactly "assets" in the same sense as capital and skills, since a person does not really "own" the authority or the complex tasks. Nevertheless, since incumbents of such jobs do have effective control over the exercise of authority and complex tasks, and since this does confer upon them income-generating advantages, it is not too much of a stretch to fold this into the general Weberian conceptualization of class.

The most basic anchor of Weber's own analysis of class is also not primarily the question about life chances, but rather, as I will argue in more detail below, the question about broad historical variation. His specific focus on market capacities in the question about life chances is derived from his theoretical concerns about historical variation and the distinctiveness of capitalism as a highly rationalized form of market society. For many neo-Weberians, particularly those whose empirical concerns are restricted to the analysis of developed capitalist societies, the issue of broad historical variation tends to get marginalized, and thus the life-chances question in practice becomes the basic anchor for class analysis.

In Bourdieu's class analysis the life-chances question plays the most pivotal role. Broad questions of epochal historical variation or questions about social emancipation are relatively peripheral and do not impose significant constraints on the elaboration of his class concept. For Bourdieu, the crucial issues in class analysis are found in the interplay between the question about life chances and the problem of subjective identity.

Antagonistic conflict

The fourth question of class analysis adds further complexity to the underlying explanatory function of the concept of class: "What cleavages in society systematically generate overt antagonisms and conflicts?" As in the third question, this question suggests a concept of class closely linked to the causes of inequalities in economic opportunities, but here the concept attempts to identify those aspects of economic inequality that generate antagonisms of interest and thus have a tendency to generate overt conflict. Classes would not be defined simply by a commonalty of the conditions that generate economic opportunities, but by those specific clusters of common conditions that have an inherent tendency to pit people against each other in the pursuit of those opportunities. Class, here, would be contrasted on the one hand with noneconomic sources of social cleavage – such as religion or ethnicity – and, on the other hand, with nonclass forms of economic cleavage – such as economic sector or geographical region.

This question about the basis of antagonistic conflict figures especially prominently in the Marxist tradition, although class also plays a role in explaining social conflict in non-Marxist theoretical traditions as well. Weber certainly sees class as a potential basis for conflicts, but he explicitly rejects any claims that there is an inherent general tendency for class relations to generate overt conflicts. Marx, in contrast, saw conflict as an intrinsic consequence of class relations. This does not imply that Marx saw explosive class conflict as a constant feature of capitalist society, but

he certainly did believe, first, that capitalist societies would be characterized by recurrent episodes of intense struggles generated by antagonistic
class interests, and second, that there would be a systematic tendency for
these episodes to intensify over time.[7] While the aphorism "class struggle
is the motor of history" is an oversimplification of Marx's theory of historical dynamics, it does express the importance of the problem of conflict
for his concept of class.

When one of the central questions of class analysis is explaining conflict,
a concept like "exploitation" is likely to play a particularly important role.
In Marx and most neo-Marxists this concept is elaborated in terms of the
process through which labor effort is appropriated from one class by
another. In Aage Sørensen's approach to class, exploitation is elaborated
in terms of the process through which economic rents are extracted. In
both cases, conflicts of interests are not treated as contingent properties
of class but are seen as built into the very structure of class relations.[8]

Historical variation

The fifth question of class analysis centers on a broad macro-level problem: "How should we characterize and explain the variations across history in the social organization of inequalities?"[9] This question implies
the need for a macro-level concept, rather than simply a micro-level concept capturing the causal processes of individual lives; and it requires a
concept that allows for macro-level variations across time and place. This
question plays an especially central role in both the Marxist and Weberian
traditions, but the two traditions treat the problem of historical variation
in quite different ways.

---

[7] These two expectations underwrite two of the striking theoretical arguments of classical
Marxism. The thesis that capitalism will be characterized by recurrent episodes of intense
class conflict is the basis for the thesis that capitalist societies need political and ideological
"superstructures" in order to be reproduced, since in the absence of such institutions,
these explosive conflicts could not be contained. The thesis that there would be a tendency
for class struggles to intensify over time is a central part of the prediction that capitalism
will eventually be transformed through revolutionary struggle.

[8] The basic difference between Sørensen's rent-based view of exploitation and a more
Marxist labor-appropriation based view is that in the latter the material interests of the
exploiter depend upon continued, ongoing interactions with the exploited, not simply
the exclusion of the exploited from access to the rent-generating process. As discussed in
Chapter 1, I refer to the Sørensen-type of exploitation as "non-exploitative oppression."
For an extended Marxian discussion of Sørensen's approach, see Wright (2000).

[9] I have framed the question here as the problem of historical *variation* rather than historical
trajectory or historical *development*. Classical Marxism, of course, was concerned not simply
with an account of structural variations across historical *époques*, but with elaborating a
general theoretical explanation of the trajectory of historical development ("Historical
Materialism").

Within the Marxist tradition, the most significant aspect of historical variation in inequality is the ways in which economic systems vary in the *manner in which an economic surplus is produced and appropriated*. Capitalism, in these terms, is contrasted with feudalism on the basis of the specific mechanisms through which exploitation takes place. In capitalism this occurs through the ways in which labor markets enable propertyless workers to be employed by capitalists, and capitalist control over the labor process enables them to appropriate labor effort from workers. In feudalism, in contrast, the surplus is extracted from serfs through the direct exercise of coercive power by lords. Both of these ways of organizing economic relations constitute class structures because both are built on the appropriation of the economic surplus by an exploiting class, but they are qualitatively different because of the process by which this is accomplished.

For Weber, in contrast, the central problem of historical variation is the *relative salience of different forms of inequality*, especially class and status.[10] In these terms the critical contrast between capitalism and feudalism is not between two types of class structures, but between a society within which class is the fundamental basis of power and inequality, and a society within which status is the fundamental basis. While classes did exist in feudalism, since feudalism did contain markets and thus people engaged in market exchanges with different resources and market capacities, the market system was subordinated to the status order, and it was the status order which most fundamentally determined the advantages and disadvantages of lords and serfs.

The problem of historical variation also plays some role in specifying the concept of class in the analyses of Jan Pakulski and David Grusky, but in their case the central issue is the variation in the class-ness of social inequality across time *within* the history of capitalist development. For both Pakulski and Grusky, class (or "big classes" in Grusky's analysis) describes the social organization of inequality in a specific period of capitalist development, from roughly the beginning of the industrial revolution until the emergence of the postindustrial (or postmodern) era. Here the issue is not, as in Weber, the relative weight of a class order and a status order, or, as in Marx, the large-scale historical variations in forms of exploitation, but the shift from a highly structured and coherent

---

[10] The historical variation in the relative salience of different aspects of inequality is intimately bound up with a more general theme in Weber's historical sociology – the problem of *rationalization*. Class, for Weber, is the most fully rationalized form of economic inequality. For a discussion of the relationship between rationalization and class in Weber's class analysis, see Wright (2002).

system of inequality in industrial capitalism to a fragmented, crosscutting system of complex inequalities in postmodern societies.

Emancipation

The most controversial question asked by social theorists for which class is an important part of the answer is "What sorts of transformations are needed to eliminate economic oppression and exploitation within capitalist societies?" This question implies not simply an explanatory agenda about the mechanisms that generate economic inequalities, but a normative judgment about those inequalities – they are forms of oppression and exploitation – and a normative vision of the transformation of those inequalities as part of a political project of emancipatory social change.

This is the question that, I believe, most fundamentally anchors the Marxist approach to class analysis and infuses each of the other core questions with a particular set of meanings. In the context of the Marxian emancipatory agenda, the problem of historical variation includes trying to understand possible future forms of social relations within which the exploitation and oppression of capitalist class relations have been eliminated. Historical variation relevant to class analysis thus revolves around the contrast not simply between capitalism and feudalism as empirically observable historical forms of class relations, but also between capitalism and a hypothetical communism (understood as an egalitarian classless society). Similarly with respect to the problem of class conflict: characterizing the antagonistic interests embedded in class relations as "exploitation" and "oppression" suggests that the conflicts generated by those relations involve issues of social justice, not simply morally neutral material interests.[11] Within the broad agenda of Marxist class analysis, therefore, the concept of class contributes to the critique of capitalist society rather than just to description and explanation.

Because of the ideologically charged character of many of the debates over class, the alternative frameworks of class analysis that we have

---

[11] Not everyone, of course, believes that such explicitly normative questions should play such a major role in specifying concepts within sociological theory. John Goldthorpe, for one, has explicitly attacked Marxist approaches to class on precisely these grounds. In a footnote to an article in the *American Journal of Sociology* commenting on Aage Sørensen's rent-based concept of class, Goldthorpe says of the concept of exploitation that it is "a word I would myself gladly see disappear from the sociological lexicon." He adds, by way of clarification, "Its function in Marxist thought was to allow a fusion of normative and positive claims in a way that I would find unacceptable." And he concludes: "If invoking exploitation is no more than a way of flagging the presence of structurally opposed class interests that lead to zero-sum conflicts, then its use is innocuous but scarcely necessary" (Goldthorpe 2000: 1574).

reviewed often appear to be hostile camps, each trying to recruit supporters and defeat opponents. Students interested in class analysis thus often feel that they have to make a choice, to adopt one or another of these approaches to the exclusion of others. But if it is the case that these various approaches are organized around different mixes of anchoring questions, then, depending upon the specific empirical agenda, different frameworks of class analysis may provide the best conceptual menu. One can be a Weberian for the study of class mobility, a Bourdieuian for the study of the class determinants of lifestyles, and a Marxian for the critique of capitalism.

References

Abbott, Andrew, 1988 *The System of Professions: An Essay on the Division of Expert Labor*, Chicago, The University of Chicago Press.

2001 *Time Matters: On Theory and Method*, Chicago, The University of Chicago Press.

Accardo, Alain, 1997 *Introduction à une sociologie critique: Lire Bourdieu*, Bordeaux, Editions Le Mascaret.

Ainslie, George, 1992 *Piconomics*, New York, Cambridge University Press.

Akerlof, G. A., 1982 "Labor Contracts as Partial Gift Exchanges," *Quarterly Journal of Economics* 92, pp. 543–69.

Aronowitz, Stanley, and William DiFazio, 1994 *The Jobless Future*, Minneapolis, University of Minnesota Press.

Barley, Stephen R., 1995 "The Technician as an Occupational Archetype: A Case for Bringing Work into Organizational Studies," working paper, Stanford University.

Barnes, Barry, 1995 *The Elements of Social Theory*, London, UCL Press.

Barzel, Yoram, 1997 *Economic Analysis of Property Rights*, 2nd edn., New York, Cambridge University Press.

Baudrillard, J., 1988 *Selected Writings*, translated and edited by M. Poster, Cambridge and Oxford, Polity and Blackwell.

Baxter, J., and M. Western (eds.), 2001 *Configuration of Class and Gender*, Stanford, CA, Stanford University Press.

Beck, U., 1992 *Risk Society*, London, Sage.

Becker, Gary S., 1964 *Human Capital*, New York, National Bureau of Economic Research.

Bell, Daniel, 1976 *The Coming of Post-Industrial Society*, New York, Basic Books.

1987 "The New Class: A Muddled Concept," pp. 455–68 in *Structured Social Inequality*, edited by Celia S. Heller, New York, Macmillan.

Bernstein, Basil, 1971 *Class, Codes, and Control: Vol. 1, Theoretical Studies toward a Sociology of Education*, London, Routledge and Kegan Paul.

Blossfeld, Hans-Peter, 1992 "Is the German Dual System a Model for a Modern Vocational Training System?," *International Journal of Comparative Sociology* 33, pp. 168–81.

Boltanski, Luc, 1987 [1982] *The Making of a Class: Cadres in French Society*, translated by Arthur Goldhammer, Cambridge, UK, Cambridge University Press.

Bottero, W., and K. Prandy, 2003 "Social Interaction Distance and Stratification," *British Journal of Sociology* 54:2, pp. 177–97.

Bottomore, Tom, 1981 "A Marxist Consideration of Durkheim," *Social Forces* 59, pp. 902–17.

Bouglé, Célestin, 1926 *The Evolution of Values*, translated by Helen S. Sellars, New York, Henry Holt and Company.

  1971 [1927] *Essays on the Caste System by Célestin Bouglé*, translated by D. F. Pocock, Cambridge, UK, Cambridge University Press.

Bourdieu, Pierre, 1966 "Condition de classe et position de classe," *Archives européennes de sociologie* 7:2, pp. 201–23.

  1977 [1972] *Outline of a Theory of Practice*, translated by Richard Nice, Cambridge, UK, Cambridge University Press.

  1984 [1979] *Distinction: A Social Critique of the Judgment of Taste*, translated by Richard Nice, Cambridge, MA, Harvard University Press.

  1986 "The Forms of Capital," pp. 241–58 in *Handbook of Theory and Research for the Sociology of Education*, edited by John G. Richardson, New York, Greenwood Press.

  1987 "What Makes a Social Class? On the Theoretical and Practical Existence of Groups," *Berkeley Journal of Sociology* 32, pp. 1–17.

  1988 [1984] *Homo Academicus*, translated by Peter Collier, Stanford, CA, Stanford University Press.

  1990a [1980] *The Logic of Practice*, translated by Richard Nice, Stanford, CA, Stanford University Press.

  1990b *In Other Words: Essays Towards a Reflexive Sociology*, translated by Matthew Adamson, Stanford, CA, Stanford University Press.

  1991 *Language and Symbolic Power*, translated by Gino Raymond and Matthew Adamson, Cambridge, MA, Harvard University Press.

  1998a *Acts of Resistance: Against the Tyranny of the Market*, translated by Richard Nice, New York, The New Press.

  1998b [1994] *Practical Reason: On the Theory of Action*, Stanford, CA, Stanford University Press.

  2001a *Contre-feux 2: Pour un mouvement social européen*, Paris, Editions Raisons D'Agir.

  2001b [1998] *Masculine Domination*, translated by Richard Nice, Stanford, CA, Stanford University Press.

  2002 *Interventions, 1961–2001: Science sociale et action politique*, Marseilles, Agone.

Bourdieu, Pierre, and Jean-Claude Passeron, 1990 [1970] *Reproduction in Education, Society and Culture*, translated by Richard Nice, London, Sage Publications.

Bourdieu, Pierre, and Loïc J. D. Wacquant, 1992 *An Invitation to Reflexive Sociology*, Chicago, The University of Chicago Press.

Bourdieu, Pierre, Alain Accardo, Gabrielle Balazs, Stéphane Beaud, François Bonvin, Emmanuel Bourdieu, Philippe Bourgois, Sylvain Broccolichi, Patrick Champagne, Rosine Christin, Jean-Pierre Faguer, Sandrine Garcia, Remi Lenoir, Françoise Œvrard, Michel Pialoux, Louis Pinto, Denis Podalydès, Abdelmalek Sayad, Charles Soulié, and Loïc J. D. Wacquant,

1999 *The Weight of the World: Social Suffering in Contemporary Society*, translated by Priscilla Parkhurst Ferguson, Susan Emanuel, Joe Johnson, and Shoggy T. Waryn, Stanford, CA, Stanford University Press.

Bowles, Samuel, and Herbert Gintis, 1990 "Contested Exchange: New Microfoundations for the Political Economy of Capitalism," *Politics and Society* 18:2 (June), pp. 165–222.

Bradley, Harriet, 1996 *Fractured Identities: Changing Patterns of Inequality*, Cambridge, Polity.

Braverman, Harry, 1974 *Labor and Monopoly Capital*, New York, Monthly Review Press.

Breen, Richard, 1997 "Risk, Recommodification and the Future of the Service Class," *Sociology* 31:3, pp. 473–89.

Breen, Richard, and John H. Goldthorpe, 2001 "Class, Mobility and Merit: The Experience of Two British Birth Cohorts," *European Sociological Review* 17:2, pp. 81–101.

Breen, Richard, and David B. Rottman, 1995a *Class Stratification: A Comparative Perspective*, New York, Harvester Wheatsheaf.

1995b "Class Analysis and Class Theory," *Sociology* 29:3, pp. 453–73.

Breiger, Ronald L., 1982 "The Social Class Structure of Occupational Mobility," *American Journal of Sociology* 87:3, pp. 578–611.

Broom, L., and F. L. Jones, 1976 *Opportunity and Attainment in Australia*, Canberra, ANU Press.

Brubaker, Rogers, 1985 "Rethinking Classical Theory: The Sociological Vision of Pierre Bourdieu," *Theory and Society* 14:6, pp. 745–75.

Bryson, Bethany, 1996 " 'Anything but Heavy Metal': Symbolic Exclusion and Cultural Dislikes," *American Sociological Review* 61:5, pp. 884–99.

Burawoy, Michael, and Erik Olin Wright, 2001 "Sociological Marxism," pp. 459–86 in *Handbook of Sociological Theory*, edited by Jonathan Turner, New York, Kluwer Academic/Plenum Publishers.

Bureau of Labor Statistics, 1998 "Worker Displacement, 1995–98," Labor Forces Statistics from the Current Population Survey, news release, August 19, 1998, Washington, DC, US Department of Labor.

Calhoun, Craig, and Loïc J. D. Wacquant, 2002 " 'Everything is Social': In Memoriam, Pierre Bourdieu (1930–2002)," *Footnotes* 30:2, pp. 5–10.

Calhoun, Craig, Edward LiPuma, and Moishe Postone (eds.), 1993 *Bourdieu: Critical Perspectives*, Chicago, The University of Chicago Press.

Caplow, Theodore, 1954 *The Sociology of Work*, Minneapolis, University of Minnesota Press.

Carchedi, Guglielmo, 1977 *The Economic Identification of Social Classes*, London, Routledge and Kegan Paul.

Casey, Catherine, 1995 *Work, Self, and Society*, London, Routledge.

Charlesworth, Simon J., 2000 *A Phenomenology of Working Class Experience*, Cambridge, UK, Cambridge University Press.

Clark, Terry, N., 1996 "The Debate over 'Are Social Classes Dying?'," working paper, Conference on Social Class and Politics, Woodrow Wilson Center, Washington, DC.

Clark, Terry N., and Seymour M. Lipset, 1991 "Are Social Classes Dying?," *International Sociology* 6, pp. 397–410.

Clark T. N., and S. M. Lipset (eds.), 2001 *The Breakdown of Class Politics*, Baltimore, The Johns Hopkins University Press.

Coase, Ronald H., 1960 "The Problem of Social Cost," *Journal of Law and Economics* 3, pp. 1–44.

Cohen, G. A., 1978 *Karl Marx's Theory of History: A Defense*, Princeton, NJ, Princeton University Press.

1995 *Self-Ownership, Freedom and Equality*, Cambridge, UK, Cambridge University Press.

Cole, Robert E., 1979 *Work, Mobility, and Participation*, Berkeley and Los Angeles, The University of California Press.

Coleman, James S., 1990 *The Foundations of Social Theory*, Cambridge, MA, The Belknap Press of Harvard University Press.

Collins, Randall, 1979 *The Credential Society: An Historical Sociology of Education and Stratification*, New York, Academic Press.

Comte, Auguste, 1988 [1830] *Introduction to Positive Philosophy*, edited by Frederick Ferré, Indianapolis, Hackett.

Coser, Lewis A., 1992 "Introduction: Maurice Halbwachs, 1877–1945," pp. 1–34 in *On Collective Memory*, edited and translated by Lewis A. Coser, Chicago, The University of Chicago Press.

Cotreel, Allin, 1984 *Social Class in Marxist Theory*, London, Routledge and Kegan Paul.

Crook, S., J. Pakulski, and M. Waters, 1992 *Postmodernization: Change in Advanced Society*, London, Sage.

Dahrendorf, Ralf, 1959 *Class and Class Conflict in Industrial Society*, Stanford, CA, Stanford University Press.

Dixit, Avishnah, and Mancur Olson, 1996 "The Coase Theorem is False: Coase's Insight is Nonetheless Mainly Right," unpublished paper, University of Maryland, College Park, MD.

Dominitz, Jeff, and Charles F. Manski, 1997 "Perceptions of Economic Insecurity: Evidence from the Survey of Economic Expectations," *Public Opinion Quarterly* 61, pp. 261–87.

Donnelly, Michael, 1997 *Statisical Classifications and the Salience of Social Class*, pp. 107–31 in *Reworking Class*, edited by John R. Hall, Ithaca and London, Cornell University Press.

Dore, Ronald P., 1973 *British Factory – Japanese Factory*, London, Allen and Unwin.

Duncan, Otis Dudley, 1968 "Social Stratification and Mobility. Problems in the Measurement of Trend," pp. 675–719 in *Indicators of Social Change*, edited by Eleanor B. Sheldon and Wilbert E. Moore, New York, Russel Sage Foundation.

Durkheim, Emile, 1933 [1893] *The Division of Labor in Society*, New York, Free Press.

1951 [1897] *Suicide. A Study in Sociology*, translated by John A. Spaulding and George Simpson, Glencoe, IL, Free Press.

1960 [1893] *The Division of Labor in Society*, translated by George Simpson, New York, Macmillan.

1956 [1911] "Jugements de valeur et jugements de réalité," *Revue de métaphysique et de morale* 19, pp. 437–53.

1958, *Professional Ethics and Civic Morals*, translated by C. Brookfield, Glencoe, IL, Free Press.

1970a [1897] *Suicide*, London, Routledge and Kegan Paul.

1970b [1905] *La Science sociale et l'action*, edited by J. C. Filloux, Paris, Presses Universitaires de France.

Durkheim, Emile, and Marcel Mauss, 1963 *Primitive Classification*, translated by Rodney Needham, Chicago, The University of Chicago Press.

Eder, K., 1993 *The New Politics of Class*, London, Sage.

Edwards, Richard, 1979 *Contested Terrain*, New York, Basic Books.

Eggertsson, Thráinn, 1990 *Economic Behavior and Institutions*, Cambridge, UK, Cambridge University Press.

Ehrenreich, Barbara, and John Ehrenreich, 1977 "The Professional-Managerial Class," *Radical America* 11, pp. 7–31.

Emirbayer, Mustafa, 1997 "Manifesto for a Relational Sociology," *American Journal of Sociology* 103:2, pp. 281–317.

Emmison, Michael, and Mark Western, 1990 "Social Class and Social Identity: A Comment on Marshall et al.," *Sociology* 24, pp. 241–53.

Erikson, Robert, 1984 "Social Class of Men, Women and Families" *Sociology* 18:4, pp. 500–14.

Erikson, Robert, and John H. Goldthorpe, 1992 *The Constant Flux: A Study of Class Mobility in Industrial Societies*, Oxford, Oxford University Press.

Erikson, Robert, and Jan O. Jönsson (eds.), 1996 *Can Education be Equalized? The Swedish Case in Comparative Perspective*, Boulder, CO, Westview Press.

Erikson, Robert, John H. Goldthorpe, and Lucien Portocarero, 1979 "Intergenerational Class Mobility in Three Western European Societies: England, France and Sweden," *British Journal of Sociology* 33, pp. 1–34.

Esping-Andersen, Gösta, 1988 "The Making of a Social Democratic Welfare State," pp. 35–66 in *Creating Social Democracy: A Century of the Social Democratic Labor Party in Sweden*, edited by Klaus Misgeld, Karl Molin, and Klas Amark, University Park, The Pennsylvania State University Press.

Evans, Geoffrey, 1992 "Testing the Validity of the Goldthorpe Class Schema," *European Sociological Review* 8:3, pp. 211–32.

1997 *The End of Class Politics? Class Voting in Comparative Perspective*, Oxford, Oxford University Press.

Evans, Geoffrey, and Colin Mills, 1998 "Identifying Class Structure: A Latent Class Analysis of the Criterion-related and Construct Validity of the Goldthorpe Class Schema," *European Sociological Review* 14:1, pp. 87–106.

2000 "In Search of the Wage-Labour/Service Contract: New Evidence on the Validity of the Goldthorpe Class Schema," *British Journal of Sociology* 51, pp. 641–61.

Eyerman, Ron, 1994 "Modernity and Social Movements," pp. 707–10 in *Social Stratification: Class, Race and Gender*, edited by David Grusky, Boulder, CO, Westview Press.

Fantasia, Rick, 1989 *Cultures of Solidarity: Consciousness, Action, and Contemporary American Workers*, Berkeley, The University of California Press.

Featherman, David L., and Robert M. Hauser, 1978 *Opportunity and Change*, New York, Academic Press.

Featherman, David L., F. Lancaster Jones, and Robert M. Hauser, 1975 "Assumptions of Mobility Research in the United States: The Case of Occupational Status," *Social Science Research* 4, pp. 329–60.

Fenton, Steve, 1980 *Race, Class, and Politics in the Work of Emile Durkheim*, Paris, UNESCO.

Filloux, J.-C., 1993 "Inequalities and Social Stratification in Durkheim's Sociology," pp. 211–28 in *Emile Durkheim: Sociologist and Moralist*, edited by Stephen P. Turner, London and New York, Routledge.

Fortin, Nicole M., and Thomas Lemieux, 1997 "Institutional Changes and Rising Wage Inequality: Is There a Linkage?," *Journal of Economic Perspectives* 11:2 (spring), pp. 75–96.

Freeman, Richard, and James L Medoff, 1984 *What Do Unions Do?*, New York, Basic Books.

Freidson, Eliot, 1986 *Professional Powers: A Study of the Institutionalization of Formal Knowledge*, Chicago, The University of Chicago Press.

1994 *Professionalism Reborn: Theory, Prophecy, and Policy*, Chicago, The University of Chicago Press.

Geiger, Theodor J., 1932 *Die Soziale Schichtung des Deutschen Volkes: Soziographischer Versuch auf statistischer Grundlage*, Stuttgart, F. Enke.

Giddens, Anthony, 1971 *Capitalism and Modern Social Theory*. Cambridge, UK, Cambridge University Press.

1972 "Durkheim's Writings in Sociology and Social Philosophy." pp. 1–50 in *Emile Durkhiem: Selected Writings*, edited and translated by Anthony Giddens, Cambridge, UK, Cambridge University Press.

1973 *The Class Structure of the Advanced Societies*, London, Hutchinson.

1978 *Emile Durkheim*, New York, Viking Press.

1983 "Classical Social Theory and the Origins of Modern Sociology," pp. 40–67 in *Profiles and Critiques in Social Theory*, Berkeley, The University of California Press.

Goldthorpe, John H., 1980 *Social Mobility and Class Structure in Modern Britain*, Oxford, Clarendon Press.

1987 *Social Mobility and Class Structure in Modern Britain*, 2nd edn., Oxford, Clarendon Press.

1990 "A Response," pp. 399–440 in *John Goldthorpe: Consensus and Controversy*, edited by Jon Clark, Celia Modgil, and Sohan Modgil, London, The Falmer Press.

2000 *On Sociology: Numbers, Narratives and the Integration of Research and Theory*, Oxford, Oxford University Press.

2002 "Occupational Sociology, Yes: Class Analysis, No – A Comment on Grusky and Weedens' Research Agenda," *Acta Sociologica* 45, pp. 211–17.

Goldthorpe, John, and Keith Hope, 1974 *The Social Grading of Occupations: A New Approach and Scale*, Oxford, Clarendon Press.

Goldthorpe, John H., and Gordon Marshall, 1992 "The Promising Future of Class Analysis: A Response to Recent Critiques," *Sociology* 26:3, pp. 381–400.

Gordon, Milton M., 1958 *Social Class in American Sociology*, Durham, NC, Duke University Press.

Gouldner, Alvin, 1979 *The Future of Intellectuals and the Rise of the New Class*, New York, Seabury Press.

Granovetter, Mark, and Charles Tilly, 1988 "Inequality and Labor Processes," pp. 175–221 in *Handbook of Sociology*, edited by Neil J. Smelser, Newbury Park, Sage.

Grusky, David B. (ed.), 2001 *Social Stratification*, Boulder, CO, Westview Press.·

Grusky, David B., and Jesper B. Sørensen, 1998, "Can Class Analysis Be Salvaged?," *American Journal of Sociology* 103:5, pp. 1,187–234.

   2001 "Are There Big Social Classes?," pp. 183–94 in *Social Stratification: Class, Race, and Gender in Sociological Perspective*, 2nd edn., edited by David B. Grusky, Boulder, CO, Westview Press.

Grusky, David B., and Kim A. Weeden, 2001 "Decomposition without Death: A Research Agenda for a New Class Analysis," *Acta Sociologica* 44, pp. 203–18.

   2002 "Class Analysis and the Heavy Weight of Convention," *Acta Sociologica* 45, pp. 229–36.

Grusky, David B., Kim A. Weeden, and Jesper B. Sørensen, 2000 "The Case for Realism in Class Analysis," *Political Power and Social Theory* 14, pp. 291–305.

Haiku, F. A., 1948 "The Meaning of Competition," in *Individualism and Social Order*, Chicago, The University of Chicago Press.

Halaby, Charles N., and David L. Weakliem, 1993 "Ownership and Authority in the Earnings Function: Nonnested Tests of Alternative Specifications," *American Sociological Review* 58, pp. 16–30.

Halbwachs, Maurice, 1992 [1945] *On Collective Memory*, edited and translated by Lewis A. Coser, Chicago, The University of Chicago Press.

   1958 *The Psychology of Social Class*, Glencoe, IL, Free Press.

Hall, Stuart, 1988 "Brave New World," *Marxism Today* (October 24–9).

   2001 "The Meaning of New Times," pp. 859–65 in *Social Stratification: Class, Race, and Gender in Sociological Perspective*, 2nd edn., edited by David B. Grusky, Boulder, CO, Westview Press.

Hall, Stuart, and Martin Jacques, 1989 *New Times: The Changing Face of Politics in the 1990s*, London, Lawrence and Wishart.

Hauser, Robert M., and John Robert Warren, 1997 "Socioeconomic Indexes of Occupational Status: A Review, Update, and Critique," pp. 177–298 in *Sociological Methodology 1997*, edited by Adrian Raftery, Cambridge, UK, Blackwell.

Hawkins, M. J., 1994 "Durkheim on Occupational Corporations: An Exegesis and Interpretation," *Journal of the History of Ideas* 20, pp. 461–81.

Hayek, F. A., 1948 "The Meaning of Competition," in *Individualism and Social Order*, Chicago, The University of Chicago Press.

Heath, A. F., and N. Britten, 1984 "Women's Jobs do Make a Difference," *Sociology* 18: 4, pp. 475–90.

Hirsch, Fred, 1976 *The Social Limits to Growth*, Cambridge, MA, Harvard University Press.

Hollingshead, August, and Frederick Redlich, 1958 *Social Class and Mental Illness*. New York, Wiley.

Holton, Robert, 1996 "Has Class Analysis a Future?," pp. 26–41 in *Conflicts about Class: Debating Inequality in Late Industrialism*, edited by David J. Lee and Bryan S. Turner, London and New York, Longman.

Holton, Robert J., and Bryan S. Turner, 1989 *Max Weber on Economy and Society*, London, Routledge and Kegan Paul.

Holzer, Harry J., 1990 "The Determinants of Employee Productivity and Earnings," *Industrial Relations* 29, pp. 403–22.

Hout, Michael, and Robert M. Hauser, 1992 "Symmetry and Hierarchy in Social Mobility: A Methodological Analysis of the CASMIN Model of Class Mobility," *European Sociological Review* 8, pp. 239–66.

Hout, Michael, Clem Brooks, and Jeff Manza, 1993 "The Persistence of Classes in Postindustrial Societies," *International Sociology* 8, pp. 259–77.

International Labour Office, 1990 [1968] *International Standard Classification of Occupations: ISCO-88*, Geneva, ILO.

Ishida, Hiroshi, 1993 *Social Mobility in Contemporary Japan*, Stanford, CA, Stanford University Press.

Jencks, Christopher, Lauri Perman, and Lee Rainwater, 1988 "What is a Good Job? A New Measure of Labor Market Success," *American Journal of Sociology* 93, pp. 1,322–57.

Jensen, Michael C., and Kevin J. Murphy, 1990 "Performance Pay and Top-Management Incentives," *Journal of Political Economy* 98, pp. 225–65.

Joyce, Patrick, 1995 *Class*, Oxford, Oxford University Press.

Juhn, Chichi, Kevin M. Murphy, and Brooks Pierce, 1993 "Wage Inequality and the Rise in Returns to Skills," *Journal of Political Economy* 101, pp. 410–42.

Kalleberg, Arne L., and Ivar Berg, 1987 *Work and Industry: Structures, Markets and Processes*, New York, Plenum.

Kingston, Paul W., 1994 "Are There Classes in the United States?" pp. 3–41 in *Research in Social Stratification and Mobility*, vol. 13, edited by Robert Althauser and Michael Wallace, Greenwich, CT, JAI Press.

2000 *The Classless Society*, Stanford, CA, Stanford University Press.

Kohn, Melvin L., and Kazimierz M. Slomczynski, 1990 *Social Structure and Self-Direction*, Oxford, Blackwell.

Konrad, György, and Ivan Szélenyi, 1979 *The Intellectuals on the Road to Class Power*, New York, Harcourt Brace Jovanovich.

Korpi, Walter, 1983 *The Democratic Class Struggle*, London, Routledge.

Krause, Elliot A., 1971 *The Sociology of Occupations*, Boston, Little Brown.

Krueger, Alan B., and Lawrence H. Summers, 1987 "Reflections on the Inter-Industry Wage Structure," pp. 17–47 in *Unemployment and the Structure of Labor Markets*, edited by Kevin Lang and Jonathan S. Leonard, Oxford, Basil Blackwell.

Lamont, Michèle, 1992 *Money, Morals, and Manners: The Culture of the French and American Upper-Middle Class*. Chicago, The University of Chicago Press.

2000 *The Dignity of Working Men: Morality and the Boundaries of Race, Class, and Immigration*, Cambridge, MA, Harvard University Press.

Lane, Jeremy F., 2000 *Pierre Bourdieu: A Critical Introduction*, London, Pluto Press.

Laraña, Enrique, Hank Johnston, and Joseph R. Gusfield, 1994 *New Social Movements: From Ideology to Identity*, Philadelphia, Temple University Press.

Lareau, Annette, and Elliot B. Weininger, 2003 "Cultural Capital in Educational Research: A Critical Assessment," *Theory and Society* 32:5–6, pp. 567–606.

Laumann, E. O., 1973 *Bonds of Pluralism*, New York, John Wiley.

Lawrence, Paul R., and Davis Dyer, 1983 *Renewing American Industry*, New York, Free Press.

Lazear, Edward P., 1995 *Personnel Economics*, Cambridge, MA, MIT Press.

Lee, David J., 1995 "Class as a Social Fact," *Sociology* 28, pp. 397–415.

Lee, David J., and Bryan S. Turner (eds.), 1996 *Conflicts about Class: Debating Inequality in Late Industrialism*, London, Longman.

Lehmann, Jennifer, 1995 "Durkheim's Contradictory Theories of Race, Class, and Sex," *American Sociological Review* 60, pp. 566–85.

Lenin, Vladimir I., 1927 *Collected Works of V. I. Lenin*, New York, International Publishers.

Levy, Frank, and Richard J. Murnane, 1992 "U.S. Earnings Levels and Earnings Inequality: A Review of Recent Trends and Proposed Explanations," *Journal of Economic Literature* 30, pp. 1,333–81.

Lipset, S. M., 1960 *Political Man. The Social Bases of Politics*, New York, Doubleday.

Lipset, S. M., and S. Rokkan, 1967 "Cleavage Structures, Party Systems, and Voter Alignments: An Introduction," pp. 1–64 in *Party Systems and Voter Alignments: Cross-national Perspective*, edited by S. M. Lipset and S. Rokkan, New York, Free Press.

Lockwood, David, 1992 *Solidarity and Schism*, Oxford, Clarendon Press.

Love, Geoff, 1997 "The Diffusion of Downsizing among Large U.S. Firms, 1977–95: The Role of Firm Status," Ph.D. dissertation, Joint Program in Organizational Behavior, Harvard Business School, and Departments of Sociology and Psychology, Harvard University, Cambridge, MA.

Lukes, Steven, 1973 *Emile Durkheim: His Life and Work*, London, Allen Lane.

Marshall, Alfred, 1949 [1920] *Principles of Economics*, 8th edn., London, Macmillan.

Marshall, Gordon, David Rose, Howard Newby, and Carolyn Vogler, 1988 *Social Class in Modern Britain*, London, Unwin Hyman.

Marshall, T. H., 1950 *Citizenship and Social Class*, Cambridge, UK, Cambridge University Press.

Marx, Karl, 1959a [1848] "The Communist Manifesto," pp. 315–55 in *Capital, The Communist Manifesto, and Other Writings by Karl Marx*, edited by Max Eastman, New York, The Modern Library.

   1959b [1894] "Capital, Volume 3, Chapter 9," pp. 54–9 in *Capital, The Communist Manifesto, and Other Writings by Karl Marx*, edited by Max Eastman, New York, The Modern Library.

   1964 [1894] *Selected Works: Volume 1*, Moscow, Progress Publishers.

Medoff, James J., and Katherine Abraham, 1981 "Are Those Paid More Really More Productive?," *Journal of Human Resources* 16, pp. 186–216.

Meštrović, Stjepan G., 1992 *Durkheim and Postmodern Culture*, Hawthorne, NY, Aldine de Gruyter.

Mills, C. W., 1951 *White Collars*, New York, Basic Books.

1956 *The Power Elite*, Oxford and New York, Oxford University Press.

Mitchell, Daniel J. B., 1985 "Shifting Norms in Wage Determination," *Brookings Papers on Economic Activity*, Washington, DC, Brookings Institute.

Mortimer, Jeylan T., and Jon Lorence, 1995 "Social Psychology of Work," pp. 497–523 in *Sociological Perspectives on Social Psychology*, edited by Karen S. Cook, Gary A. Fine, and James S. House, Boston, Allyn and Bacon.

Mouzelis, Nicos, 1993 "The Poverty of Sociological Theory," *Sociology* 27, pp. 675–95.

Müller, Hans-Peter, 1993 "Durkheim's Political Sociology," pp. 211–28 in *Emile Durkheim: Sociologist and Moralist*, edited by Stephen P. Turner, London and New York, Routledge.

Murphy, Raymond, 1988 *Social Closure: The Theory of Monopolization and Exclusion*, Oxford, Clarendon Press.

Myles, John, Garnett Picot, and Tedd Wannell, 1988 "The Changing Wage Distributions of Jobs," *Canadian Economic Observer* 4, pp. 4.2–4.12.

Nakane, Chie, 1970 *Japanese Society*, London, Weidenfeld and Nicolson.

Nelson, Robert L., and William P. Bridges, 1999 *Legalizing Gender Inequality: Courts, Markets, and Unequal Pay for Women in America*, Cambridge, UK, Cambridge University Press.

Nisbet, Robert A., 1952 "Conservatism and Sociology," *American Journal of Sociology* 58, pp. 167–75.

North, Douglass, and Robert P. Thomas, 1973 *The Rise of Western Capitalism*, New York, Cambridge University Press.

Olson, Mancur, 1965 *The Logic of Collective Action*, Cambridge, MA, Harvard University Press.

Ossowski, S., 1963 [1958] *Class Structure in the Social Consciousness*, London, Routledge.

Pahl, R. E., 1989 "Is the Emperor Naked? Some Questions on the Adequacy of Sociological Theory in Urban and Regional Research," *International Journal of Urban and Regional Research* 13, pp. 709–20.

Pakulski, J., 2001 "Class and Politics" pp. 36–49 in *The Breakdown of Class Politics*, edited by T. N. Clark and S. M. Lipset, The Johns Hopkins University Press.

2004 *Globalizing Inequality*, Sydney, Allen and Unwin.

Pakulski, Jan, and Malcolm Waters, 1996a *The Death of Class*, London, Sage Publications.

1996b "The Reshaping and Dissolution of Class in Advanced Society," *Theory and Society* 25:5, pp. 667–91.

1996c "Misreading Class as Status: A Reply to Our Critics," *Theory and Society* 25, 731–6.

Parkin, Frank, 1971 *Class Inequality and Political Order: Social Stratification in Capitalist and Communist Societies*, New York, Praeger.

1979, *Marxism and Class Theory: A Bourgeois Critique*, New York, Columbia University Press.

1992 *Durkheim*, Oxford, Oxford University Press.

Parsons, Talcott, 1949 *Essays in Sociological Theory, Pure and Applied*, Glencoe, IL, Free Press.

1954 "An Analytical Approach to the Theory of Social Stratification," pp. 69–88 in *Essays in Sociological Theory*, Glencoe, IL, Free Press.

1967 *Sociological Theory and Modern Society*, New York, Free Press.

1968 [1937] *The Structure of Social Action*, New York, Free Press.

1970 "Equality and Inequality in Modern Society, or Social Stratification Revisited," pp. 13–72 in *Social Stratification: Research and Theory for the 1970s*, edited by Edward O. Laumann, Indianapolis, Bobbs-Merrill Company.

Pearce, Frank, 1989 *The Radical Durkheim*, London, Unwin Hyman.

Perkin, H., 1989 *The Rise of Professional Society*, London, Routledge.

Peterson, Richard A., and Roger M. Kern, 1996 "Changing Highbrow Taste: From Snob to Omnivore," *American Sociological Review* 61:5, pp. 900–7.

Piore, Michael J., and Charles F. Sabel, 1984 *The Second Industrial Divide: Possibilities for Prosperity*, New York, Basic Books.

Pope, Whitney, and Barclay D. Johnson, 1983 "Inside Organic Solidarity," *American Sociological Review* 48, pp. 681–92.

Portes, Alejandro, 2000 "The Resilient Importance of Class: A Nominalist Interpretation," pp. 249–84 in *Political Power and Social Theory*, vol. 14, edited by Diane E. Davis, Amsterdam, JAI Press.

Poulantzas, Nicos, 1974 *Classes in Contemporary Capitalism*, London, Verso.

1975 *Classes in Contemporary Capitalism*, London, New Left Books.

Prandy, Kenneth, 1999 "The Social Interaction Approach to the Measurement and Analysis of Social Stratification," *International Journal of Sociology and Social Policy* 19, pp. 215–49.

Przeworski, Adam, 1985 *Capitalism and Social Democracy*, Cambridge, UK, Cambridge University Press.

Resnick, Stephen, and Richard Wolff, 1987 *Knowledge and Class*, Chicago, The University of Chicago Press.

Ricardo, David, 1951 [1821] *On the Principles of Political Economy and Taxation*, Vol. 1 of *The Works and Correspondence of David Ricardo*, edited by Piero Sraffa, Cambridge, UK, Cambridge University Press.

Roemer, John, 1982 *A General Theory of Exploitation and Class*, Cambridge, MA, Harvard University Press.

1986 "Should Marxists Be Interested in Exploitation?," pp. 260–82 in *Analytical Marxism*, edited by John E. Roemer, New York, Cambridge University Press.

Rouanet, H., W. Ackermann, and H. Le Roux, 2000 "The Geometric Analysis of Questionnaires. The Lesson of Bourdieu's *La Distinction*," Bulletin de méthodologie sociologique 65, pp. 5–18.

Ryan, William, 1971 *Blaming the Victim*, New York, Orbach and Chambers.

Ryscavage, Paul, and Peter Henle, 1990 "Earnings Inequality Accelerates in the 1980's," *Monthly Labor Review* 113:12, pp. 3–16.

Rytina, Steven, 2000 "Is Occupational Mobility Declining in the U.S.?," *Social Forces* 78, pp. 1,227–76.

Sartori, G., 1969 "From the Sociology of Politics to Political Sociology," pp. 65–100 in *Politics and the Social Sciences*, edited by S. M. Lipset, New York, Oxford University Press.

Saunders, Peter, 1989 "Left Write in Sociology," *Network* 44, pp. 3–4.

Schneider, Louis, and Sverre Lysgaard, 1953 "The Deferred Gratification Pattern," *American Sociological Review* 18:2, pp. 142–9.

Scott, J., 1996 *Stratification and Power*, Cambridge, UK, Polity.

Shavit, Yossi, and Hans-Peter Blossfeld (eds.), 1993 *Persistent Inequality: Changing Educational Attainment in Thirteen Countries*, Boulder, CO, Westview Press.

Shils, E., 1968 "Deference," pp. 104–32 in *Social Stratification*, edited by J. A. Jackson, New York, Cambridge University Press.

Simmel, Georg, 1908 *Soziologie*, Leipzig, Duncker & C. Humblot.

Simon, Herbert, 1957 "The Employment Relation," pp. 24–45 in *Models of Man*, New York, Wiley.

Smith, Adam, 1991 [1776] *The Wealth of Nations*, Amherst, NY, Prometheus.

Smith, Philip, and Jeffrey C. Alexander, 1996 "Durkheim's Religious Revival," *American Journal of Sociology* 102, pp. 585–92.

Solow, Robert M., 1979 "Another Possible Source of Wage Stickiness," *Journal of Macroeconomics* 1:2, pp. 79–82.

Sørensen, Aage B., 1983 "Processes of Allocation to Open and Closed Positions in Social Structure," *Zeitschrift für Soziologie* 12, pp. 203–24.

1991 "On the Usefulness of Class Analysis in Research on Social Mobility and Socioeconomic Inequality," *Acta Sociologica* 34:2, pp. 71–87.

1994 "The Basic Concepts of Stratification Research: Class, Status, and Power," pp. 229–41 in *Social Stratification: Class, Race, and Gender in Sociological Perspective*, edited by David B. Grusky, Boulder, CO, Westview Press.

1996 "The Structural Basis of Social Inequality," *American Journal of Sociology* 101:5, pp. 1,333–65.

1998 "On Kings, Pietism and Rent-seeking in Scandinavian Welfare States," *Acta Sociologica* 41:4, pp. 363–76.

2000 "Toward a Sounder Basis for Class Analysis," *American Journal of Sociology* 105:6, pp. 1,523–58.

Sørensen, Jesper B., and David B. Grusky, 1996 "The Structure of Career Mobility in Microscopic Perspective," pp. 83–114 in *Social Differentiation and Social Inequality*, edited by James N. Baron, David B. Grusky, and Donald J. Treiman, Boulder, CO, Westview Press.

Spenner, Kenneth I., 1995 "Technological Change, Skill Requirements, and Education: The Case for Uncertainty," pp. 81–137 in *The New Modern Times: Factors Reshaping the World of Work*, edited by David B. Bills, Albany, State University of New York Press.

Stanworth, M., 1984 "Women and Class Analysis: A Reply to John Goldthorpe," *Sociology* 18:2, pp. 159–70.

Stewart, A., K. Prandy, and R. M. Blackburn, 1980 *Social Stratification and Occupations*, London, Macmillan.

Swartz, David, 1997 *Culture and Power: The Sociology of Pierre Bourdieu*, Chicago and London, The University of Chicago Press.

Swift, Adam, 2001 *Equality, Freedom and Community*, Cambridge, UK, Polity.

Therborn, Göran, 1988 "A Unique Chapter in the History of Democracy: The Social Democrats in Sweden," pp. 1–34 in *Creating Social Democracy: A Century of the Social Democratic Labor Party in Sweden*, edited by Klaus Misgeld, Karl Molin, and Klas Amark, University Park, The Pennsylvania State University Press.

Thompson, E. P. 1966 [1963] *The Making of the English Working Class*, New York, Vintage Books.

Thompson, K., 1982 *Emile Durkheim*, London and New York, Tavistock/ Routledge.

Tiryakian, Edward A., 1975 "Neither Marx nor Durkheim . . . Perhaps Weber," *American Journal of Sociology* 81, pp. 1–33.

Tocqueville, A. de, 1945 [1862] *Democracy in America*, London, Longman.
2000 [1835] *Democracy in America*, New York, Bantam.

Treiman, Donald J., 1977 *Occupational Prestige in Comparative Perspective*, New York, Academic Press.

Tullock, Gordon, 1980 "The Transitional Gains Trap," pp. 211–21 in *Toward a Theory of the Rent Seeking Society*, edited by James S. Buchanan, Robert D. Tollison, and Gordon Tullock, College Station, TX, Texas A&M University Press.
1989 *The Economics of Special Privilege and Rent Seeking*, Boston, Kluwer Academic Publishers.

Tumin, M. M., 1953 "Reply to Kingsley Davis," *American Sociological Review* 18, pp. 372–84.

Turner, Bryan S., 1988 *Status*, Philadelphia, Open University Press.
1990 "An Outline of a Theory of Citizenship," *Sociology* 24:2, pp. 189–217, 190.
1996 "Capitalism, Classes and Citizenship," pp. 254–62 in *Conflict about Class*, edited by D. J. Lee and B. S. Turner, Harlow, Longman.
2001 "The Erosion of Citizenship," *British Journal of Sociology*, 52:2, pp. 189–209.

Van Maanen, John, and Stephen R. Barley, 1984 "Occupational Communities: Culture and Control in Organizations," *Research in Organizational Behavior* 6, pp. 287–365.

Visser, Jelle, 1988 "Trade Unionism in Western Europe: Present Situation and Prospects," *Labour and Society* 13, pp. 125–82.

Wacquant, Loïc J. D., 1991 "Making Class: The Middle Class(es) in Social Theory and Social Structure," pp. 39–64 in *Bringing Class Back in: Contemporary and Historical Perspectives*, edited by Scott G. McNall, Rhonda F. Levine, and Rick Fantasia, Boulder, CO, Westview Press.
2002 "From Slavery to Mass Incarceration: Rethinking the 'Race Question' in the US," *New Left Review* 13, pp. 41–60.

Warner, W. Lloyd, Marchia Meeker, and Kenneth Bells, 1949 *Social Class in America*, New York, Science Research Associates.

Waters, M., 1991 "Collapse and Convergence of Marxist Theory," *Theory and Society* 20, pp. 141–72.

Watts Miller, W., 1996 *Durkheim, Morals and Modernity*, London, UCI Press.

Weber, Max, 1968a [1946] *From Max Weber*, translated by Hans H. Gerth and C. Wright Mills, London, Routledge and Kegan Paul.
1968b [1922] *Economy and Society*, Berkeley, The University of California Press.
1968c [1946] "Class, Status and Power," pp. 180–95 in *From Max Weber: Essays in Sociology*, translated by Hans H. Gerth and C. Wright Mills, New York, Oxford University Press.
1978 [1922] *Economy and Society*, 2 vols., edited by Guenther Roth and Claus Wittich, Berkeley, The University of California Press.

Weeden, Kim A., and David B. Grusky, 2002 "Class Structuration in the United States," working paper, Department of Sociology, Cornell University.

Weininger, Elliot B. 2002 "Class and Causation in Bourdieu," pp. 49–114 in *Current Perspectives in Social Theory*, vol. 21, edited by Jennifer Lehmann, Amsterdam, JAI Press.

Wesolowski, W., 1977 *Klasy, warstwy i wladza*, Warsaw, PWN (translated as *Classes, Strata and Power*, London, Routledge, 1978).

Wilensky, Harold L., 1966 "Class, Class Consciousness, and American Workers," pp. 12–44 in *Labor in a Changing America*, edited by William Haber, New York, Basic.

Wolff, Edward N., 1995 *Top Heavy: A Study of Increasing Inequality of Wealth in America*, Washington, DC, Brookings Institution.

Wright, Erik Olin, 1978 *Class, Crisis and the State*, London, New Left Books.
    1979 *Class Structure and Income Determination*, New York, Academic Press.
    1980a "Class and Occupation," *Theory and Society* 9, pp. 177–214.
    1980b "Varieties of Marxist Conceptions of Class Structure," *Politics and Society* 9:3, pp. 323–70.
    1982 "The Status of the Political in the Concept of Class Structure," *Politics and Society* 11:3, pp. 321–52.
    1985 *Classes*, London, New Left Books/Verso.
    1996 "The Continuing Relevance of Class Analysis," *Theory and Society* 25, pp. 697–716.
    1997 *Class Counts: Comparative Studies in Class Analysis*, Cambridge, UK, Cambridge University Press.
    2000 "Working-Class Power, Capitalist-Class Interests and Class Compromise," *American Journal of Sociology* 105:4 (January), pp. 957–1,002.
    2002 "The Shadow of Exploitation in Weber's Class Analysis," *American Sociological Review* 67, pp. 832–53.

Wright, Erik Olin, Andrew Levine, and Elliott Sober, 1993 *Reconstructing Marxism*, London, Verso.

Wright, Erik Olin *et al.*, 1989 *The Debate on Classes*, London, Verso.

Wrong, D., 1976 [1964] *Skeptical Sociology*, New York, Columbia University Press.

Zabusky, Stacia E., and Stephen R. Barley, 1996 "Redefining Success: Ethnographic Observations on the Careers of Technicians," pp. 185–214 in *Broken Ladders: Managerial Careers in the New Economy*, edited by Paul Osterman, Oxford, Oxford University Press.

Zeitlin, Irving M., 1968 *Ideology and the Development of Sociological Theory*, Englewood Cliffs, NJ, Prentice Hall.

Index

Abbot, Andrew, 62, 66, 109
Abraham, Katherine, 148
Accardo, Alain, 109
Ackermann, W., 88
Ainslie, George, 135
Akerlof, G. A., 39
Alexander, Jeffrey, 53
asset-specificity, and class, 37

Barley, Stephen, 62
Barnes, Barry, 61
Barzel, Yoram, 121, 128, 129, 132
Baudrillard, Jean, 177
Beck, Ulrich, 169
Becker, Gary, 142, 163
Bell, Daniel, 122, 163
Bells, Kenneth, 122
Bernstein, Basil, 71
Blossfeld, Hans-Peter, 50, 64
Boltanski, Luc, 106
Bottero, Wendy, 168
Bottomore, Tom, 53, 54, 55
Bouglé, Célestin, 58
Bourdieu, Pierre, 59, 71, 78, 143, 163,
    168, 169, 177, 184, 186
  capital in, concept and varieties, 87–9
  causal complexity in, 108–10
  causal role of class in, 110–13
  class agency in, 92–5, 113–17
  class analysis in, 3, 82–118
  class and status in, 84, 95
  class structure in, 86–90
  classificatory conflicts in, 95–102
  constructivist dimension of class in, 115
  culture and class in, 97
  discursive construction of class in, 103
  field in, concept of, 95
  gender and class in, 110–13
  habitus and class in, 90–2
  symbolic power in, 102–7, 117–18
  symbolic violence in, 95–102
Bowles, Sam, 29, 140, 143

Bradley, Harriet, 68
Braverman, Harry, 142
Breen, Richard, 3, 31, 39, 47, 48, 50,
    187
Breiger, Ronald, 43
Bridges, William, 75
Britten, N., 48
Brooks, Clem, 66
Brubaker, Rogers, 82, 169
Burawoy, Michael, 4

Calhoun, Craig, 82
capital
  class and, in Bourdieu, 87–9
  composition of, 88
  volume of, 88
capitalism, class relations in, 11, 190
Carchedi, Guglielmo, 5
Casey, Catherine, 61, 64
citizenship, and class, 164
Clark, Terry, 51, 153, 170, 178
class
  ambiguity in academic discussions, 2
  ambiguity in popular imagination, 1–2
  and alienation, 59
  and asset-specificity, 37
  and attitudes and lifestyles, 78;
    in Bourdieu: see habitus
  and citizenship, 164
  and democracy, 164
  and education, 163; see also education
  and gender, 164–5; in Bourdieu, 58
  and inequality, 121–8; multiplicity of
    causes, 162–3, 171–3
  and labor contract, 37, 38
  and life chances, 32–3, 122, 130, 134–6,
    185–8
  and market, 33
  and occupational associations, in
    Durkheim, 56–7, 62–3
  and occupations, in Durkheim, 61–2
  and race, 164–5

207